THE CONTAGIOUS CO

'A must-read for the modern marketer'
Fernando Machado, CMO, Burger King

'If you work in marketing, or if you're simply fascinated by the effect creative ideas can have, this book is a must-read. Full of the most compelling and disruptive ideas, it offers a practical framework to ignite exceptional ideas'
Stephan Loerke, Chief Executive Officer, World Federation of Advertisers

'A brilliant riposte to those who believe that all modern advertising is soulless, mechanical and computerized'
Rick Webb, COO of TimeHop, co-founder of The Barbarian Group, author of *Agency: Starting a Creative Firm in the Age of Digital Marketing*

'Few have had their finger on the pulse of marketing in this brave new landscape quite like Paul Kemp-Robertson and the team at Contagious'
Mark Tutssel, Executive Chairman & Chief Creative Officer, Leo Burnett Worldwide

'Contagious has an encyclopaedic knowledge of what cutting edge creative is. Of the digital world and technologies that are fuelling creativity. He is also one of the best minds and nicest people in our industry. What a treat to have access to all that in this wonderful book'
Carter Murray, Worldwide CEO, FCB

'In this world of ever louder and more irrelevant marketing crap, *The Contagious Commandments* is a clear, practical and compelling guide to creating brilliant campaigns that really stand out and get people to engage'
Alain Groenendaal, President & CEO, Grey Group Europe

'Here is the bible for brands built in a more modern age. This fantastic book details the most enthusiastic communications campaigns; ones where consumers, fans and punters jump for joy and share with glee. Don't leave home (for work) without it'
James Kirkham, Head of Copa 90

'Contagious are world-class in their ability to create communications that capture the imagination of your consumers and in this invaluable book they teach you how'
Ian Wilson, Senior Director of Global Digital Marketing Development, Heineken

ABOUT THE AUTHORS

Paul Kemp-Robertson co-founded the now globally renowned creative and strategic intelligence resource, Contagious, in 2004. Previously, he worked in commercials production and was part of the launch team behind the marketing creativity magazine *Shots* before going on to become editor, and was later Leo Burnett's worldwide director of creative resources. Paul has written for publications including *Business 2.0* and the *Guardian* and his TEDGlobal talk on alternative currencies has been viewed over one million times. He has a Masters degree from the University of London.

Chris Barth is lead strategist at Contagious, where he oversees a wide variety of projects for brands and agencies in North America, including trend briefings, research reports, creative capabilities training, innovation workshops and collaborative strategic initiatives. Prior to joining Contagious in 2013, Chris worked as a staff writer at *Forbes*, where he also produced Steve Forbes' Intelligent Investing interview series, which featured conversations with global leaders in economics, business and investing. In the past, he has also been a freelancer at *Rolling Stone*, an editorial producer at Major League Baseball Advanced Media, and a consultant at Arcadia Solutions.

THE CONTAGIOUS COMMANDMENTS

TEN STEPS TO
BRAND BRAVERY

PAUL KEMP-ROBERTSON AND CHRIS BARTH

BUSINESS

PENGUIN BUSINESS

UK | USA | Canada | Ireland | Australia
India | New Zealand | South Africa

Penguin Business is part of the Penguin Random House group of companies
whose addresses can be found at global.penguinrandomhouse.com.

First published by Portfolio 2018
Published in Penguin Business 2019
001

Copyright © Paul Kemp-Robertson and Chris Barth, 2018

The moral right of the authors has been asserted

Set in 12/14.75 pt Dante MT Std
Typeset by Jouve (UK), Milton Keynes
Printed and bound in Great Britain by Clays Ltd, Elcograf S.p.A.

A CIP catalogue record for this book is available from the British Library

ISBN: 978–0–241–32897–2

www.greenpenguin.co.uk

This book is dedicated to exceptional ideas.

CONTENTS

CONTENTS

INTRODUCTION

Imagine, for a second, that the person next to you in whatever bookstore, airport, or living room you've picked this book up has just coughed. Or sneezed. Or generally expelled some sort of germ that threatens to ruin the better part of next week.

Chances are you'd step away, consider washing your hands, or mutter an instinctive curse or prayer, depending on your disposition. Contagion, typically, is not something we want to tangle with.

But in marketing (and entertainment, media, and many other fields), contagion is something to seize upon and amplify. Brands thrive on it. It is a cheap ticket to extensive reach. The same mechanism that causes an ill-judged tweet to derail a career enables a lo-fi video to persuade millions of strangers to pour buckets of ice over their heads. It makes brand ideas that will spread like wildfire. These contagious things can be beautifully filmed creative stories that earn a place in pop culture. They can be innovative public-relations campaigns that champion social causes. Or they can be a livestream of a potato slowly growing in a pile of sand (trust us; it's coming).

In an age where expensive ads can be blocked but billions of eyeballs can be reached for free on people's smartphones, contagious thinking is more valuable than ever. Marketers unable to create contagious ideas will quickly find themselves over and out – overspending on advertising and, potentially, out of a job.

Advertising isn't dead, but it needs to take some lessons from the flu.

WE ARE (COUGH) CONTAGIOUS

Contagious launched in 2004, in the middle of a marketing maelstrom; a time of historic change. Mobile was beginning to get smart, social media was primed to explode, and people's relationships with brands were becoming a whole lot more interactive and opinionated. New media had created new behaviours, enabling the audience to run ahead of the advertiser.

The communications industry needed a fresh guidance system, to make sense of all the change and disruption. Contagious was devised as a triple-headed guide – business intelligence resource, quarterly journal, and marketing advisory service – to help its clients navigate the immediate future of marketing.

Our purpose as a company is to ignite exceptional ideas. Contagious's services are designed for marketers seeking competitive edge through creativity and innovation. We interrogate the world's most exceptional marketing and disruptive trends to help our clients achieve winning ideas, fast. We believe in the maxim that creativity is the last legal means to gain an unfair advantage over the competition.

Since its launch, the company has become a world-class authority on the future of marketing and the power of creative leadership. Fascinated by the stuff people choose to care about and feel compelled to share, we've created a platform to explore alternative advertising ideas, to assess the impact of emerging technologies, and to champion a greater sense of purpose for brands.

WE'D LIKE TO MAKE YOU CONTAGIOUS

So why should you read this book? For one, it's chock full of the most compelling and disruptive ideas the advertising industry has devised in this millennium. Whether you're in the mood for an ingenious activation from a Guatemalan shoe retailer, an oddball vending machine for a Japanese coffee brand, internet-connected underwear, or a radio station for dogs, we've got it all. If you work in the marketing industry or are simply fascinated by the effect creative ideas exert on culture as well as business, you'll find plenty to chew on here.

More than just creative inspiration, though, this book is a practical guide: ten clear and simple commandments that will enable you to create and share successful, contagious ideas. Honed over the most intense decade of change and disruption in the advertising universe, this decalogue for today lays out a clear framework to set you on the path to better and more effective ideas, both in marketing and beyond.

Creating contagious ideas requires breaking long-standing paradigms and well-worn category norms. Picture a beer ad. Is there a party or maybe a sports game, men bantering, women giggling and a culminating shot of either the bottle or a freshly poured pint, sparkling with condensation and a tiny bit of brew frothing over the lip? Adhere to the category codes and the ad practically writes itself. For shampoo it's even simpler, a paradigm enforced by brand handbooks around the globe: always include a 'spin, swish and smile', in which the woman starring in the commercial turns to the camera, flips her freshly washed hair, and flashes a brilliant grin. Perfectly generic, perfectly forgettable.

Think of the hundreds or thousands of advertisements you encounter every day on the television or your tablet, on your commute to work, or in front of your PC that follow these category codes. How many can you remember? Just as our immune systems consistently win the battle against predictable and ubiquitous germs, our brains' defences tune out banal ideas and stale executions. People have developed a cognitive immunity to most marketing.

This book provides ten strategic imperatives to developing creative ideas that avoid these codes and shatter such norms – and consequently bring about more contagious outcomes by penetrating people's defences in a positive way. By following these commandments, you'll unlock ideas that move from audience to audience under their own power, enabling your brand to become part of the cultural conversation. Although creating such ideas cannot be done by rote, there *are* precedents and guidelines to create purposeful initiatives that resonate with real people. We hope to help you do just that.

THE TALE OF THE ARGENTINEAN AD MAN

Stories lie at the heart of all infectious ideas, and two stories sparked the formation of Contagious as a business. The first comes from Buenos Aires, the capital of Argentina. It's 1998. A shiny new neighbourhood, branded as Madero Este, has been built at Puerto Madero, a former industrial district by the river. It comprises the country's first Hilton hotel, an apartment block, office buildings, mall and cinema complex. To promote the new neighbourhood, wealthy developer Alberto L. González approaches one of the country's most celebrated creative directors, Jorge Heymann. 'Here's $4 million,' he says. 'We need an advertising campaign to drive awareness and attract people to this new city within the city. Come back to me with some ideas.'

Just as any self-respecting creative director would do when handed such an ambitious and high-profile brief, Heymann spent time interrogating the product. He visited Puerto Madero at various times of day and night to get a feel for this ambitious, gleaming new place. But when he turned up to pitch his advertising ideas to the business magnate, he came empty-handed. He told González: 'Sir, you don't need an ad campaign. You need . . . a bridge.'

By looking at Madero Este through the lens of a consumer, Heymann realized that it felt too disconnected from the main hub of the city to be an attractive proposition for would-be visitors. The river was a psychological barrier as much as a physical one. Sure, he could easily have churned out the usual array of billboards, print ads, radio and TV commercials. But if people had to take two buses, commit to a circuitous walk or pay the expense of a taxi, they wouldn't be in the mood for much shopping and socializing by the time they got to the new hotspot. No amount of advertising sheen would solve that. But a bridge would.

Not just any bridge, though.

Heymann felt that this upstart new district that had changed the map of Buenos Aires needed something bold and iconic. It needed a story. The bridge ought to be contagious; a landmark that people talked about, that generated media buzz and column inches – an ambitious design that would serve as the advertising campaign, with the benefit of lasting far longer than a conventional twelve-week media plan. It would be both an artery and an artwork. Something that would immediately connect Madero Este to its customer base and bring the fledgling neighbourhood to life.

Knowing that fame begets fame, Heymann printed a business card with the developer's logo and his own name on it and flew to Spain to convince Santiago Calatrava, one of the world's most iconic architects, to take on the brief. The result? Puente de la Mujer, a stunning and unique pedestrian footbridge connecting Puerto Madero to the rest of Buenos Aires. The city got an amazing new landmark and the shops, apartments, offices, cinema, hotel, and restaurants of Madero Este got lots of customers. At $6 million, the project cost 50 per cent more than the original marketing and media budget, but the return on investment was exponentially higher. In the book *The New Waterfront: A Worldwide Urban Success Story*, authors Ann Breen and Dick Rigby describe it as one of the most successful waterfront renewal projects in the world.

That great twentieth-century philosopher Elvis Presley once urged us all to 'Walk a Mile in My Shoes', and the Argentinean ad man did just that (although it's unclear if they were blue suede). By exploring Puerto Madero on foot, rather than drafting up some ad layouts in his office on the other side of town, the creative director got inside the mind of the target audience. He anticipated their reactions by plotting their journey. And his creative brain landed on an alternative response to the traditional marketing brief.

It sounds obvious, but marketers sometimes need to leave their desks and data dashboards to get inside the lives of the people who buy their products and services. Helping marketers use new approaches to find creative solutions is what Contagious was born to do.

THE TALE OF ANCIENT MEXICAN SCROTUMS

A second story helped to shape Contagious. When researching a question posed by a multinational food-and-drinks client – 'Can a brand ever be truly empathetic?' – Paul stumbled across this tale of extreme empathy. (Please stay with us on this one!)

In Western religious societies, childbirth is explicitly connected with Original Sin. In biblical terms, the pain and suffering associated with labour is seen as a natural punishment for female transgression. Things didn't go according to plan in the Garden of Eden, Eve got hornswoggled by the snake, and so God passed judgement, condemning Man to sustain life through hard labour and Woman to create new life through painful childbirth. This belief was so entrenched that early anaesthesia was routinely withheld from women during childbirth, since 'descendants of Eve' were 'supposed' to suffer.

One of the few societies to take a contrary view, however, were the Huichol of Mexico. These descendants of the Aztecs believed that the burden of childbirth should be shared. To do so they created an ingenious – and extremely empathetic – solution (men: get ready to wince). During labour, the expectant mother would hold on to a rope that was tied to her male partner's scrotum. With each painful contraction, she would instinctively give the string a yank, so that her partner – positioned above her in the rafters of a house or the branches of a tree – could share both the pain and, ultimately, the spiritual joy of the experience.

Now, we're not suggesting that anyone involved in building brands should go to such extreme lengths in order to empathize with their customers. But Contagious does encourage marketers to build the capacity to (metaphorically) 'feel their tugs' and follow Elvis's sage advice to get inside someone's mind to better anticipate their needs.

Mass media can be efficient at spreading a product message at scale, and can generate a strong emotional reaction, but at Contagious we also believe that to benefit fully from any degree of loyalty or interest shown by a consumer, brands should use their unique clout – be it media muscle or creative armoury – to bring about positive change. To create utility. To shape experiences that would otherwise be out of reach or unavailable. In our frequently frenetic and bewildering world, brands have started to fill some of society's vacuums by acting as advisors, concierges, problem solvers, educators, and entertainment providers.

FEEL THEIR TUGS

'Feel Their Tugs' would certainly make an appropriate slogan for T-shirts slipped into marketing conference tote bags, but the Mexican Huichol story and the tale of the advertising brief that became a bridge both get to the heart of why Contagious was created as a business, born on the back of a beer mat in a London gastropub.

Traditional marketers expend much energy on mapping out 'the customer journey' – plotting consumers' typical daily behaviours in order to figure out the most appropriate 'contact points'. In plain English: to find places where brands can target people with advertising messages. As the 'Feel Their Tugs' analogy suggests, Contagious instead advocates that brands identify the 'pain points' in the customer journey, and provide solutions, services, facilities, information or experiences to solve or ease them. This is a different, more empathetic mindset to the traditional advertising approach that adopts an almost militaristic approach to communicating a message to consumers; which probably explains why words like 'campaign', 'target', 'bombard', 'guerrilla', 'penetration', and 'stealth' are common in the standard marketing dictionary.

Obviously, price and product performance are major factors in purchasing decisions, but when brands behave in such intuitive, productive ways, it increases the likelihood of establishing a more tangible connection (or, in marketing speak, a 'reason to believe') compared with a standard, transient advertisement.

Delta Airlines felt its passengers' tugs when it resolved a typical passenger anxiety – the fear of a suitcase getting lost en route – by adding a feature to its mobile app enabling customers to track the exact whereabouts of their luggage from the moment it leaves the check-in desk. The Bank of Åland felt its customers' tugs when it reshaped its identity as a sustainability-focused financial institution. Safaricom addressed cultural tugs by turning its mobile-phone balance into an ad-hoc banking system in Kenya. The following pages are full of such examples of brands paying attention to their customers' problems, adding a dose of creativity to their solution, and reaping the benefits.

THE CONTAGIOUS COMMANDMENTS

'Feel Their Tugs' is a canny slogan, but a tad socially awkward. Let's be honest, it's not always appropriate to begin business conversations with images of lassoed scrotums. But it did plant a seed that ultimately led to us writing the Contagious Commandments: our ten steps to successful marketing, future fitness, and brand bravery. The commandments – forged over more than a decade of writing, speaking, and thinking about the changing marketing industry, through more than fifty issues of our quarterly printed journal, and innumerable hands-on sessions in the trenches with Contagious clients – are what we believe to be the hallmarks of contagious companies; a set of principles and provocations to make brands fit for the future.

// **ONE / Have an Organizing Principle /** Figure out why your business exists – both for you and for the people you serve. Don't get distracted by short-termism and faddish trends. Your organizing principle should be a clear manifestation of your company's reason for being, the central tent pole on which the very fabric of your company hangs.

// **TWO / Be Useful, Relevant, and Entertaining /** The original contagious commandment, circa 2005. Fundamental, but somehow still often overlooked. If you're asking someone to invest time and energy into the content, services, and experience your brand offers, you'd better be sure what you're giving back has value.

// **THREE / Ask Heretical Questions /** When was the last time you asked questions about the fundamental nature of your organization? Brave marketers champion awkwardness and embrace dissent. They question and question and question until they get to the true heart of an issue. And, perhaps most importantly, they empower others in their company to do the same.

// **FOUR / Align with Behaviour /** Resist the urge to reinvent the wheel or build a walled garden far away from where consumers actually operate. Instead, collaborate. Identify existing patterns and behaviours and figure out how your brand can build on them, rather than distracting from them.

// FIVE / Be Generous / Don't ask what's in it for you, ask what's in it for them. The best advertising isn't always advertising. Ease the friction, solve the pain points in the customer journey, and leave the world a better place after your campaign than it was before.

// SIX / Join The 5% Club / Test and learn. 'Fail Forward Fast' is not a cliché for nothing. Divert a percentage of your production budget, your media budget, your award-show budget to experimentation. Be optimistically curious: failure sucks, but only if you don't learn something from it.

// SEVEN / Prioritize Experience Over Innovation / Good technology is no excuse for a bad idea. Innovation may garner a brief PR boost, but unless that innovation is delivering superior customer experience, it won't help you in the long run. Technology should serve creativity, not the other way around.

// EIGHT / Weaponize Your Audience / Turn people into media. Leverage their voices to shout you out from the mountain tops. Your audience is powerful and vocal – invite them to influence your brand's direction and behaviour, and give them tools and assets to spread the word about what you're up to.

// NINE / Make Trust Sacred / Reputation is a micro-economy with far-reaching repercussions for your business. Cultivate trust with your consumers so they'll see you as a partner or ally. Step one: never forget that data is a manifestation of the lives of living, breathing people. Treat it with respect.

// TEN / Be Brave / Studies show that the brains of business people subliminally equate creative ideas (i.e. the new and risky) with poison, vomit, and agony. But! Creative work is six times more effective than non-creative work. We must prioritize creativity to cut through the cognitive immunity of jaded consumers. Brief bravely for that creativity. Empower courage.

In the following pages we unpack and expound on these commandments. Study them, and we think your brand, company or clients will be stronger. But of course we know that the advertising industry's most precious commodity is time, and the unit of currency is attention. Agencies spend thousands of hours devising ingenious ways to trigger a reaction inside the scant seconds it takes to scroll past a Facebook post or to hover over the 'Skip Ad' button on YouTube.

So, yes, we get it: many of you work in the most horologically challenged industry on the planet, yet there's a heap of information being hurled at you inside these pages. Therefore, to aid the time-crunched reader, we have presented each commandment in two versions: latte and espresso.

The full versions are, metaphorically speaking, a luxurious latte, foaming inside a glazed ceramic cup, to be consumed at leisure while reclining on a vintage leather sofa. At the end of every commandment comes the espresso version: its essence distilled into a short, sharp hit. Two minutes, and you'll get the gist; you'll have enough to explain to your boss or your team what the core ideas and key takeaways are.

Plus, at Contagious, we've got a few tricks up our sleeve – frameworks, tools, and diagrams that will help you take the insights from a commandment and put them to work in your own business. Keep an eye out for those throughout the book.

PART ONE
CREATING A CULTURE

HAVE AN ORGANIZING PRINCIPLE

According to a much higher authority than the mere mortals writing this book, commandments are not necessarily a place to get fancy. 'Thou shalt not kill' isn't exactly digging deep for rules about comportment, is it? Thus, our first commandment is both blatantly obvious and incredibly important. Before doing anything else, you must understand why your company exists in the world.

As Jack Ma, founder of Chinese e-commerce giant Alibaba, wrote to shareholders in a 2017 letter, 'We have responsibilities beyond business results. When I started Alibaba eighteen years ago, my partners and I asked ourselves not how to build a successful company, but why we want to build this company in the first place.' The mission that grew out of that conversation – to make it easier to do business anywhere – has enabled smart, adaptive decision-making in pursuit of long-term success in a fast-evolving world.

Within your organization you may have your own term for this. Maybe you call it a 'North Star' or a 'purpose' or the 'big idea' or a 'mission statement' or your 'why'. Maybe you have a poster tacked up next to your computer monitor with a numbered list of company values. At Contagious, we like the term 'organizing principle'.

We're not dogmatic about this phrase, by any means, but it does have a few helpful attributes. It doesn't have the automatic association with social good that the word 'purpose' does. It doesn't drag people into mechanical sales conversations like 'why' often can. It doesn't reek of jargon like 'North Star'. Instead, it's direct and clear about what it does: your organizing principle is a thesis around which your company or brand can radiate and rally. It is a central belief that drives everything you do, from internal policies to external communications.

Feel free to mentally substitute your term for 'organizing principle' throughout. We reckon it will still be relevant. But also don't hesitate to ditch yours and think in terms of an organizing principle. We think you'll like the way it works.

WE EXIST TO NOT SELL YOU THINGS

Organizing principle, literally writ large, became an audacious message against Black Friday, the day-long festival of shopping that American capitalism has given the world, in 2011. There, right on the front section of *The New York Times*, was a full-page ad by outdoor-clothing manufacturer Patagonia. 'DON'T BUY THIS JACKET', screamed the headline, accompanied by a picture of the brand's best-selling R2 fleece. The copy below the jacket explained how our modern consumption culture is depleting the Earth's resources, and detailed the effect this particular item of clothing has on the environment: how each one produced needs 135 litres of water, and generates twenty-four times its final weight in carbon dioxide emissions.

The stark words didn't come without a call to action though. Patagonia took the opportunity to explain its Common Threads Initiative, with the programme's five Rs (Reduce, Repair, Reuse, Recycle, Reimagine) detailing a pact between the company and its customers, to work in tandem to move towards 'a world where we take only what nature can replace'.

Common Threads launched in September of that year, when

Patagonia and eBay debuted a resale website where people could buy pre-owned Patagonia clothing and gear. Once customers made the pact, the brand would elevate their attempts to find new homes for their gear through a special auction section on eBay. Patagonia's VP of environmental affairs and communication, Rick Ridgeway, introduced the site's aims, and the partnership with eBay, echoing eBay CEO John Donahoe's statement: 'The greenest product is the one that already exists.'

It was a stunningly bold step for a manufacturer to tell people not to make unnecessary purchases of its products, especially during the feeding frenzy of Black Friday. But the Common Threads Initiative follows on from Patagonia's long list of environmental programmes and promises. It managed to pull off this initiative by proving its dedication to the cause, which resonated with its outdoorsy, environmentally aware consumers. According to Bloomberg's Kyle Stock, 'In 2012 – which included about nine months of the "buy less" marketing – Patagonia sales increased almost one-third, to $543 million, as the company opened fourteen more stores. Last year [2013], revenue ticked up another 6 per cent, to $575 million. In short, the pitch helped crank out $158 million worth of new apparel.' Ironic, to be sure, but one hopes those sales came at the expense of less environmentally focused competitors.

This isn't a shallow corporate social responsibility campaign, or a cynical publicity grab. Patagonia is causing change in communities through activism by encouraging its customers – which it refers to as 'constituents' – to consume less, to be more conscientious of what they buy, and even elect individuals to help bring this about at a governmental policy level, with a 'Vote the Environment' push designed to help people choose local policies that are environmentally friendly. Over forty years, by tearing apart its business multiple times, the company has developed a stronger philosophical core. It wants to be a transformative force.

Patagonia has found an organizing principle. A central belief. A powerful perspective that goes way beyond a charitable donation or a single campaign. *This is the reason it exists.*

'Whenever companies tell you what their mission statement is, you can kind of see the ennui in their eyes,' Ridgeway says. 'Patagonia's different, because the mission guides the business. And it guides me, on a short- and long-term basis, to make the decisions I make. It really is the reason the company succeeds.'

That mission statement? 'Build the best product, cause no unnecessary harm, use business to inspire and implement solutions to the environmental crisis.'

With this organizing principle in hand, Patagonia can go about its business in the world with confidence that it's staying true to itself and not starting down garden paths. In the past few years the brand has:

// launched a $20 million investment fund to support responsible and like-minded start-ups bringing positive change to the environment.
// created a beer, under its Patagonia Provisions label, that is made using Kernza, a grain that doesn't require pesticides, uses less water than wheat, and 'acts like a sponge for carbon', according to label head Birgit Cameron.
// announced it would give people store credit in exchange for their used Patagonia clothing, which the brand would then wash (in an eco-friendly waterless process), repair, and resell at low prices.
// led the charge of outdoor apparel companies to pull a lucrative annual conference out of the state of Utah after the state's government failed to support the protection of Bears Ears National Monument.
// posted a call to action titled 'The President Stole Your Land' after President Trump rolled back federal recognition of 85 per cent of the Bears Ears lands, and announced that the company would sue Trump in court, stating: 'Protecting public lands is a core tenet of our mission.'

Is Patagonia a venture capital company? A brewery? A thrift store? A lobbyist? A protest organizer? In some ways, it's all of the above. At its core, though, it remains an outdoor-apparel brand. But because the brand's clear organizing principle is understood both internally and externally, none of these efforts strikes us as out of place. It all makes sense. Companies with strong philosophical (and often ethical) foundations are able to develop bold ideas that would make their competitors' sales pitches shrink. An organizing principle gives ideas, and brands, their spine.

START WITH WHY

The power of having a clear understanding of not just what you do but why you do it isn't a new or novel concept, of course. Chances are you've heard Simon Sinek's TED Talk, the third most viewed talk in TED's history, or read one of his enlightening books on the concept of 'starting with why'.

'People don't buy what you do, they buy why you do it,' says Sinek. 'Very, very few people or organizations know why they do what they do. And by *why* I don't mean "to make a profit". That's a result. It's always a result. By *why*, I mean: What's your purpose? What's your cause? What's your belief? Why does your organization exist? Why do you get out of bed in the morning? And why should anyone care? As a result, the way we think, we act, the way we communicate is from the outside in, it's obvious. We go from the clearest thing to the fuzziest thing. But the inspired leaders and the inspired organizations – regardless of their size, regardless of their industry – all think, act and communicate from the inside out.'

This inside-out thinking is a powerful concept that can't be overstated, especially for those tasked with communicating the value of a brand to a broad audience. By peeling back the layers of *what* a brand is or *what* consumers want, eventually we get to *why* a brand exists and *why* consumers choose them. Marketers should be like a curious child, asking 'why' over and over until they uncover universal truths (or drive their parents/bosses to madness).

Asking why, and drilling down to root causes, is key to unlocking insights about your brand and about your customers. And by combining those insights to create a holistic yet simple picture of why your brand exists in the lives of its customers, you can drill down to an organizing principle that will drive your marketing from the inside out. From the foundation of an organizing principle you can build both impactful social good campaigns (see Bayer's HeroSmiths box on pages 25–6) and light-hearted stunts with equal success. With an organizing principle at its core, an idea gives employees, suppliers, partners, and customers alike a reason to believe.

An organizing principle forces you to examine your priorities, take a position, and plant a flag in the ground. As legendary ad man and DDB co-founder Bill Bernbach summed it up: 'If you stand for something, you will always find some people for you and some against you. If you stand for nothing, you will find nobody against you, and nobody for you.'

A TALE OF TWO BRANDS: UBER VS LYFT

We recently saw a neatly packaged side-by-side display of organizing principles as differentiating factors. Uber and Lyft had established themselves as the clubhouse leaders in the competitive ride-sharing space, with Uber a fair bit ahead of the pack. On the expertise and reliability side of things, the two brands were virtually identical. Both services delivered on-demand rides with connected navigation and payment consistently in cities around the world.

But *why* do the two brands do what they do? Let's take a look at their stated missions:

Uber: *Transportation as reliable as running water, everywhere and for everyone*

Lyft: *To reconnect people through transportation and bring communities together*

Slightly different, no? And while neither is inherently 'better' than the other, these missions give each brand a unique perspective on events and a unique position in the eyes of potential customers. Essentially, these organizing principles help people choose between two very similar brands. And they give people within the brands easy access to a lens through which to make decisions quickly.

This was illustrated in January 2017, when President Trump announced an apparently racially motivated ban on travellers from seven nations entering the US. Protesters stormed JFK airport in New York, and the yellow taxi cab drivers went on strike in solidarity. Uber and Lyft had a decision to make. Reaching into their back pockets and pulling out their handy organizing principles, they made different decisions. Lyft stopped car services at the airport. Uber turned off its surge pricing and asked passengers to be patient if wait times were extended, an action many interpreted as strike-breaking.

The backlash was quick and ruthless. On social media, a movement under the hashtag #deleteuber erupted, encouraging people to delete the app, which a reported 200,000 people did, punishing the brand for its misaligned mission. Lyft, sensing an opportunity to double down on its own mission, published an open letter and donated $1 million to the American Civil Liberties Union. 'We created Lyft to be a model for the type of community we want our world to be: diverse, inclusive, and safe,' wrote founders John Zimmer and Logan Green.

In February, the month following the movement, Lyft registered a 7 per cent uptick in its customer base, largely driven by users fleeing Uber. It was a stark example of the way an organizing principle can resonate.

As Ben Boyd, president of practices and sectors at communications marketing agency Edelman, told us: 'First-mover advantage and scale can create inoculation for a period of time, but eventually trust trumps convenience.' Eventually, people pick the brand with the organizing principle they relate to.

Uber, of course, wasn't killed by the deletion movement. The service retains a sizeable lead over its competition, attracts plenty of venture capital and continues to grow. But later the same year it also fired its founder/CEO and went to great pains to rehabilitate its image as a company. Perhaps a sign that it's wising up to the importance of principles – or fear that the next movement could hurt even more.

THE BENEFIT OF 'ORGANIZING PRINCIPLE'

Another brand that has nailed the value of an organizing principle is Volvo. The brand is often cited as a marketing success for its ownership of the word safety in the minds of consumers. But Volvo's organizing principle actually takes the idea of keeping people safe a step further. Their mantra? 'Everything We Do Starts with People.'

It's an interesting organizing principle for a car brand, given that it doesn't mention anything about speed, luxury, style, transportation, or even cars. Instead, it reminds both those working for the company and its customers that Volvo is a company committed to the safety of people, brought to life through its cars. As far back as its founding in 1927, this commitment has been a part of the brand's DNA. 'Cars are driven by people,' wrote co-founders Assar Gabrielsson and Gustaf Larson. 'The guiding principle behind everything we make at Volvo, therefore, is – and must remain – safety.' In fact, the pair started the company because foreign cars were not safe enough for Sweden's narrow, twisting, and often-snowy roads.

After briefly losing focus – for example, regrettably billing its 2011 S60 as 'the naughty Volvo' – the brand recentred itself around its more staid messaging. It brought its people first, cars second principle back to the forefront in 2013, highlighting Volvo's role in keeping people safe. Intoned one advertisement: 'Some say cars are all about going fast, some say cars are all about looking cool. They aren't wrong. But our main passion is to help our drivers and their loved ones to live longer.'

Although automobiles remain Volvo's primary focus, this sort of organizing principle allows the brand to pivot as the automotive landscape shifts. Take, for example, its partnership with Swedish start-up Albedo100 to create a product called LifePaint, a paint product that sprays on clear but reflects brightly when hit with light. The paint, initially designed to help drivers avoid reindeer on dark Nordic highways, became Volvo's offering to the cycling community, with the brand aiming to minimize collisions between cars and cyclists in London.

Introduced with an online video and distributed for free from six London bike shops over a weekend in March, LifePaint was a hit. 'In the first hour we hit nearly 1 million visitors on our site,' Hollie Newton, the creative director at Grey London who worked on the campaign, told Contagious. 'Every single can disappeared in under seventy-two hours. And people were selling it on eBay.' Now Grey is working on rolling out LifePaint across global markets, including the US, Germany and South Africa. Having such a strong perspective on the brand's purpose, and its role in consumer lives, allows Volvo to be creative in how it reaches people around the world.

Australian vodka brand 42Below positions itself as the purest vodka in the world, thanks to its source: pure, soft New Zealand spring water. Organizing around that idea, the brand found an intriguing way to communicate with consumers very close to the point of purchase – in pub toilets. Working with Botanical Distillery and communications agency Colenso BBDO, the Bacardi-owned brand gathered up used lemon slices from the bottom of Martini glasses around the country and turned them into soap, aptly called Recycled Lemons Eco Soap. The liquid soap was then bottled and distributed for customers' use and sachets were handed out with drinks.

Along with the soap, 42Below published amusing messages about how the substance tied back to the brand's core organizing principle of purity. Read one verbiage-packed coaster:

> As you know, we're on a small rock hurtling through space and we've only got the one, so stuffing it up would be quite a problem, especially for us at 42Below. Why? Because we make the purest vodka on the planet, so if anyone sullies our little island paradise with their filthy emissions and pollution, our vodka might start tasting terrible, like gin. But we're not going to let that happen. Because from now on, as well as making super tasty vodka, we're doing some planet-saving hippie eco-stuff. We're taking all the leftover bits of lemon from the drinks in this bar and recycling them to create 42Below Recycled Cocktail Lemons Eco Soap, which means when you drink 42Below you won't just look cool (if you're already cool looking), but you'll smell good, and feel good, as well as totally save the planet and all mankind. Bit of an overpromise you say? This is marketing, you can't lie. 42Below. Keeping our planet pure to keep our vodka pure.

According to the agency, over 10,000 kilograms of lemons were recycled into 21,000 bottles of soap. The campaign reached 42.5 million people globally, and sparked a 20 per cent sales increase of 42Below in bars.

BRING YOUR ORGANIZING PRINCIPLE TO WORK

One of our favourite examples of organizing principle brilliance comes from Mars's billion-dollar pet food brand, Pedigree.

Legendary ad man Lee Clow – perhaps best known for earning the trust of oft-curmudgeonly control freak Steve Jobs when it came to Apple's advertising – identified a very simple organizing principle for Pedigree while working with the brand at TBWA\Chiat\Day: 'Dogs Rule.' Not 'Pedigree food is better than the rest' (dog food, after all, is a heavily commodified category). Not 'Your dog loves us.' Quite the opposite: we love dogs. Dogs rule.

The realization and statement caused a stark shift at Pedigree, which up to that point hadn't even allowed employees to bring their dogs to work. It caused the brand to re-evaluate not only its messaging but also its entire way of doing business.

'We're for dogs,' a Pedigree campaign intoned soon after. 'Some people are for the whales. Some are for the trees. We're for dogs. The big ones and the little ones, the guardians and the comedians, the pure breeds and the mutts. We're for walks, runs and romps. Digging, scratching, sniffing and fetching. We're for dog parks, dog doors and dog days. If there were an international day for dogs, to celebrate their contribution to the quality of life on earth, we'd be for that too. Because we're for dogs.'

Since Clow's realization in 2005, Pedigree's organizing principle has evolved slightly, but the core idea stays the same. Today on their website you'll see the statement that resembles Volvo's mission, 'Everything we do is for the love of dogs.' Pedigree is an advocate for all things dog, an idea that moves the brand beyond the sale of pet food and expands its mission to include things like dog adoption drives and games to teach kids how to play safely with dogs. In Pedigree's world, having a four-legged friend in your life is unequivocally a good thing, and anything the brand can do to make that possible is in bounds.

This core idea allows the brand free rein to execute interesting campaigns and initiatives only tangentially tied to the sale of pet food. A few of our recent favourites:

// Found, an app that uses geo-targeted display ads on mobile phones to reunite owners with their lost dogs.

// Doggelganger, an adoption website that matched photos of people with shelter dogs who look like them, playing on the idea that dogs often look like their owners.

// K9FM, a New Zealand radio station designed to entertain lonely dogs while their owners are out of the house.

// The Pedigree Adoption Drive, which has donated millions of dollars to dog shelters and rescue organizations.

// A Brazilian Tinder campaign proving that men with dogs are more likely to be marked as attractive than men without dogs.

// SelfieStix, an attachment that allows owners to clip a dog treat directly above their phone's camera, ensuring attentive pups and therefore better selfies.

// The Child Replacement Programme, a tongue-in-cheek campaign urging New Zealand parents whose kids have recently left for university to replace their offspring with a dog.

Like the Patagonia examples given earlier, these campaigns are wildly diverse in platform, content, audience, and execution. But because they all tie back to that central tenet – being fundamentally dedicated to dogs – they enable Pedigree to present a consistent front to users, no matter where or how they encounter the brand.

FINDING A BROADCAST SIGNAL

Principles that are truly believed throughout organizations enable brands to play different roles in the same market. Rather than a cacophony of noise about who makes the best pair of shoes or shorts, you end up with Nike speaking to the motivated athletes, Adidas to culture creators, Rapha to cycling die-hards. And in categories where organizing principles aren't well defined, brand identities often fade away.

Take, for example, the beer category. Remember that clichéd ad we mentioned in the intro? Beer brands are some of the biggest spenders of advertising money, but it's a wildly commoditized sector at the same time. That's the situation Colenso BBDO – the same agency responsible for some of Pedigree's most off-the-wall work – had with DB Export, a New Zealand brewery and one of Heineken's brands. 'They didn't really have an established brand history. In terms of advertising, they had been doing quite a bit of superficial, stereotypical beer advertising – think beaches, parties and so on,' says Paul Courtney, Colenso BBDO's chief operating officer.

To find DB Export's reason for being, Courtney and his team studied the brewery's founder, inventor Morton Coutts. A bit of an eccentric, Coutts built his own X-ray machine at age twelve and became the first person to broadcast a radio signal across the equator at thirteen, according to DB Export. Turning to slightly more inebriating pursuits, Coutts took over the family brewery and invented what he called the continuous fermentation system – a brewing system where ingredients are added to one end and beer extracted from the other, with fermentation happening in between.

'While a lot of the time brands are looking forward, sometimes the answer is in your history. That's just brand building 101 – know where you come from,' says Courtney. Drawing on Coutts's legacy, the agency launched a new positioning for DB Export: Made By Doing. 'You know that point when you're sitting around with your friends over a few beers and you say: "We should make this happen" or "We can change the world" and everyone's full of enthusiasm?' asks Courtney. 'Our brand stands for the ones that go on and do it.'

MADE BY BREWING

In May 2015 DB Export launched its first campaign under the Made by Doing tagline – an ambitious product, of sorts, called Brewtroleum. Says Courtney, 'One of the team landed on one brewery in the States that turns beer waste into biofuel and we thought that was pretty genius. We knew it had been done on a small scale but never on a broader scale or in New Zealand, and we started looking at ways to make it happen.'

Partnering with New Zealand petroleum company Gull, DB Export created a biofuel using ethanol derived from yeast left over after the brewing process. The fuel emits 8 per cent less carbon than traditional petroleum, delivers the same performance, and can be used in all petrol engines. And after hundreds of calls, Colenso BBDO was able to rig up what Courtney calls 'a beautiful supply chain', from brewery to distiller to fuel company to car.

With Gull as a partner, DB Export cooked up a whopping 300,000 litres of Brewtroleum and sold it at all sixty Gull stations around New Zealand's North Island. The brewer ran TV and digital ads, calling on people to drink DB Export and 'save the world', by keeping a steady stream of brewery waste products flowing into that beautiful supply chain. Drinkers also got a discount on the fuel when purchasing DB Export beer.

In a declining category, the new alignment with a noteworthy cause – backed up with some pretty substantive innovation and creativity – resulted in a 10 per cent sales increase for the brand, according to the agency. Since then, the brand has adapted the campaign to have a more serious and educational tone, and has sold subsequent batches of Brewtroleum around New Zealand.

LIGHTNING IN A BOTTLE

Sensing they had a hit on their hands with the Made by Doing organizing principle, DB Export and Colenso BBDO doubled down on the strategy the following year, with a campaign dubbed the Beer Bottle Sand Machine.

Did you know that construction-grade sand is a much sought-after resource in this great world of ours? And that modern-day sand mafias are slowly robbing beaches and riverbeds around the world? Vince Beiser, writing in *The New York Times*, describes the global wreckage being wrought by our insatiable thirst for sand to make materials like concrete:

In India, river sand mining is disrupting ecosystems, killing countless fish and birds. In Indonesia, some two dozen small islands are believed to have disappeared since 2005 because of sand mining. In Vietnam, miners have torn up hundreds of acres of forest to get at the sandy soil underneath. Sand miners have damaged coral reefs in Kenya and undermined bridges in Liberia and Nigeria. Environmentalists tie sand dredging in San Francisco Bay to the erosion of nearby beaches.

We had no idea – until DB Export brought it up, at least.

The brewery, again working with Colenso BBDO, created a machine that instantly turns empty beer bottles into sand substitute. It sounds like science fiction: when a bottle is inserted, a laser triggers a wheel of tiny steel hammers, which reduce the vessel to tiny glass particles in just five seconds. Then, a vacuum system removes silica dust and plastic labels, leaving behind 200 grams of sand substitute. Designed for easy transportation between bars and events, the machines weigh just 300 kilos and are two metres tall.

Once the sand substitute is created, it's shipped off to Drymix, New Zealand's biggest producer of bagged concrete, which struck a two-year deal to sell a DB Export branded 'eco-concrete' through New Zealand's biggest home-improvement retailer. Plus, Beer Bottle Sand is being supplied to national road-building projects, commercial and residential construction, and even golf bunkers, reducing the country's dependence on beach-derived sand.

Executing this kind of campaign fulfils DB Export's mission of bringing crazy, late-night, at-least-two-sheets-to-the-wind ideas to life. It gives the brand an organizing principle in the world beyond selling beer and making money. And it gives consumers a reason to pay attention to the brand, to believe in its identity and to reach for it on the shelf.

Did you know that there are 2.44 million people in the United States with the last name Smith? Or that, on average, someone in the US has a heart attack every forty-two seconds? Pharmaceutical company Bayer, which owns the trademark for Aspirin, took those two seemingly unrelated facts and combined them to create a campaign dubbed The HeroSmiths.

Aspirin has been shown to mitigate the effects of a heart attack if chewed while the attack is occurring. Having one on hand can literally be a life-saver. So Bayer, whose organizing principle is 'Science For A Better Life', decided to target the most common last name in the country and encourage people with the surname Smith to carry Aspirin at all times, giving them the chance to help someone in the future.

During the first portion of the campaign, 1,800 Smiths, all living in the town of Fort Smith, Arkansas (which has a high rate of both the name Smith and heart attacks), were given a 'HeroSmith' kit, containing a coupon for Bayer Aspirin and a branded carrying case. Others – Smith or not – could pledge online to carry Aspirin and receive a case of their own in return. An inspiring film led the campaign for the brand.

Says Larry Gies, chief strategy officer of Energy BBDO, who developed the campaign, 'The primary objective was to expand the brand's relevance, and that meant making sure people knew about the life-saving power of Aspirin. It's something that can obviously have a dramatic effect on your life if you are able to prevent or mitigate the effects of a heart attack while it's happening. It was about making Aspirin more relevant, but also making sure that more people know what Aspirin can do.'

BUILDING AN ORGANIZING PRINCIPLE

Every year at Contagious, we conduct something called the Genius Survey. The concept is simple: we approach top marketers, business experts, founders, and academics across Europe, Asia, Africa, and the Americas and ask them a single question: what is the biggest challenge facing businesses over the next twelve months? It's a fascinating peek at what people at the top of their respective games are thinking about. And almost every year it's a reminder that most businesses face similar challenges, no matter what their sector, geography or size.

In 2017 the answer to this question rang loud and clear: businesses need to earn back consumer trust. Rachel Botsman, an author and lecturer at Oxford University's Saïd Business School, has written extensively about collaborative consumption and trust. She highlighted systemic changes in the way trust is built, telling us:

> Trust underpins so much of our lives, so many of our transactions, it's vital we understand the changed mechanics of building it. Technology is rewriting the rules and creating what I call 'distributed trust', trust that works across huge networks of people, organizations and intelligent machines. Blockchain technologies, for example, allow people who might otherwise not trust one another, to transfer huge assets directly and transparently, and without mediation from a third party such as a lawyer or bank.
>
> Or take the rise of crowdfunding, social media, peer-to-peer lending, Massive Open Online Courses (MOOCs) and dozens of other person-to-person agreements that bypass traditional middlemen. They all point to the same profound shift: we've stopped trusting institutions, yet started trusting strangers. It means the old conventions of how trust is built, managed, lost and repaired – in brands, leaders, entire systems – are being turned on their head.

We'll examine more closely how important building and protecting trust is for brands in the ninth commandment, where we talk about making trust sacred. But a similar flip may also be happening in how organizing principles are built, with mission statements driven as much by a brand's consumers as by brands on their own. Obviously, not every brand will rely on its customer base to tell it what to believe – in fact, that may be unwise for the majority of brands – but for some, it can be revelatory.

SHARED PRINCIPLES

Take, for example, Airbnb. In talking about shifts in reputation-building, Botsman asked somewhat rhetorically, 'Why is it that people no longer trust their bank but can be persuaded to offer their house to strangers?'

For one, Airbnb relies on the masses – combined with strict vetting and insurance, of course – to build that belief in the brand. As people travel the world, staying in each other's homes, they build relationships, share advice, and leave reviews. The result is a rock-solid community built *around* a brand, but *by* its customers.

Already well established in the advertising industry thanks to his successful stint as CMO at Coca-Cola, Jonathan Mildenhall uncovered this idea when he joined Airbnb as CMO in 2014. He told us he asked the brand's co-founder, Brian Chesky, 'What is the value that you're creating in the world?' Chesky's response? 'I genuinely believe that every time I go and stay in a stranger's house, I leave as a friend. And because of that, wherever I travel, I feel a deep sense of belonging.'

BELONGING AT THE CORE

That idea of belonging quickly became Airbnb's organizing principle. The brand redesigned its logo in 2014 with references to a heart, a person, a location marker, and an 'A' for Airbnb. James Greenfield, who led the logo redesign at DesignStudio, called it 'a universal symbol of belonging'. In 2016, after a third-party review of the brand uncovered inherent biases that ran counter to the idea of belonging, Airbnb made a concerted effort to improve inclusion on the platform, increase diversity in its workforce, and make employees aware of unconscious biases. The brand now requires all members to sign a Community Commitment, pledging to treat all others with respect and without judgement or bias.

The realignment has been transformational for the brand and its marketing. A striking ad during the 2017 Super Bowl broadcast the mission to the world, with close-up photos of people's faces overlaid with text saying, 'We believe no matter who you are, where you're from, who you love, or who you worship, we all belong. The world is more beautiful the more you accept.'

Rather than coming across as hollow in a time when many brands felt forced to take a stand for social causes, the sentiment felt natural because the mission is fundamentally tied to the product's success. 'A lot of brands can be purpose-driven, but acceptance is in the core principles of the business,' says Tony Högqvist, Airbnb's executive creative director. 'If you close doors, if you don't accept people, our business will not grow.'

To that end, the brand continues to emphasize acceptance, belong-ing, and community. When the US loosened its Cuban embargo in 2015, Airbnb paid for travellers' stays in its properties for a week to celebrate. An initiative called Open Homes allows hosts to offer their spaces for free to people in need in times of tragedy or emergency. When people of colour identified bias on the platform using the hashtag #airbnbwhileblack, the company responded with policies, features and training to prevent discrim-ination. And as the company expands on its core service with offerings like Trips, wherein people can book local experiences around activities rather than lodging, Airbnb is leaning on its organizing principle of belonging, relying on community members to connect with travellers. In June of 2017 it announced a €5 million Community Tourism fund to preserve local trad-itions and landmarks through non-profits, charities, and community groups.

'I've had the privilege of working for lots of highly popular brands, but I've never experienced a company whose mission is so clearly articulated,' James Goode, managing director of Airbnb's in-house creative team, told Contagious about the principle's influence inside the brand. 'I understand that mission, I understand how that relates to the business, I understand how it relates to the user, I understand how it relates to the community of hosts. I can get behind it and it's something I can use to guide my daily work.'

FINDING YOUR JACKET

Organizing principles need not grow directly from the core product your brand offers. A final case study illustrates a perhaps more inten-tional method of determining an organizing principle, although the outcome still results in warm fuzzies. The Bank of Åland, a small Finn-ish bank in the centre of the Baltic Sea region, faced a problem familiar to many other banks: people didn't feel any particular affinity for it at best and didn't trust it at worst.

Mathias Wikström, CEO of the bank's ad agency, RBK Communica-tion, put it bluntly when we spoke with him in 2016: 'All key performance indicators for brands and brand attributes for banks are at an all-time low.' He joked that people were more inclined to trust gun smugglers than bankers.

To turn the tide, Åland and RBK charged themselves with this brief:

How can we position the bank with an activity well-grounded in the organizations, abilities and values that will enable communication, sense of urgency and progress? More specifically, the bank's chief administrative officer, Tove Erikslund, called Wikström and put him on the spot.

'We don't have a jacket,' said Erikslund, inspired by Patagonia's impactful Black Friday ad. 'If they [Patagonia] can take responsibility from an environmental perspective, why can't a bank do it too?' Working with the World Wildlife Fund in Sweden and Finland, the bank confirmed the market opportunity: 65 per cent of people would change banks if there were a climate-smart alternative.

For two decades, Åland had been funding environmental projects through a line of so-called 'Environmental' savings accounts. The bank pledged to match 0.2 per cent of the deposits with donations of its own money to environmental initiatives. But there wasn't a direct local tie or area of focus.

'When the client came to us, we understood that there's a huge potential here but we needed to focus on something close to Bank of Åland,' says Wikström.

CLOSE TO HOME

Looking at its customers, the bank noted a heightened awareness and concern, particularly with regard to the health of the Baltic Sea. Hoping to take a leadership position on an issue of importance to its target market, while simultaneously establishing a new organizing principle and raison d'être for the bank, Åland founded the Baltic Sea Project, funding great ideas to enact change in the Baltic Sea, inspiring and enabling passionate change-makers in small projects around the region and positioning the brand as a partner.

'We made it easier for people to submit their ideas and get them funded. We didn't want to say "Bank of Åland is saving the Baltic Sea", we wanted to say, "Let's save the Baltic Sea together",' says Wikström. Beyond simply funding others to do the work as part of a single campaign (two examples of one-off purpose marketing are featured in the boxed sections of this chapter), Åland looked for ways to bake the organizing principle into the DNA of how the bank did business.

'From a brand perspective we wanted to raise awareness, establish Åland as a player and position it as a responsible, personal and ambitious brand. We wanted to come up with something that corresponds with those values,' says Wikström. 'From a business perspective it was about establishing a stronger position in the marketplace and putting the company on top of people's minds.'

To emphasize its environmental focus, Bank of Åland introduced a biodegradable credit card, dubbed the Baltic Sea Card, replacing the plastic chip cards for select accounts. 'We wanted to create consumer engagement on a level that every time people open their wallets to pay for something, they would be reminded about their environmental responsibilities for everyday actions,' says Wikström. Mastercard, which partnered with the bank on the cards, even agreed to put its logo on the back, to let the message stand alone on the front. The card was such a hit that the bank soon made it the default for all accounts.

ÅLAND AS ALLY

On top of that, Åland realized it could use its unique position as a financial institution to help customers make decisions more closely aligned with their values. To that end, Bank of Åland worked with KPMG's sustainability consulting division and Mastercard to develop the Åland Index, a report card of sorts that ties financial transactions to environmental impacts, calculating a carbon cost for each credit-card user. Åland customers receive their monthly carbon footprint along with their credit-card bill, and are encouraged to offset this environmental impact by making changes in their consumption and behaviour or by donating the estimated carbon footprint amount to a local or global environmental initiative.

Not only that, the brand has put its money where its mouth is, open sourcing the index so that other banks can adopt it if they so choose. Says Wikström:

You can also say that we did it for protection. One way to protect your idea is to give it away, when you are smaller than many of your competitors. There is no better way of protecting the Åland Index than opening it to everyone else. This is also in line with the ambition of the client in general. If we are going to create change, we need to collaborate.

The campaign – and the brand's new organizing principle – was a hit, resulting in a 186 per cent increase in brand awareness, a 14.6 per cent year-over-year increase in environmental savings account deposits, and an invitation to present at the UN. The Åland Index was launched as a mandatory case study in the Stockholm School of Economics by Sweden's minister for financial markets and consumption. And the bank drew enough corporate interest that it is developing business accounts, which it previously didn't offer.

AGILE LONG-TERMISM

Beyond simply offering a guiding light for your company and brand, an organizing principle enables what we like to call 'agile long-termism', a mindset and operating framework that are essential to succeeding in the modern world. Agile long-termism means keeping your eyes on the prize, but being adaptive and flexible in the short term. Think of yourself as the driver of a car. You set out with a destination in mind, but along the way you may slow down in treacherous conditions, stop to refuel, or swerve to avoid an accident. The end goal never changes, and you react to stimuli along the way in a manner you believe will best get you there. That is agile long-termism.

Keeping a long-term focus has never been harder. You're perhaps familiar with the so-called 'Marshmallow Test', first administered by Walter Mischel at Stanford in the late 1960s. In the experiment, a child is left alone in a room with a single marshmallow and told that they can either eat it immediately or hold out until the experimenter returns, at which point they'll receive a second marshmallow. Companies face this same test of willpower regularly: we decide whether to harvest short-term gains or maintain a longer horizon with the potential of increased gains in the future. And to make matters worse, shareholders often play the role of devil, sitting on our shoulder yelling about short-term priorities.

This is a poisonous environment. 'The Economic Implications of Corporate Financial Reporting', a 2004 study by the National Bureau of Economic Research, found that 78 per cent of executives – nearly four in five – admit to sacrificing long-term value to smooth earnings. Despite knowing that it will damage their company in the long-run, CEOs and CFOs trim back R&D and innovation budgets, skimp on marketing, and delay starting new projects in order to pacify the shareholders. They take their marshmallow and feed it to a stranger who owns stock.

Smart companies understand this trap. Back in 2004, when filing for IPO, Google's founders Larry Page and Sergey Brin called out the long-term/short-term tension explicitly. 'Outside pressures too often tempt companies to sacrifice long-term opportunities to meet quarterly market expectations,' they wrote. 'Sometimes this pressure has caused companies to manipulate financial results in order to "make their quarter". In Warren Buffett's words, "We won't 'smooth' quarterly or annual results: If earnings figures are lumpy when they reach headquarters, they will be lumpy when they reach you."'

No surprise that Alphabet, Google's parent company, is one of the most valuable companies in the world.

'Our business environment changes rapidly and needs long-term investment,' wrote Brin and Page later in that same letter. It's a sentiment that appears oxymoronic. If a landscape is constantly changing, long-term planning seems almost foolhardy. But in reality, it's the only way to survive. Build a vehicle that will withstand and adjust to bumps in the road, while driving straight on toward a steady destination.

SYSTEM ONE AND SYSTEM TWO

In *Thinking, Fast and Slow*, behavioural economist Daniel Kahneman describes two systems operating in our brains, creatively named System One and System Two. System One makes quick, small, instinctual decisions almost like a reflex. System Two, on the other hand, makes a more limited number of careful, considered decisions. Every day these systems coordinate to help us navigate the world.

The same should be true of your company. System Two thinking is your organizing principle – a well-thought-out and fully articulated mission that need not be revisited and revised regularly. System One is your day-to-day decision-making brain, which reacts and responds quickly and confidently to whatever challenges may arise. System One is guided by System Two. As Kahneman described in an Edge master class in 2011, '[System Two] is like an editor who has a quick look at the copy that's coming in from [System One], and sends it to the printer.'

Marketers play tug of war daily between long-term brand building and short-term sales goals. But thinking of these two goals not as competing with but as complementary to each other is a powerful mindset shift. As the CMO of an e-commerce giant recently said in a Contagious work session, the fact that some marketers still see sales as an unrelated silo and not an integral part of their job is crazy.

WALK THE LONG WALK

Defining an organizing principle is very different from actually living it in your company every day, at all levels of your organization. As Nick Worthington, creative chairman at Colenso BBDO, told Contagious, 'It's easy for those of us who lead and are aware of these values to assume that everybody is aware of them and what they mean . . . You have to reinforce these values constantly. You have to use them on a daily basis.'

More than simply talking about company values or slapping them on a poster, leadership must establish measurable goals against their long-term organizing principle. Without long-term goals, marketers often default to the closest and easiest metrics, chasing shiny objects or short-term needle fluctuations rather than maintaining a steady course.

'Unless the marketer has a very clear idea of what their campaign intends to achieve, it's all too easy to fall back on the short term and driving sales,' Nigel Hollis, chief global analyst at Millward Brown, told Contagious.

Matt Edgar, the head of design at NHS Digital in the UK, compares it to looking at the moon in the night sky but becoming distracted by the clouds rushing in front of it. While the moon appears stationary compared with the clouds, in fact it is moving more than 2,000 miles an hour while the clouds crawl at a slower comparative pace. Similarly, we are distracted by short-term results that seem more pressing and important, letting them obscure the much more important and weighty long-term brand building we aspire to do. As Edgar says:

> Short-termism is a broad trend across business, but it is especially acute with marketing because of the delusion, perpetuated by digital thinking, that we can achieve everything we need to in an instant. This simply results in transient sales effects, not embedded sustainable change. Our best hope is that the current mood change towards digital channels and metrics will bring about a renewed respect for traditional channels and metrics, which have been proven to deliver long-term growth.

ON THAT LONG WALK, BE READY TO SIDESTEP OBSTACLES

Long term, long term, long term. But also: short term. Paradoxical, we know. But, of course, businesses cannot survive without short-term successes and must react to a changing environment. Remember the car analogy? When we come across a road closure, we must find alternative routes, taking a detour from the planned path, even though the final destination remains constant.

This is adaptive thinking, defined by James W. Lussier and colleagues at the US Army Research Institute for Behavioral and Social Sciences as 'the cognitive behavior of an officer who is confronted by unanticipated circumstances during the execution of a planned military operation'. Ditch the military ideas and you're left with a fairly common business challenge. We make plans, and unexpected problems arise, forcing us to adapt on the fly.

Writing in the *Harvard Business Review*, Lindsay McGregor and Neel Doshi talk about their work studying this sort of adaptive thinking. They asked 2,823 Americans if they had the ability to find new ways of working in their day-to-day jobs. A mere 27 per cent said yes.

It's easy to see how that happens. It's tempting to solidify an organizing principle by establishing a set of rules and best practices to guide every decision made in your company, locking in a way of thinking and acting that is absolute. In reality, though, your organizing principle should be articulated well enough to serve as a guide that enables adaptive fast-twitch decisions based on the challenge presented. McGregor and Doshi use the example of a call centre, where employees were trained to follow a script in order to resolve customer questions and complaints. To test the power of adaptive thinking, they took an experiment group from the call centre and implemented a number of new measures: weekly problem-solving meetings, co-location with management, focus on skill-building (rather than deficiency identification), and regular performance reflection.

'The change in performance was observable. Within four months, our pilot teams had more than doubled the close rates of the other teams. The pilot team made more adjustments to their approach, and members shared what worked more proactively with colleagues . . . Maintaining great performance over the long term will require organizations to also emphasize adaptive performance,' write McGregor and Doshi.

FLY SLOWLY, ADJUST QUICKLY

In 1976, aviation pioneer Paul MacCready set his sights on something called the Kremer Prize, which offered £50,000 to anyone who could complete a flight on a figure-eight-shaped course more than a mile long using a human-powered aircraft. Where previous competitors attempted the course in wooden aeroplanes designed for height and speed, MacCready took a different approach. He and his team decided to fly slow and low, prioritizing light plastic materials that could be quickly rebuilt. While other teams often took months to refigure and rebuild their planes after a failed attempt or crash, MacCready and co. could quickly iterate after a failure and try again.

Between July 1976 and August 1977 MacCready's team attempted the course 222 times. On the 223rd attempt, pilot Bryan Allen completed the course in a plastic plane dubbed the Gossamer Condor, taking home the prize.

Like MacCready and his Gossamer Condor, companies must have an unwavering vision and explore innovative and iterative ways to reach that goal. Experiment, fail, adjust, and try again. Fly slowly, but adjust quickly.

A clear organizing principle manifests across the actions and communications of an organization, unlocks potential, enables clear decision-making, and empowers creative bravery. It gives employees a reason to be passionate. It gives customers a reason to pay attention. And it gives brands purpose beyond profit.

Figure out why your company exists. Organize around that principle. Give your employees permission to experiment and iterate in support of that principle. It's not a magic bullet, but it is a necessary step to building a brand for the long haul. Have an organizing principle, and the next nine commandments will be much more straightforward than if your brand is a rudderless ship whose direction is decided by shifting winds.

HAVE AN ORGANIZING PRINCIPLE / ESPRESSO VERSION

'We are stubborn on vision. We are flexible on details.' So said Amazon founder Jeff Bezos on a shareholder conference call in 2011. That mindset gets to the crux of an organizing principle. Companies must understand why they exist in the first place, establish that long-term vision and, in doing so, unlock the ability to be agile and adaptive in the short term. A clear organizing principle – a statement of purpose that fits on a T-shirt or can be scrawled in a few words on a postcard – becomes an evergreen guide that enables fast decisions in the short term and ongoing creativity in pursuit of long-term success.

Working with our clients at Contagious, we often point to three origination points for organizing principles: brand, team, and customers. DB Export and Airbnb looked to their brands and brand histories to identify their organizing principle, which gave them a reason to connect externally with prospective customers. Pedigree did some soul searching by looking at its team and created an organizing principle that started as a reason to believe internally about the brand's purpose. And Bank of

Åland looked to its customers to develop its organizing principle, in turn creating a reason for people to pay attention.

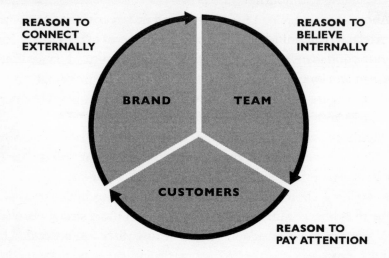

These three lenses provide a starting point for brands that feel unanchored, drifting in a sea of possibilities without a guiding light. Beyond the obvious purpose of making a profit, what does your brand actually stand for? Why was your brand founded? Why do your employees believe in the company's potential? Why do customers choose your offering over the competition?

None of these work on their own – an organizing principle must make sense for brand, employees, and customers alike in order to truly succeed. Figure out what makes your brand magic, for anyone and everyone involved.

After you've started to rough out your organizing principle, run through this checklist:

- **//** Are you conflating short-term 'purpose' with long-term principles?
- **//** Does your organizing principle feel authentic, unique, and relevant?
- **//** Are you being honest and transparent with yourself and your consumers about why and how your brand operates?

If you answer those questions correctly (no, yes, yes, if you need a cheat sheet) then you're ready to print that sucker on a T-shirt. Use it as a guide along your journey.

Above all else, having a fully articulated and clearly defined organizing principle will unlock avenues of creativity and opportunities for conversation. It gives you a reason to be brave, and a compass for both short-term and long-term decision making.

BE USEFUL, RELEVANT, AND ENTERTAINING

Once you've nailed down your organizing principle, it's time to focus on being useful, relevant and entertaining. A tree can fall in the forest *and* make a sound, but unless someone has reason to pay attention, it doesn't much matter.

Guess what? In the grand scheme of things, nobody cares about your idea. *No one*. We're sorry. It might be the best idea since the electric guitar, but when looked at from afar, the population who care even a little bit about it amounts to a rounding error.

Think of it this way: in the thirty seconds you've taken to read this far down the page, something like 8 million text messages have been sent, 2 million videos have been watched on YouTube, 500,000 swipes have been made on Tinder, and 2.5 million queries have been searched on Google. A cacophony of notification bubbles and alert vibrations pop, buzz and vie for our attention. If you're trying to share an idea across this landscape, on one hand it's great: there's a global canvas open to you. But on the other, you face a kind of option paralysis: there are many, many ways to tell your story – and many, many more ways for people to not hear it. Why would they go out of their way to hunt down your ad campaign or message?

Of course, that's a bleak way of looking at things. The silver-lining searcher would put it this way: if you can attract even a tiny fraction of people to pay attention to your idea, you're incredibly lucky and on the road to success. How do you do that? By being relevant, useful, or entertaining. Preferably all three.

DON'T BLOCK ME, BRO

From the earliest days of advertising, whether this be the soles of prostitutes' sandals in ancient Greece being imprinted with the words 'follow me' or primordial jingles played on bamboo flutes in China, marketers have relied on a single commodity: attention. Newspapers drew readers' attention through hard-hitting journalism and then sold that attention to brands wanting to hock their wares. Television programmes drew audiences' attention through entertainment and storytelling . . . and then sold that attention to brands wanting to hock their wares. Internet sites drew audiences' attention through games and communities and knowledge, cats, and boobs . . . and then sold that attention to brands wanting to hock their wares. You get the idea.

Over the last decade that attention landscape has changed dramatically, thanks largely to technology. Rather than owning captive audiences, platforms and publishers have begun renting them – and the conduits for rental have catered to their audiences by enabling them to avoid the advertising. Scott Galloway, clinical professor of marketing at the New York University Stern School of Business, describes advertising as 'the tax that poor and technically illiterate people pay'. According to a report from PageFair, use of ad-blocking software on internet browsers surged 30 per cent in 2016. Put into real numbers, there were 615 million devices blocking commercial messages at the end of 2016: that's more than the combined populations of the United States, Japan, Germany and the UK.

Most advertising is 'still based on this idea that we can buy consumers' time', says P. J. Pereira, co-founder and chief creative officer of award-winning advertising agency Pereira & O'Dell. 'That truth is no longer unbreakable.'

In 2013 Pereira & O'Dell blurred the line between advertising and entertainment for its clients Intel and Toshiba. Rather than steal inter-ruptive moments of time from people engaged with other program-ming, they put the brand in the director's chair and created their own entertainment. *The Beauty Inside*, a six-part film directed by Drake Dore-mus, launched on Facebook and YouTube, centred around a main char-acter named Alex, who woke up each morning with a different face and body. Still, no matter his outward appearance, he was the same on the inside. Armed with a Toshiba Portégé Ultrabook, he shared his story with the world. What's more, a global casting call let audience members audition to play these different versions of Alex by uploading home-made videos. Selected members were then woven into the story's fabric, becoming an integral part of the action.

In just eight and a half weeks, *The Beauty Inside* amassed nearly 70 million views. Toshiba reported a 360 per cent sales lift in the following weeks. The campaign took home three Grand Prix awards at the Cannes Lions International Festival of Creativity, the annual adver-tising awards festival, in the Film, Cyber, and Branded Content catego-ries. And what's more, *The Beauty Inside* won an Emmy for Outstanding New Approach to a Daytime Series.

'Content is becoming more and more an important part of the strategy for the client to reach out to this audience,' said Pereira of the campaign. 'They can see the difference it makes if instead of interrupt-ing consumers with a "pitch" they attract them to a lighter, but deeper message they actually enjoy.' Create content that has value on its own, instead of simply within the context of a more worthy-of-attention property, and people won't block it – in fact, they'll seek it out.

Premium services have reacted quickly to the advertising allergy that people have developed. Publishers are putting ad-free content behind paywalls. Even YouTube, the pioneer of everyone's favourite pre-roll ad format, has embraced the idea of an ad-free walled garden with YouTube Red. You won't see a traditional ad on Netflix – instead, the brand makes its moolah on subscription fees and the odd (and occa-sionally pretty darn blatant) product-placement deal.

But the insidious avoidance of your brilliant idea goes much further than installing AdBlock. As Nikki Usher Layser, an assistant media studies professor at George Washington University, told *NY Magazine*, 'We have always surrounded ourselves with people who agree with us [and] sought information we agree with, but there was at least a chance for serendipity.'

Today, thanks to the increasingly algorithmic filter bubbles that surround us, we're much more likely to see things we agree with – or that artificial intelligence thinks we'll be interested in – rather than getting an unbiased slice of the world. It becomes harder to break out of our patterns of behaviours, and we are blind to actions outside of our filter bubble. From a brand perspective, if people aren't already in your world, it's increasingly unlikely they'll accidentally find their way there.

Warning: an audience paying a subscription fee doesn't always react terribly kindly to brands being clunkily shoehorned into the narratives of their favourite shows. In May 2017 Australian viewers of *Designated Survivor* flocked onto Twitter to decry as 'cringeworthy', 'worst ever', and 'blatant' a particularly awkward seven-second sequence featuring an FBI agent firing up a carefully focused Ford app interface on her mobile phone in order to start the ignition of her gleaming car nearby in order to check the fuel level. When the action then cuts to a lingering shot of the car's dashboard, complete with AN OBVIOUS FORD LOGO, the drama suddenly feels like it's lurching directly into the visual cues of a typical TV commercial. A Subway sandwich plug on American television reboot *Hawaii Five-O* in 2012 was so ridiculous that a YouTube clip of it has racked up 1.5 million views.

FROM PULL TO PUSH

In the last decade or so we've moved from a *pull* to a *push* media culture. Contagious began in the twentieth century's mature-media paradigm: everyone watched the same television programmes, read the same newspaper and magazine articles, and experienced a narrowly outlined spectrum of passive media. Today's push culture, in contrast, has caused a decline in the default. From watching just a handful of

TV channels, people can now subscribe to millions of YouTube channels. Rather than reading their local newspaper, they opt in to niche newsletters and follow Facebook pages. Media has become fractured.

These consumers want content on their own terms. Rather than seeking out channels and asking if there's anything useful or relevant or entertaining there, we expect those pieces of content to find us when they have something worth paying attention to. As Zach Seward, executive editor of online publication *Quartz*, says, 'Pull media has quickly been replaced by push media . . . Information – status updates, photos of your friends, and sometimes even news articles – come at you; they find you.'

In order to earn that attention and get people to agree to your push, ideas must in some measure be useful, relevant or entertaining. One of those three is good. Two is better. Sometimes, an idea can be all three.

FILM IN THE FRIENDLY SKIES

In the United States, airlines consistently score low in customer satisfaction surveys. In 2014 the American Customer Satisfaction Index placed them just above the IRS, the US tax authority, in the public's affections. Put simply, people hate airlines. When carriers resort to physical force to remove innocent passengers from overbooked flights (United), or cancel thousands of flights at short notice due to a staff rotation error (Ryanair), it's easy to see why. And yet, despite this predisposition, relevant, useful ideas have brought glimmers of hope for brands in this deeply unloved sector.

One of those annoying little scenarios that spoils many a long-haul flight is when you misjudge the length of a movie, meaning you miss the end because the plane's entertainment system has to shut down during final descent. In 2016, to mark thirty-six years of partnership with the Cannes Film Festival, Air France launched a service to counter this, by allowing passengers to continue watching movies after their flight. The 'Cinema to Go' service was designed with agency BETC in Paris and was available on flights from Los Angeles (home of Hollywood) to Paris Charles de Gaulle airport for the length of the film festival. This meant customers were able to watch a selection of former Cannes award-winning films on their tablet, phone or computer after their flight.

For passengers who weren't flying from California to France, the curated Cannes selection was also available on all long-haul Air France flights throughout the festival month. By creating a valuable service that continued after the flight, Air France found a way to extend customer interaction with its brand. And choosing an LA-to-Paris route brought its Cannes Film Festival partnership to the attention of just the right people.

This idea is useful, relevant and, depending on the film chosen, entertaining as well. Usually, customer interaction with an airline ends when the customer gets off the plane. The customer journey often begins earlier, with online check-in, meal choices, and even browsing entertainment, but it rarely stretches past landing – unless the airline loses a passenger's bags. By providing a service that tackles a specific pain point in the airline customer journey – missing the last fifteen minutes of *Fast & Furious 7* – Air France has given its customers a good reason to continue interacting with its brand well past the usual cut-off point.

EMOTIONAL BAGGAGE

Earlier, in 2012, US airline Delta used another major customer pain point – losing your bag – to promote its mobile app, by including a feature whereby passengers can track the location of their luggage, from the check-in desk onwards.

In an online video to promote the app, the airline fits six cameras into a suitcase and sends it on a flight from Atlanta to New York. Along the way it passes along a series of conveyor belts; through a Transportation Security Administration scanning area (no photography allowed); and is transferred to and from the aircraft in luggage vehicles. It gets handled (carefully) by a number of airport staff and is picked up again at baggage reclaim. Within two weeks, the video had been viewed nearly 850,000 times.

The app's feature allows Delta passengers to scan their bag tag and track their luggage's status throughout the journey. It can be used during their flight, and shows where they are able to reclaim it at their destination airport. Delta's app also allows customers to check updates to flight and boarding times, check in and receive a QR-code boarding pass, view/change seats and rebook cancelled flights, as well as including a plethora of travel and airline information.

Delta's video was useful *and* entertaining. Consumers now habitually check the delivery status of everything from Amazon packages to their Domino's pizza, and baggage provides a similar timeline of real-time data. Of course, this particular feature is more about ensuring peace of mind and satisfying curiosity than providing a practical service – there's not much the app can do once your bag has boarded the wrong flight. But alongside the genuine utility of checking in and changing seats via smartphone, there's a lot of incentive for passengers to download the app – especially if they're frequent flyers.

'The only source of sustainable competitive advantage is your ability as an enterprise to innovate and to stay in touch with the needs of your customers,' Tim Mapes, Delta's senior vice-president of marketing, told Contagious. 'Staying really close to customers and looking at how their needs are constantly evolving disallows any kind of respect for the status quo.' Delta understood the need to be relevant to its customers in every moment, in order to build services they would actually use.

For brands outside the travel sector, Delta's app and video also provide an important case study in how to use different media to draw attention to an unseen journey, whether it's the product's provenance, manufacturing processes or behind-the-scenes customer service. If you've never seen it before, even a grey suitcase on a conveyor belt can be thrilling to watch. You'll find more on how these unseen processes can build customer affinity in the ninth commandment, Make Trust Sacred.

While consumers might find an onboard film choice entertaining, and might get some small pleasure from taking the conveyor-belt view through the bowels of an airport, one final airline idea is about pure delight, and sticking it to the man.

No-frills South African airline kulula.com wanted to position itself as price leader in the local airline sector. As an underdog, it sought to harness the hysteria around the 2010 World Cup in South Africa, while poking fun at the draconian rules and regulations FIFA put in place to govern advertising and marketing during the tournament period. Kulula.com wasn't an official sponsor, so it wasn't allowed to link itself officially to the World Cup in its communications.

Instead, the airline embarked on a national pricing campaign for the event with press, radio and banner ads trumpeting its 'Unofficial National Carrier' status. FIFA took exception, filing a lawsuit, but the public rallied behind the brand. On April Fool's Day, kulula trademarked the sky with its own set of rules and potential infringements in a mock legal document released to the press. Finally, when the competition began, it ran a press ad offering free flights to anyone named Sepp Blatter (FIFA's president at the time). The brand then fulfilled that promise . . . by flying a Boston terrier by the name of Joseph ('Giuseppe') Blatter around the country, documenting his progress on their blog and social media.

FIFA was already widely resented for extracting significant payments from government deals and for insisting on the construction of brand-new stadia – most of which became underutilized 'white elephants' after the event – in a country with some of the biggest income disparities on the planet. The idea of a feisty, local airline thumbing its nose at a global giant resulted in massive local and international coverage and over R3 million (£160,000/$220,000) of free publicity. Kulula saw a 33 per cent increase in ticket sales on a total campaign investment of only R1.5 million.

SERVICES AS MARKETING

Entertainment has long been synonymous with ads. Ask anyone on a British street to name their favourite Christmas advert, or anyone on an American sidewalk for their favourite Super Bowl spot, and they'll no doubt be able to rattle off a few examples that made them laugh or pulled on their heartstrings. But useful? That's another idea entirely.

And yet, recent years have shown both the ability and the *need* for branded communications to serve a useful purpose in people's lives. We call it service design as marketing, where branded utilities serve as a simultaneous provider of value and deliverer of message.

Take, for example, a recent campaign from Nissan, where the car brand paired up with renewable energy supplier Ovo in the UK to become part of a literal utility. Here's the situation: when UK households running on solar power produce more energy than they use, the excess can be sold back to the National Grid. In the evenings, when there's more demand for electricity but no sunshine to power solar cells, those same households have to buy back the energy from the grid. Clever solar enthusiasts have found a solution to this problem, though: home batteries, which help balance the gap in supply and demand.

To help accelerate the adoption of home battery storage in the UK, Nissan has partnered with Ovo for a vehicle-to-grid (V2G) service. The offering combines Ovo's Solar Store (home battery and software) and Nissan's xStorage Home systems, essentially letting Nissan Leaf vehicles serve as additional battery capacity. Ovo customers who bought the new Nissan Leaf from January 2018 were able to connect to the grid to charge at low-demand periods when power is cheap, and they could use the energy stored in their car at home or work when costs are higher – or sell it back to the grid at peak times for about four times as much as they paid for it.

The collaboration means the energy supplier automatically recharges the car when prices are low, and Ovo estimates the V2G reuse service could save customers an average of £590 per year. A reason to buy a Nissan Leaf sure sounds like marketing to us. But it's also a useful service that can save customers money and make their energy management easier at the same time.

BRAND AS CONCIERGE

Another car brand, Volvo, has brought the idea of branded utility, or usefulness, to life via a concierge service that delivers value directly to owners through a dedicated app. When a Volvo owner wants to refuel, wash their car, or have their vehicle serviced, the Volvo Concierge Services app allows them directly to order vetted professionals to visit either their home or wherever is convenient. The app gives service providers a single-use digital key, meaning the owners don't even have to be around to hand over their keys for their car to be serviced or cleaned. (Volvo has also used a similar principle to enable retail deliveries to be made to owners' cars, to save them having to wait at home.)

'Volvo Concierge Services will mean that you never have to stand out in the rain to fill your car again,' said the president and CEO of Volvo Car USA, Lex Kerssemakers, in a press release. 'At Volvo Cars our mission is to make life less complicated, and this is a great example of how in-car technology can be used to deliver this.'

Imagine that. Marketing that makes life less complicated.

To add heft to this shift toward services, in September 2017 Volvo acquired the car valet and concierge start-up Luxe, taking the automaker deeper into Silicon Valley. Atif Rafiq, Volvo's chief digital officer, echoed the words of his CEO:

> Our vision is a future in which technology simplifies life so you never have to stop at a petrol station, go to a car wash or even take your car in for service ever again. The acquisition of Luxe is a step towards realizing that ambition . . . The technology behind Luxe provides the company with advanced algorithms in the areas of routing, logistics planning and arrival time prediction . . . As more of our cars are connected, the availability of digital services becomes a critical part of the process of selecting a new car. Simplification of experience and placing control directly into the hands of the consumer is what today's technologies enable, and what defines our vision in the digital space.

Uber has pursued similar utilities to drive adoption of their car service. In 2015 the start-up announced a partnership with Practo, the most popular medical practice search engine in Asia. Users who booked their first appointment via Practo in Singapore, India, Indonesia, and the Philippines were given a code that would unlock two free rides – there and back for the doctor's appointment. A later integration involved Ride Reminders, as well, a feature where Uber notified patients an hour before their meeting about their upcoming journey, to make sure they didn't miss their appointment.

As many Uber customers use the service on the fly, it was a smart way to show that Uber vehicles can be booked in advance. And for Practo, it was a way to position the brand as being on the patient's side, considering not just their medical needs but the entire experience of visiting a doctor.

One brand collaboration that nailed the holy trinity of useful, relevant, and entertaining was a 2017 effort by Lyft and Taco Bell that saw the taxi service quite literally serving customers in their time of need. To make it easy for hungry revellers to get their grub at the end of a night out, Lyft passengers riding between the hours of 9 p.m. and 2 a.m. in Southern California could select Taco Mode, instructing their driver to make a detour through the Taco Bell drive thru lane. Taco Bell provided in-car menus and incorporated its branding into the Lyft app and vehicles. And the Cool Ranch icing on the cake? Passengers also received a complimentary Doritos Locos Taco with their order. Useful, relevant, and entertaining, wrapped up in a crunchy taco shell.

EXPANDING THE RELATIONSHIP

Usefulness alone does not a brand make, however. No matter how good you are at delivering utilitarian value to people, at some point they will begin to demand more. First-mover advantage may get you out of the gate with a head start, but competitors always catch up. That's when entertainment and creativity can give you an additional edge.

Street artist Banksy, advocating for the legalization of graffiti, once invited people to imagine 'A city where everybody could draw whatever they liked. Where every street was awash with a million colours and little phrases. Where standing at a bus stop was never boring. A city that felt like a party where everyone was invited.' If we imagine that city as the world of brands (admittedly a bit ironic, given Banksy's hatred for advertising), it's easy to imagine why the entertaining ones have an advantage in attracting attention.

For years the world of weather forecasting has been a boring bus stop – all utility, with very little entertainment. Most weather-reporting services rely on the same data sets and projection models. They deliver their prognostications in the same style and format. You get your forecast from whatever app you happened to download or site you happened to search, and you move on with your life.

Until Poncho the Weather Cat, that is. Launched initially as an email and text service, Poncho was a chatbot that delivered the weather with pizazz and personality. Oh, and GIFs. Poncho used the same data sources as all the other folks, but wrapped that data with those 'million colours and little phrases' Banksy referenced and turned the morning forecast into a party where everyone was invited. As platforms like Kik, Facebook Messenger, and Slack gained prominence, and people became accustomed to interacting with bots, Poncho quickly found new ways to entertain – thanks to a team of writers that made sure the information Poncho delivered to users is punchy, fun, and entertaining, in addition to useful.

'What most bots don't take into account is that you've usually got more questions after you've received the information they're peddling. And, beyond that, they ignore what probably brought you to talk to them in the first place: boredom,' wrote Ashley D'Arcy, a senior editor at Poncho (yep, a senior editor at a weather-forecasting service), in a post on blogging platform Medium:

> Poncho works because when you go off topic, Poncho goes there with you, and then he brings you back. It's a chatbot that's actually chatty. Everything in the bot is imbued with Poncho's sensibility . . . Poncho is at home in your messaging app because he feels like your friend.

Although forecasting didn't prove lucrative, being relevant to consumers did. In 2018, Poncho was acquired by social media ecommerce beverage company Dirty Lemon, to 'build a frictionless conversational platform' and 'advance the future of conversational interfaces.'

Being entertaining, in addition to being useful, allows brands the ability to engage in new spaces. To interrupt without feeling interruptive. To continue conversations with consumers beyond the initial transaction. And perhaps most importantly, entertainment gives people a reason to seek you out ahead of your competition.

CONTEXTUAL RELEVANCE

OK, but what about relevance. Surely if something is useful, it must by definition be relevant as well, right? Well, yes. But the relevance we talk about frequently at Contagious goes beyond utility to include something much more important. Context.

On the web, famed MIT computer scientist Alan Kay is often credited with the aphorism 'Context is worth 80 IQ points.' He didn't actually say those words (he argued 'perspective' or 'point of view' was what amounted to that intellectual boost), but he was a strong believer that a good idea, or a smart student, when nurtured in the right context, could achieve greatness. We believe the same is true for advertising.

Miguel de Cervantes agrees, no doubt. 'La mejor salsa del mundo es la hambre,' he said through Teresa, one of his characters in *Don Quixote*. The best sauce in the world is hunger. When put in the right context, even the middling can become phenomenal.

So what is context? Well, in short, context is everything. And everything is context.

'Jacked Up', a 2017 State Farm Insurance commercial made by DDB Chicago, brilliantly riffs on this idea, with two characters reciting the same lines of dialogue while looking at a car: 'Is this my car? What?! This is ridiculous! This can't be happening!' In one scene, it's a teenage girl looking at her first car in the driveway. In the other, it's a businessman whose car is on blocks after its wheels have been stolen. Context – everything happening outside of the dialogue – tells the story.

From a brand perspective, 'context is everything' can be a daunting proposition. So think of it instead as the confluence of internal and external factors that led to a consumer interacting with you in a given moment. The person's internal context forms one side of the equation: their personality, their intent, their habits and past experiences. The other side of the equation is external: weather, place, time, current events, and more. Anyone who has designed digital experiences knows that digital context – what device someone is using, whether they're logged into an account – is just as real a consideration.

In 2012 Guatemalan shoe store Meat Pack used a relevant offer to snatch customers directly out of the stores of their rival retailers. Working with agency 4 AM Saatchi & Saatchi, the brand introduced Hijack, a new feature of the Meat Pack app used by customers. Hijack identified any shop selling the same brands as Meat Pack and used GPS to identify whenever someone with the app entered one of those locations. As soon as customers entered, the app would pop up a time-sensitive discount at the nearest Meat Pack store. Discounts started at 99 per cent and decreased by 1 per cent every second, meaning customers literally ran out of competitors' stores and made a beeline to Meat Pack.

The agency reported that 600 sneakerheads tested their sprinting speed in just one week, including one customer, Pedro Rodriguez, who made the mad dash from a rival store in eleven seconds to secure an 89 per cent discount. We'd bet Pedro and many of the other customers went into non-Meat Pack shoe shops with their app open and their legs ready to run after hearing about the campaign. If that visual isn't entertaining, we don't know what is.

RELEVANCE RETAIL

While vending machines in the US and Europe have historically sold snacks and drinks, a new breed of machine has emerged recently, particularly in airports. No doubt you've seen these new automated kiosks offering whatever you forgot to pack on your plane journey: inflatable travel pillows, phone chargers, headphones, and even make-up.

In 2017 clothes retailer Uniqlo even installed 'Uniqlo To Go' vending machines stocked with wardrobe staples in ten airports and shopping malls across the US. The machines offered travellers a variety of garments, including men's and women's HeatTech thermal tops and Ultralight down jackets – exactly the type of items that would save the day if you failed to pack for cooler weather, or left a couple of crucial layers at home.

This is relevance retail. Vending machines, with their small footprint, can be geographically positioned to serve customers in hyper-specific contexts, meaning their offering is much more likely to appeal to passers-by. In the years since Contagious first started out, we've seen every variation of vending machine possible, trying to capitalize on this relevance. Here are just a few:

// Minute Maid lemonade brand Limon Y Nada set up vending machines in water and theme parks across Spain that sold the drink for increasingly lower prices as the temperature outside got hotter, making the drink even *more* appealing as its relevance rose.
// Coffee brand Douwe Egberts created a machine that gave out free cups of joe to yawning individuals and positioned it near jet-lagged travellers at O. R. Tambo International airport in South Africa.
// L'Oréal Paris installed an interactive vending machine in the New York City subway, with sensors that would detect the dominant colours in an outfit and recommend eye, lip, and nail products that either complemented or clashed with the clothes, available for immediate purchase.
// Coca-Cola, a big fan of vending machine stunts, created a 3.5 metre-high machine that required people to climb on a friend's shoulders to reach the slot, but rewarded people with two Cokes for the price of one.
// Sportswear giant Nike turned sweat into a digital currency by installing a vending machine in New York City stocked full of sportswear such as socks, T-shirts, and hats that eschewed cash and instead only accepted Nike+ FuelBand points, earned by working out with the brand's fitness tracker.

For people who have travelled through Japan, the recent popularity of vending machines will come as little surprise. Vending machines are a much more integral part of the Japanese retail mix, with over 5 million installed across the country, or roughly one unit for every twenty-three citizens. That's the highest density of vending machines in the world, per the Japan Vending Machine Manufacturers Association.

One of the most off-the-wall examples of contextual marketing we've come across in the near decade and a half Contagious has been around is from that vending-machine mecca, where consumers are much more comfortable and accustomed to interacting with these machines. Coca-Cola-owned ready-to-drink coffee brand Georgia (we told you Coke loves vending machines!) wanted to strengthen engagement between loyal fans and its vending machines in order to influence their purchasing habits and raise the likelihood of them buying a drink.

Working with Tokyo-based agency Dentsu, Georgia (one of Coca-Cola's twenty-one brands that grosses more than $1 billion in sales) launched a mobile app that makes buying a drink from a vending machine more like visiting your favourite neighbourhood coffee shop.

Users could register the vending machine they regularly visited and choose one of six virtual 'cafe managers'. Each time the customer visited the machine, that avatar would interact with them, welcoming them by name and sending personalized messages based on purchase history. For example, the manager thanked people for buying a second cup of coffee in a day, and would remark on it being a sunny day or recommend that you carry an umbrella if the weather forecast called for rain.

Dentsu reported that the app was downloaded more than 460,000 times, and 68.5 per cent of users felt more attached to the brand following their experience. Plus, 41 per cent of people who used the app ended up visiting other nearby vending machines more often as well. The app also hit the top of Google Play's entertainment app charts in Japan and became the country's top free iTunes app.

THE NEXT WAVE

Improvements in payment, mobility, and even supply-chain management technology are creating cascading evolution in the vending machine / relevance retail world. In the US, start-up Bodega launched in 2017 with the goal of installing pantry boxes around cities, replacing corner stores with computer vision recognition and electronic payment boxes that required no staff. 'Eventually, centralized shopping locations won't be necessary, because there will be 100,000 Bodegas spread out, with one always a hundred feet away from you,' co-founder Paul McDonald told *Fast Company*. Perhaps because its name was seen as a shot across the bow at beloved urban institutions, the start-up was widely met by ridicule.

In China, however, the automated small-scale retail revolution is already in full effect. Start-up BingoBox, for example, offers portable small-scale convenience stores that require no staff and are open 24/7. One of the first to market, thanks to a 'launch and learn' approach, this unmanned convenience chain is powered by messaging app WeChat. Its container-like units are fitted with wheels for ease of transportation and carry a range of everyday items, from drinks to snacks to noodles. Users simply open the door to the BingoBox through WeChat, choose from over 800 products in stock, and pay for their purchases using the messaging app or Alibaba Group's popular Alipay platform. Computer vision tech makes sure customers don't try to walk out with a five-finger discount, and remote customer service is available around the clock.

The company launched in February of 2017 and had 158 locations in China within eight months, with aspirations for 5,000 stores by the end of 2018 (and 100,000 by 2020!). The stores cost a quarter of a typical bricks-and-mortar retail store to set up, require only four people to run forty stores, and can be moved to areas of high demand when necessary.

Recognizing the potential at the confluence of unmanned retail and relevant offerings, a number of other businesses are starting to compete in this space, particularly in China. Start-up Wheelys is designing self-driving pop-up shops that can literally move to wherever a customer wants to buy something, with variable inventory based on what's relevant to a given location. French retail giant Auchan, an early partner of BingoBox, has launched its own branded mini-store called Auchan Minute. 'We are providing hyper-connected Chinese consumers with a solution that is in line with their buying,' said Ludovic Holinier, executive chairman of Auchan Retail China. And China's biggest drinks manufacturer, Hangzhou Wahaha Group, has signed a contract to roll out 1 million (a million!) automated TakeGo stores in the next decade.

Vending machines, once relegated to break rooms and bowling alleys, have morphed into the front lines of the retail wars, driven by a need for brands to be relevant to consumers.

RELEVANT TO MY INTERESTS

It has become a gag to remark online that something is 'relevant to my interests'. But brands that hit that sweet spot (often with something that is also useful and entertaining) have indeed found success in creating habits among their consumers.

Take, for example, Spotify's Discover Weekly playlist feature, which analyses your taste in music, compares it to other Spotify users with similar tastes, and recommends adjacent songs you might not have heard. By surfacing music new to the user, Spotify provides a helpful service. By taking the user's taste as a guide, Spotify ensures that the playlist is relevant. And by cross-referencing against the listening habits of people with similar tastes, Spotify guarantees the resulting product will be entertaining. Within ten weeks of the feature's soft launch in 2015, more than 1 billion tracks had been streamed via Discover Weekly, and it quickly became the backbone of many more personalized and relevant playlists generated on an ongoing basis by Spotify.

'After a while it became very clear that we have created a Monday habit, a ritual for our users,' said Will Page, Spotify's director of economics, of Discover Weekly in a talk at 2016's Convergence Conference. 'We have created a random event (you don't know what you're getting); a regular event (happens every Monday); and a reinforcing event (cheers you up on a Monday).'

Relevance and personalization are increasingly interchangeable terms, and it should be no surprise to anyone in the marketing world that demand for personalization is on the rise. As Ben Perkins, head of consumer business research at management consulting firm Deloitte, put it in a 2015 report, 'Businesses who do not offer an element of personalization risk losing revenue and customer loyalty over the longer term as customers increasingly demand personalization.' Market researcher Forrester, for its part, discovered that 77 per cent of consumers have chosen, recommended or paid more for a brand that provides a personalized service or experience. Stats aside, it's common sense: products that are closer to our personal interests are more relevant to us, and consequently more appealing.

BIO-RELEVANCE

Recently a slew of start-ups have taken this idea even further, drilling into the DNA of relevance, quite literally. Thanks to technology, partial genome sequencing has dropped to costs that make it possible at the consumer level. Perhaps predictably, the health and wellness industry has pounced, sensing an opportunity for hyper-relevance.

Take, for example, Habit, a Californian start-up that uses customers' DNA to create bespoke diet plans. Users send in samples of their saliva and blood, which are analysed to create an individual nutritional profile. Then, the company creates a tailored nutrition plan that specifies the exact amounts of carbohydrates, proteins and fat the person's body needs to function optimally. Another start-up, Vinome, analyses a person's DNA and then matches them with wines selected especially to match their palate. 'Genes affect your senses of taste and smell, which in turn influence your wine preferences. Why not let your genes help you discover wines you'll love?' the start-up asks.

Helix, a start-up from San Francisco (California seems to be a hotbed for this field), hopes to become the 'app store' for this sort of genomic brand relevance. Like its competitors, the company provides genome sequencing to individuals. But it also stores that data and shares it with other brands at the user's request. (Remember, though: with great data comes great responsibility, a concept we explore further in the ninth commandment.) The idea is that, via Helix, any brand can create tailored DNA products and services without having to sequence someone's genome themselves. The company's first collaboration shared genome data with National Geographic, who then gave people more information about their family history.

'We wanted to spark innovation by being an open platform that allows any partner or developer to build DNA into their products using software alone,' Justin Kao, Helix's co-founder and SVP, told Contagious. 'We're building the first open platform in this space, similar to what Apple and Google did for mobile.'

Relevance isn't just about context. It can also be about keeping up with the world around your brand. In 2016 McDonald's realized its Happy Meals weren't connecting with young people in Sweden because the kids had no interest in the toys. 'We developed an insight: the relevance of the Happy Meal is not based on the competitive offering, it's based on the culture of play, and the culture of play has moved on. The task that we set ourselves was around how we can modernize the Happy Meal and turn it into a progressive play experience,' said Erik Årnell, who worked on the brand as a regional planner at DDB Stockholm. The solution? Happy Meal packaging that customers could disassemble along perforated markings and fold into a Google Cardboard-like headset. The so-called 'Happy Goggles' could then be used to play a virtual reality skiing game called Slope Stars.

MAKE THEM AN OFFER THEY CAN'T REFUSE

We opened this commandment by giving you the brutal, honest truth: in the grand scheme of things, nobody cares about your idea. But we'll leave you with a glimmer of hope. Of course, everybody cares about *some* idea. We all have a favourite book or movie or song. And yes, we even have favourite brands and favourite ads. There's a jingle or three stuck in most people's heads. And we use branded services on a daily basis to improve our lives, whether we want to admit it or not. Without Google Maps, we'd quite literally be lost.

So if everybody cares about *some* idea, the trick is simply to make sure that it's *your* idea. And how do we do that? Say it with us: Be useful, relevant, and entertaining. People will use products that work well. They will pay attention to pertinent messages. They will tune in to content that makes them laugh or fills them with suspense. We're quite selfish beings after all.

BE USEFUL, RELEVANT, AND ENTERTAINING /
ESPRESSO VERSION

This should be common sense. After all, the currency of the advertising business is attention, and we all change the channel or glaze over when an ad that doesn't strike our fancy is broadcast into our lives. Marketing that doesn't connect emotionally, doesn't provide value, and doesn't relate to our interests is quickly buried in the sands of time.

We are, in the words of UK television marketing body Thinkbox, meerkats, with our heads on a swivel, constantly switching platforms or flicking our eyes from one screen to the next in search of whatever is most likely to resonate. To make matters worse, as the media landscape fractures and new competitors hop over low barriers to entry, the meerkats have more to look at than ever before.

So we have to be useful. We have to be relevant. And we have to be entertaining.

Now, we reckon very few creative directors or CMOs set out with a brief to be useless, irrelevant, and boring. Yet thousands of hours are spent in agencies honing and fine-tuning the execution of work that is

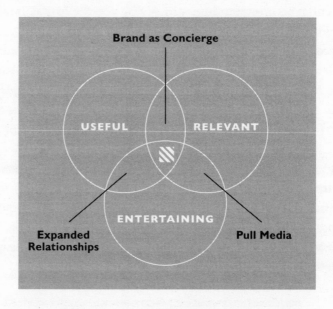

just that. Unless these goals are explicitly stated and revisited through the development process, they're often left on the cutting-room floor as a bland piece of work is bought by a risk-averse client, comfortable blending in with the white noise of category clichés.

At Contagious, we think of useful, relevant, and entertaining as overlapping circles, each made stronger by a connection to another. Creating marketing that nails one circle is good. Marketing that fits in an overlap area is even better. It's in the common ground that marketing efficiencies emerge. When your brand and its messaging are useful and relevant, all of a sudden you function as a concierge – say, a fuelling service that meets drivers when their tanks run dry or a store that moves to where you are, selling exactly the product you need when you need it. Relevant and entertaining marketing, like a personalized weekly playlist, creates a tractor beam of pull media that brings people to you rather than relying on push spending. Adding entertainment to useful services turns transactions into deeper relationships, building a moat against competitors attacking on a single front and maybe even making your customers smile at the forecast of a rainy day.

And that sweet spot in the centre? That's the Contagious logo. Marketing that is simultaneously useful, relevant, and entertaining fires on all cylinders. It grabs attention, exceeds expectations, and builds brand affinity. It is truly contagious.

Throughout the process of making a campaign, or even a single piece of collateral, ask yourself:

// What need is this addressing?
// Why will this matter to my audience at the specific time they will encounter it?
// If this weren't an ad, would it hold up as standalone entertainment?

If you can't answer at least two of those convincingly, think about how to change your idea or execution so that you can. And if you keep finding yourself falling short, try an even simpler idea: write USEFUL, RELEVANT, ENTERTAINING on the top of your creative briefs. We bet it'll change the results you'll see.

ASK HERETICAL QUESTIONS

There's no such thing as a stupid question, or so the saying goes. But in reality, we're rarely encouraged to pipe up in the boardroom or on the conference call with an unrelated musing or painfully honest question about our business.

And yet. Sometimes these ridiculous, awkward, borderline-heretical questions can lead to ideas so compelling they can't be avoided. Contagious ideas frequently come from where we least expect them. From thoughts that we had previously considered daft or too risky. Maybe even taboo. And when you find them, odds are no one else is competing in the same area.

In the first commandment we encouraged you to ask *why* it is you do what you do. Once you've settled that, and established your core purpose, it's time to challenge yourself with more provocative, unpredictable questions.

Are there any queries so crazy or heretical that if you asked them in a meeting with your colleagues, your career might as well be over? Or your team would mock you endlessly? Maybe it's a dirty secret about why customers *really* choose your product. Maybe it's asking whether a fundamental tenet of your business is outmoded and needs to be put to pasture. Perhaps your company needs to leap into a non-adjacent product category. Maybe it's just wondering if you really *could* grow potatoes on Mars (see box on pages 75–6). Our advice to you is: chase those ideas. Ask those questions. And for the love of God, convince your colleagues to chill out and do the same.

Media intellectual Marshall McLuhan talked about the importance of questions in a world where there is an ever-expanding amount of content and data. 'In a global information environment, the old pattern of education in answer-finding is one of no avail: one is surrounded by answers, millions of them, moving and mutating at electric speed,' he said in 1970. 'Survival and control will depend on the ability to probe and to question in the proper way and place.'

Asking heretical questions is one of the key steps to coming up with contagious ideas.

THE VALUE OF QUESTIONS

The urge to ask questions is drilled out of us at a young age, as we memorize our times tables, the capital cities of the world, and how to calculate sines and tangents. Odds are you don't use that calculus or geographical knowledge frequently in your day job. But you probably use inquisition to get to great ideas.

Ronald D. Vale, a professor at the University of California, wrote about the importance of questions in a 2013 issue of *Molecular Biology of the Cell*, of all places. 'Identifying a good question and being able to articulate it well is not just an exercise for high school students, but is also a key skill in becoming a successful scientist. A grant proposal often receives a poor score not because the proposed experiments are poorly conceived, but because the questions being asked are not interesting or not clearly articulated,' he wrote. In short: ask better questions, get better results.

Hal Gregersen, executive director of the MIT Leadership Center, talks frequently about the value of questions and how they can drive past obvious solutions to more creative pathways. He calls it catalytic questioning. He suggests an exercise called 'question storming', wherein people trying to solve a problem generate at least fifty questions about the challenge they're facing. Halfway through, Gregersen told the American business magazine *Fast Company*, people often lose steam. 'People say: "I don't have any more questions, I am stuck." Keep going, because it's that pass forward that can sometimes give you some of the greatest questions.'

Gregersen is the mind behind the 4–24 Project, which encourages leaders to set aside four minutes every twenty-four hours to ask better questions and understand the questions they're facing that day. 'Doing this not only helps us think more innovatively, but more introspectively,' he writes.

ASKING THE HARD QUESTIONS

Asking heretical questions isn't just about plumbing the depths of the obvious, or asking off-the-wall questions that lead to interesting executions. Sometimes, at their most heretical, these questions must be brutally honest. Uncomfortable. Painful, even.

Some of the world's biggest and most successful companies continue to flourish precisely because the capacity to debate awkward provocations is baked into their culture. It's something Facebook recognizes and openly confronts. 'If we don't create the thing that kills Facebook, someone else will,' declares a headline inside the *Little Red Book* – an internal handbook explaining the company's mission, history, and culture to new employees published as a limited edition to celebrate the social media giant clocking up 1 billion users in late 2012. 'Embracing change isn't enough,' the book argues. 'It has to be so hardwired into who we are that even talking about it seems redundant. The internet is not a friendly place. Things that don't stay relevant don't even get the luxury of leaving ruins. They disappear.'

Is there an inconvenient truth within your brand, threatening to take it down? An elephant in the room that everyone refuses to acknowledge? A sacred cow that will lead you into obscurity?

In our decade-plus of working with clients around the world, Contagious has come into contact with brands of all sizes, in myriad sectors and various geographies. And a shocking percentage of those clients have elephant-sized blind spots when it comes to what's holding their brand back. We've worked with athletic-apparel makers who refuse to say their competitors' names out loud in the office, global FMCG companies that avoid using their rivals' colours in any form, and legacy brands that refuse to entertain the notion that a start-up could become a legitimate threat.

Much more refreshing are the honest conversations with clients who are willing to admit their weak spots. These people are still energized about their own brands, confident in their ability to win in the long term. But they understand that ignoring issues is not the best way to do so.

QUESTIONS THAT PULL THE FIRE ALARM

In 1968 Columbia University researcher Bibb Latané and New York University researcher John Darley did an experiment that resulted in a paper called 'Group Inhibition of Bystander Intervention in Emergencies', now colloquially known as the smoke-filled room experiment. In the study, Columbia students were asked to fill out a questionnaire about life on an urban university campus. Some filled the form out alone, some in groups of three, and some unknowingly solo with two actors playing indifferent participants. As they filled out the questionnaire, the room they were seated in began to fill with smoke, coming through a hole in the wall. By the completion of the experiment period, the room was so full of smoke it obscured vision in the room.

The results of the study were illuminating. Participants who were alone in the room were often inquisitive, investigating where the smoke was coming from, and 75 per cent of them left the room to report the smoke to the administrators of the questionnaire. When participants were grouped in threes, at least one person reported the smoke 38 per cent of the time – and took nearly twice as long to do so as the solo participants. When solo participants were placed with two actors instructed to ignore the situation entirely, they reported the smoke only 10 per cent of the time.

In their consequent article, Latané and Darley wrote about these findings, noting that those who chose not to report the smoke often justified it by inventing causes for the fog other than fire – steam, air conditioning vapours, and even (in two cases!) 'truth gas'. The researchers cite an obvious and powerful 'report-inhibiting effect of other bystanders', an idea they later explored further in a book titled *The Unresponsive Bystander: Why Doesn't He Help?* When more people are present (particularly people who seem unaware or unbothered), individuals are less likely to act to help a victim. But interestingly, the study seems to prove that the bystander effect applies even when the *bystander* is the victim.

Flash back to our heretical questions. There's a chance you work for a brand where the room is slowly filling with the smoke of declining sales, decreasing brand equity, or increasing competition. And there's a chance the people seated to your right and your left seem unconcerned by the smoke, unwilling to cause a scene by investigating. Heretical questions are your fire alarm. By turning to the people around you and saying 'Do you see this? Couldn't this be really bad for us?' you give yourself and your colleagues an excuse to act, to get up, run out of the room, and return with an extinguisher.

'WHY DOES OUR PIZZA SUCK?'

In 2007 Domino's Pizza was seated in a room that was slowly filling up with smoke. This wasn't your Italian eatery woodsmoke, though. It was a rancid, burning cloud coming from reviewers and customers. People just didn't like the pizza. And sales were in the dumps. Slipping standards and mediocre products were increasingly being rejected by a public emboldened by the emergence of online reviews.

People inside the brand took a deep breath, steadied themselves, and pulled the fire alarm. Why does our pizza suck, and how can we fix it?

Flash forward two years, to April 2009. Overnight, the company was rocked by the first major food-safety scandal of the social-media era. Video footage emerged on the web of two employees from a store in North Carolina tainting food and laughing about it. Over a million people watched the video in just three days, confirming their deepest fears about fast food.

The most infamous quote, from thirty-one-year-old Kristy Hammonds (who was later fired, sued, and prosecuted), couldn't be more disgusting: 'In about five minutes [the food will] be sent out on delivery where somebody will be eating these . . . little did they know that cheese was in his nose and that there was some lethal gas that ended up on their salami. Now that's how we roll at Domino's.'

As the scandal unfolded, pundits clucked over the possibility that two minimum-wage workers would undo years of work at a mega-brand. But Domino's moved quickly. 'There were two people, two idiots I think our spokesperson called them, and I think consumers recognized that. We were up front with it, and we moved on,' Russell Weiner, who'd been in the CMO role at Domino's eight months at that point, told Contagious. '[The public] recognized that these two aren't like the thousands of other Domino's employees.'

As luck would have it, the crisis proved to be a perfect precursor to the brand's renaissance, thanks to the fire drill it was wrapping up.

PIZZA TURNAROUND

In October 2009 Domino's arrived at its creative agency, Crispin Porter + Bogusky, with the new and improved pizza it had been working on. To come up with a way to promote it, CP+B used its tried-and-tested format for generating ideas that resonate in culture: begin the advertising brief as if it were the headline of a press release celebrating the effort's success. Here's the brief they wrote:

// Domino's reinvents their pizza from the crust up.
// Tension: I know exactly what to expect from Domino's: mediocre pizza delivered fast.
// How can we launch Domino's pizza in an unexpected way that proves our taste credibility, thus re-establishing Domino's iconic status?

Being genuine in responding to the video scandal had worked well for the brand. 'We were honest in our anger and our approach. And I think people could sense that,' Domino's vice-president for communication, Tim McIntyre, told the *Wall Street Journal*. So Domino's took the same approach with its pizza pies, placing the elephant in the centre of the room and shining a spotlight on it.

The result of that brief is a now-legendary campaign called

Pizza Turnaround. Launched with a four-minute-long video showing employees watching focus groups reviewing Domino's pies, the campaign didn't shy away from confronting the awkward truths. 'Domino's pizza crust, to me, is like cardboard,' says one focus group participant. 'Mass produced, boring, bland pizza,' says one internet reviewer. 'The sauce tastes like ketchup,' reads one complaint.

'You can either use negative comments to get you down or you can use them to excite you and energize your process of making a better pizza. We did the latter,' says Patrick Doyle, the brand's president at the time, in the spot.

Then comes the turnaround. The tone shifts from a massive mea culpa to a corporate re-energizer for in-house consumption, complete with employees chanting ('WHO ARE WE? DOMINO'S PIZZA!') and shots of the test kitchen humming with activity. The takeaway for the consumer? 'We have changed *everything*. Now it tastes better.'

As consumers tried the new pizza and engaged with the brand on Facebook and Twitter, taste was a major – positive and negative – talking point. Domino's paid careful attention to the relationships initiated by customers, and explained different options they had to customize their food, getting feedback on delivery times and quality, all with courtesy and care.

The Turnaround campaign made big media waves: it featured on over 400 local TV stations and grew the company's audience by 80,000 Facebook fans – a sizeable number back in 2009. At the campaign's height, one image from a franchise location pictured a sales-tracking chart on the wall: the line showing increasing revenue climbed off the chart, onto the wall and then onto the ceiling, having run out of space to register the gains.

Anecdotal evidence became exceptional results: in May 2010 Domino's announced a year-on-year increase of 14.3 per cent in first-quarter same-store sales, while Pizza Hut's grew by 5 per cent and Papa John's shrank by 0.4 per cent. If you bought $100 of Domino's stock on 21 December 2009, the day the Pizza Turnaround video went up on YouTube, it would have grown to be worth more than $2,500 just eight years later. By confronting a problem head-on and asking borderline blasphemous questions about the company that would have been easier to ignore, the brand revitalized its core product and messaging. Does our pizza suck? How can we fix it? How do we show people we have changed? These sorts of questions led to a new pizza recipe, birthed an iconic ad campaign, and laid the groundwork for the future of the Domino's brand.

It's all fine and good to invest two years of time and resources into righting a listing ship. But what if you just want to inject a little life into your product on the cheap? That was the plan for sixty-seven-year-old brand Shreddies, a latticed-wheat cereal that originated in Canada. Working with Ogilvy, Toronto, the square – both literally and figuratively – brand convinced Canuck consumers to view the cereal from a new angle by, well, putting the cereal at a new angle. With tongue planted firmly in cheek, the Diamond Shreddies campaign rotated the cereal 45 degrees and then created packaging extolling the new-and-improved, innovative design.

Following a soft launch, the campaign was followed by a competition allowing ten customers to win a diamond using unique codes found on the side of the packet. TV, print, and poster ads supported an online campaign that claimed Diamond Shreddies were more flavourful and crunchier. And when one customer jokingly complained that he'd bought a packet of Diamond Shreddies and was disappointed to find that only half the packet contained diamonds and the rest were merely squares, the brand introduced the 'combo pack' to Canadian shelves (66 per cent diamonds, 33 per cent squares). Proof that silliness as a marketing tool can actually work: sales rose 18 per cent following the 'ground-breaking' relaunch.

'WHAT IF WE CLOSED ALL OUR STORES ON THE BUSIEST DAY OF THE YEAR?'

Essentially, the smoke-filled room experiment is what millions of parents have fought against with the sage advice, 'Just because everyone else is doing it doesn't mean you have to.' Even though everyone else is sitting in a smoky chamber doesn't mean you can't run out the door.

That's the situation outdoor gear and apparel retailer REI found itself in recently. Black Friday, the day after Thanksgiving, is the biggest shopping day of the year in the US. It's known for crack-of-dawn store openings and throngs of consumers racing through Walmart like hordes of locusts stripping crops in a field. But REI, like its counterpart Patagonia, whose 'Don't Buy This Jacket' Black Friday campaign we detailed in the first commandment, is about preservation, not consumption. In fact, the company is a cooperative, owned by employees and members rather than a slave to stock-market stakeholders. So why did REI participate in this retail orgy? Was it putting profits before passion?

The brand answered that question with authority with #OptOutside, a mega-successful campaign in which REI closed its retail locations and stopped accepting online orders on Black Friday, urging people to get outside instead.

Here's how it worked: in October 2015 REI announced that it wouldn't condone the annual shopper swarm. Instead, it encouraged people to opt out and #OptOutside. The Seattle-based retailer gave its 12,000 employees a paid vacation day, closed its online store for the day, and routed web visitors to a campaign site. There, people could enter their location to see suggestions for nearby national parks to visit or trails to hike.

Visitors to the site could share their decision to #OptOutside by choosing from a set of scenic images (or uploading their own), and adding a branded fill-in-the-blank filter that said 'This Black Friday I'll be . . .' To activate influencers and get people talking about the campaign, REI even distributed freeze-dried, trail-ready rations of Thanksgiving foods for people too busy hiking to gather around a dinner table.

Ben Steele, the company's senior vice-president and chief creative officer, recounted the conversation that led to the campaign to *Forbes*:

> In the midst of a big holiday brainstorming session, the head of our merchandising group said, 'We could never do it, but what if we close on Black Friday?' Obviously, at face value it seems crazy, but it was all about giving our people the day off and inviting others to join us. Part of this job is about storytelling, but when you can take an action and show people rather than just telling them, it can be really powerful.

'I have to admit it was a bit shocking, but the more we thought about it, the more excited we got about it as an idea,' CEO Jerry Stritzke told CBS. 'One, that our associates would love [the idea], but two, as a co-op, we have 5 million members that love the outdoors. We just really believe they would get into it as well.'

OPTING IN TO OPTING OUT

The consumer response was impressive: 1.4 million people – 70 per cent of whom were under the age of thirty-five – opted outside on Black Friday, using the REI hashtag. The campaign earned 3,400 media placements and trended on Instagram and Twitter for two and three days, respectively. In perhaps the most interesting barometer of brand-equity building, the retailer reported a 92 per cent increase in job applications during the fourth quarter of 2015. Oh, and REI had its second straight year of double-digit growth.

Perhaps even more interestingly, REI started a wave that saw nearly 200 other retailers join in and close their own doors. That sparked the brand to double down on the strategy in 2016 and 2017, working to get others involved: 275 organizations and brands teamed up with the co-op in 2016, including one effort in New York wherein Subaru donated cars to enable city-dwellers to take their dogs (or shelter dogs) into the great outdoors. In 2017 the brand expanded on its activity search engine, helping people find ways to get outside near them. Stritzke, announcing the third iteration of the campaign, noted than more than 8 million people had joined in during the first two years.

In many ways, the original question spawning the campaign seemed more heretical than it actually was: REI's shoppers are probably not typically the types to indulge in the Black Friday binge; and there is some evidence that points to shopping merely being redistributed to other days when stores are closed on Thanksgiving and Black Friday.

But more importantly, the question followed on from REI's purpose. By finding an unexpected way to activate against that organizing principle, and following through fully, REI built brand equity and stood out from the pack.

ASKING DUMB, OBVIOUS QUESTIONS

Beyond the hard, heretical questions, we believe there's a ton of value in asking *dumb* questions. Or questions that, at first blush, seem almost naive. What if we close our store on its busiest day? Why can't I buy a plane ticket at the grocery store? Why don't we let people stay in our hotel for free if no one else has booked the room? You'll find brilliant campaigns developed in response to these types of questions throughout this chapter.

A fair amount of the smartest writing on the value of questions comes from thinkers in the education field – perhaps because that institution has a tendency to drill curiosity out of its wards. Regardless, writing in the National Association of Elementary School Principals' publication, *Leadership Compass*, in 2000, educator Jim Force talked about the value of dumb questions: 'Dumb questions, the kind children ask but most adults know better than to ask, are born out of a desire to understand, out of curiosity not expectation,' he wrote. 'They stem from our imagination and are designed to engage us in thought. Dumb questions are simple questions that probe the obvious, and simultaneously challenge and direct our thinking.'

Dr David C. Funder, professor at the University of California Riverside, agrees with this line of thinking. In an essay titled 'Naive and Obvious Questions' in the fourth volume of *Perspectives on Psychological Science*, he writes about the need for psychology researchers to loosen their briefs (not like that, get your mind out of the gutter). 'Elegantly designed, tight little studies that measure one behavior in two behavioral conditions in pursuit of the test of a focused hypothesis are the current state of the art,' he wrote in 2009. These super-specific studies often result from resource constraints, and lead to researchers' detailed but uninteresting results.

We would argue that sometimes the same could be said about advertising. Too often we direct our creative energies towards laser-focused, platform-specific ideas. When was the last time you stepped back and looked at your efforts from 35,000 feet? Have you questioned the basic fundamentals of your marketing recently?

'The moral of this story for all aspiring researchers: Never, ever assume that a study or a finding is so obvious that somebody "must have" done or found it already,' writes Funder. 'Many of the most interesting and even important studies you can do may be hidden in plain sight.'

'WHAT IF WE SOLD UGLY FRUITS AND VEGGIES?'

Food waste – that is, food that is grown, raised or prepared that never makes it into someone's mouth – is responsible for around 8 per cent of global carbon emissions. So says Paul Hawken, editor of *Drawdown*, a book and project dedicated to providing a hundred concrete, ranked and measured steps to reverse the process of climate change:

> A third of the food raised or prepared does not make it from farm or factory to fork. Producing uneaten food squanders a whole host of resources – seeds, water, energy, land, fertilizer, hours of labor, financial capital – and generates greenhouse gases at every stage – including methane when organic matter lands in the global rubbish bin . . .
>
> In regions of higher income, willful food waste dominates farther along the supply chain. Retailers and consumers reject food based on bumps, bruises, and coloring, or simply order, buy, and serve too much.

French grocer Intermarché saw this happening first hand. Explains Guillaume Le Gorrec, an ex-strategist at Marcel, Paris, who worked with the supermarket:

> Because we buy calibrated fruit and vegetables, slowly the non-calibrated ones don't get sold. It's a human basic instinct: when you have two products – one that's weirdly shaped or one that's perfect, you go for the good-looking one. In our mind, there's a connection: if it's better looking it's better tasting, so that was the main thing to overcome. When you see an ugly carrot – and trust me I've seen some pretty ugly carrots – you don't want to eat it yet you don't know why.

To combat this omnipresent food waste – which often happens even before produce reaches the end consumer – Intermarché ran an experiment. Dubbed 'Les fruits et légumes moches' (inglorious fruits and vegetables), the initiative shook up the supply chain and filled produce bins with ugly and misshapen fruit. The retailer then sold those former outcasts to consumers, at a price 30 per cent cheaper than their perfect-looking counterparts.

The experiment was supported with a cheeky advertising campaign extolling the virtues of these unique fruits and veggies. 'A grotesque apple a day keeps the doctor away as well,' reads one, next to a picture of a contorted apple. 'A hideous orange makes beautiful juice,' says another, alongside a photo of a particularly gnarly navel orange.

'Intermarché wants to bring down the cost of living through minimizing food waste. We thought about how we could change behaviours starting from this point. We wanted to do something light-hearted and joyful because it's everyone's fault and no one's fault; it's a cultural thing,' says Le Gorrec.

The grocer tested the hypothesis that people would still buy this oddly formed produce at a discount in a single store. Then in ten stores. Then in twenty. And finally, in all stores nationwide. The advertising campaign started locally in low-cost media channels like print, radio, and PR. (The brand sent baskets of ugly fruit and vegetables to journalists with recipes for soups and smoothies.) As it grew, Intermarché even took its messaging to TV.

'The press campaign helped in terms of awareness, but once it was in store, it became real; people could actually touch the produce so it's more than a campaign. The combination of a campaign and the in-store activity worked: you have to be real and show action, not just talk about food waste,' says Le Gorrec.

The brand sold 1.2 tonnes of misshapen fruit and vegetables per store in the first two days they were available, often selling out before the supplies could be replenished. In-store traffic, driven by the creative campaign, grew by 24 per cent, and overall sales of produce in Intermarché grew by 10 per cent. In the end, the campaign reached more than 13 million people in France through social and earned media (branded message spread that doesn't rely on paid advertising). And perhaps the best sign of success: competitors Monoprix, Auchan and Leclerc all adopted similar practices in their own stores.

'We were really happy about it,' says Le Gorrec of the copycats. 'If Intermarché can be at the beginning of something that changed the category, it's perfect.'

Can you make a potato famous? That was the brief given to Will Rust, a regional executive creative director at OgilvyOne, Dubai, by the Peru-based International Potato Center. He responded with some questions of his own, he told Contagious:

> I was with a focus group of agricultural scientists in Peru. I had a bunch of questions to ask them: how would we explain what you do to a five-year-old? How do you want to be remembered when you're gone? Could we grow potatoes somewhere they've never been grown before? Could we grow them on another planet? . . . When I asked if we could grow potatoes on Mars, they said, 'Yes, potentially.'

Working with a cross-disciplinary team of experts in agriculture, plant breeding, astrobiology, medicine and physics, OgilvyOne came up with a robust plan for the project. A 'super-potato' was bred from the hardiest of the International Potato Center's 5,000-strong bank of variants. Under guidance from NASA, a hermetically sealed 'CubeSat' was built to recreate conditions on the red planet, including atmospheric pressure, CO_2 levels, light, radiation, and arid soil from Peru's Pampas de la Joya desert. And, perhaps most importantly, the team prepared for the worst. 'That's one of the things with working with scientists: they're prepared for failure permanently,' says Rust.

With the super-potato planted and sealed inside the CubeSat, a live feed from cameras inside the hermetically sealed container was relayed to the project website, so the world could see whether it would grow. And more than 100 million people tuned in to watch. Says Rust, 'The news went to about 400 international news networks and for a week all that happened on the live stream was cameras failing and nothing growing. Those were the most stressful days of my life.'

Remarkably, the experiment lived up to the expectations built by Matt Damon in *The Martian*, and the universe's most famous potato broke triumphantly through the soil. The new variety of climate-resistant potato, named 'Unique', has already been deployed in climate-crisis areas in Bangladesh, and will be part of NASA's planned Mission to Mars, set to launch in the 2030s. All because of one silly question.

THINK-FRIENDLY TO THINK DIFFERENT

Writing online for *Forbes*, contributor Rodger Dean Duncan uses the term 'think-friendly questions', to describe the type of useful queries that lead to creative answers. Rather than questions with easy, direct, often one-word answers, these urge the answerer to ponder an actual solution. Often that solution is brilliant and obvious in retrospect. Of course people will happily pay less money for produce that tastes exactly the same.

Duncan cites the example of inventor Edwin Land taking photos on a walk with his young daughter. 'Why can't we see the pictures right now?' the girl asked, perhaps an earlier predecessor of the 'Why isn't this a touch screen?' question many parents get today. The question sparked Land to work out a way to transfer images directly from the camera lens onto photosensitive paper. The Land Camera was produced by Polaroid in 1948, and would go on to define the company, compelling millions of people to shake pieces of special paper in hopes of seeing their instant photo even a few seconds sooner.

Steve Jobs himself sang Land's praises in a 1985 interview published in *Playboy*. 'The man is a national treasure. I don't understand why people like that can't be held up as models: This is the most incredible thing to be – not an astronaut, not a football player – but *this*.'

Why *can't* we see the pictures right now? In 1948 that question led to the Polaroid camera. A few decades later, it might have led Land to the digital camera. In a few more decades, it might lead to technology that implants photographic memories directly into our brains. But without the question, it's harder to find the answer.

'WHY CAN'T YOU JUST STAY IN YOUR HOTEL ROOM IF IT ISN'T RESERVED FOR SOMEONE ELSE?'

Maybe you've been there. It's 11.55 a.m., you're frantically packing your bag in a hotel room to get out before the 12 p.m. checkout deadline, miffed at the front desk for not granting your request for a late checkout. Why do I have to leave exactly at noon? It's not like there's a crowd of people in the lobby clamouring for a room! Plus, it's a Tuesday. There's probably not even someone staying in this room tonight!

Art Series Hotels, a group of three boutique hotels in Melbourne, Australia, feels your pain. That's why the brand promised guests that if they called the front desk between 8 a.m. and 11 a.m. during a quiet month when the hotel was rarely fully booked, they were guaranteed a late checkout – at the very least. In fact, if no one else was slated to check in after you, the hotel invited you to stay an additional night, free of charge.

'In a hotel that's not full, why can't people stay for a few more hours or even another night?' That's the question Adam Ferrier, co-founder of Melbourne agency Naked, asked to spawn the campaign, called Overstay Checkout:

> When we presented [the client] an idea that changed their business model – in a manner that could be turned on and off with ease – they were really interested . . . It used the principles of behavioural economics to reframe its existing assets (empty rooms) into something that consumers could access if lucky enough. This created extra interest in the hotel and in staying there. It solved the problem of what hotels do with excess inventory.

Overstay Checkout was a hit. With the initial goal of selling an additional 1,000 hotel rooms above expected occupancy, Art Series ended up selling 1,550 in just four weeks. Of course, many of those rooms didn't bring in extra revenue on their own, since they were free. But through the campaign, the hotel generated an additional $37,214 in room-service orders. After all, if you're staying in a hotel for free, you might as well spring for a bottle of room-service bubbly or a raid on the mini fridge. Overall, on a budget of $80,000, the campaign achieved an ROI of 359 per cent and generated global media coverage valued at $1.5 million. Not too shabby.

'We love it because it's "pure" marketing: creating extra value in existing assets. People stayed for extra nights up to around a week. And then they spent more in hotel ancillary services,' Ferrier told Contagious.

Just as Art Series Hotels recognized that unoccupied rooms could be a boon to guests, Icelandair has turned a negative part of travel, killing time in an airport between flights, into a desirable feature of a journey. Since 1960 the airline has allowed passengers on transatlantic routes to add a stopover in Iceland for as long as seven days, without any additional charge. Instead of sleeping uncomfortably on plastic chairs or wandering zombie-like through the Duty Free shop before changing planes, travellers can take a few days to explore Reykjavik or see the Blue Lagoon.

Working with creative agencies Brooklyn Brothers, London and Islenska, Reykjavík, in 2016 the brand further enhanced those stopovers by adding a local human guide, through the Stopover Buddy Service. Travellers availing themselves of the stopover perk could sign up online to be paired up with Icelandair employees, including flight attendants, pilots, and even the CEO, to have some local guidance on making the most of their stop. Flight attendant Margret, for example, showed guests the hottest (pun intended) geothermal springs, while her colleague Inga taught guests to cook traditional Icelandic fish dishes. CEO Birkir Hólm Guðnason took travellers sledding or skiing.

According to travel-data tracker Sojern, the campaign sparked a 35 per cent increase in searches during the first two weeks, and a sustained 18 per cent boost over a five-month period.

Following the campaign's success, in 2017 the brand introduced the Stopover Pass, which offered travellers access to theatre and music experiences in Iceland.

FINDING BLUE OCEAN

Asking ridiculous and heretical questions about the very fundamental aspects of your brand, business, or industry can help identify untapped opportunities where competition is limited. INSEAD professors W. Chan Kim and Renée Mauborgne call this area of unchallenged opportunity 'blue ocean'.

'In blue oceans, competition is irrelevant because the rules of the game are waiting to be set,' they write in their book *Blue Ocean Strategy*. 'Instead of focusing on beating the competition, you focus on making the competition irrelevant by creating a leap in value for buyers and your company, thereby opening up a new and uncontested market space.'

'There are two ways to create blue oceans,' wrote Kim and Mauborgne in the *Harvard Business Review* in 2004, describing the theory. 'One is to launch completely new industries, as eBay did with online auctions. But it's more common for a blue ocean to be created from within a red ocean when a company expands the boundaries of an existing industry . . . A blue ocean strategic move can create brand equity that lasts for decades.'

'WHY CAN'T YOU BUY AIRLINE TICKETS AT THE SUPERMARKET?'

In 2015 Air France-KLM's low-cost airline, Transavia, answered a seemingly dumb question – 'Why can't you buy airline tickets at the supermarket?' – and found itself in a bit of blue ocean.

'We needed to stand out from the crowd of airline offers,' Marco Venturelli, at the time chief creative officer at Transavia's agency, Les Gaulois in Paris, told Contagious. 'If you research an airline online, you're suddenly floating in a sea of banner ads. So we thought, let's take it somewhere where we'd be on our own terms.'

Looking to boost the brand's familiarity in the dog-eat-dog low-cost airline market, Les Gaulois thought through Transavia's challenges and opportunities. An earlier campaign, where people could exchange unwanted items for aeroplane tickets on eBay, had shown the brand it could succeed by emphasizing just how inexpensive its flights were in a fresh and interesting way. But accessibility remained a challenge.

'Tickets are so cheap that everybody has the means to buy a ticket with Transavia,' says Venturelli. 'The most important thing wasn't to sell tickets, but to make people really understand, in comparison with other objects, just how cheap a ticket is.'

Behavioural economists would call it price anchoring – tying the purchase of an airline ticket to a low-cost item makes it seem more approachable in the eyes of a potential consumer. So finding an everyday low-cost purchase and turning it into a plane ticket would be a gold mine. Transavia Snack Holiday was born.

HOP, CHIP, AND JUMP

Transavia's brilliant idea was to create snack packaging that doubled as an aeroplane ticket to a low-cost destination. A €35 packet of crisps would buy you a one-way ticket from France to Barcelona, a €40 bag of gummy bears would take you to Lisbon, or a €40 cereal bar would get you to Dublin. Simply walk into your local Carrefour supermarket, buy the snack, and then enter the code found inside the packaging to redeem your ticket and choose your outbound flight. The goodies were also found in Selecta vending machines and MK2 cinemas in Paris.

Brilliant idea, logistical nightmare. 'We presented the idea, everybody loved it, and then we had to try to understand how we could even enter into this world of supermarkets that we didn't have any connection with,' says Venturelli.

The list of reasons to say no was long. Transavia had to figure out how to make the snacks, since no companies were interested in selling their snacks under someone else's brand. They had to secure insurance, on the off chance the food made someone sick. They had to find retail partners willing to invest time and space into the atypical product.

And then there was the question of scale. Transavia made 3,000 tickets available for sale through the campaign – a huge number of aeroplane seats, but a drop in the bucket when it comes to producing potato chips. 'All of the deals we had to sign were way bigger than we needed,' admits Venturelli, who noted that extra boxes of snacks circulated around the agency for months after the campaign.

Despite all of the reasons to say no, however, the brand and agency persisted, creating a campaign that earned media, built notoriety for Transavia, and (admittedly, only for a week) sold aeroplane tickets alongside breakfast cereals and loaves of bread.

Building on the success of Snack Holidays, the team concocted a similarly off-the-wall idea in 2017. For a week, in Lyons, Nantes, and Paris, Transavia partnered with Uber to add a new transit option for city dwellers stuck in the grind: UberEscape. One simply needed to click on the option in the app to find last-minute, low-cost flights from their nearest airport. Users could select a flight and book it through Transavia, and the price of the ticket would be added to their Uber fare – which happened to be taking them to the airport. Les Gaulois reported that the UberEscape tickets sold out within a few hours each day they were available.

HOW TO GET PAST OBJECTIVE DISQUALIFIERS

In *Apples, Insights and Mad Inventors: An Entertaining Analysis of Modern Marketing*, former WPP director Jeremy Bullmore writes about what he calls the 'Kuala Lumpur Question'. He describes a competitive pitch process in which a client is choosing between five advertising agencies:

> 'Tell me,' says the potential client, now halfway through the fifth impressive presentation, 'Do you have an office in Kuala Lumpur?'
>
> It is possible, I suppose, that access to an office in Kuala Lumpur is indeed of cardinal importance to this client. It is very much more likely, however, that the client is searching with something approaching desperation for an apparently respectable reason for the elimination of at least one of the candidate agencies. However trivial it may be, he needs an Objective Disqualifier.

This concept of an objective disqualifier, something you can point to and say 'we can't because of this', is pernicious throughout advertising. We find objective reasons to reject creativity. And nowhere is this more clear than when asking heretical questions. Could we close our stores on the biggest shopping day of the year? No, because we'll lose revenue. Can we admit our pizza isn't high quality? No, we'll lose sales. Can we give people free hotel nights? No, think of the cleaning costs.

Design firm IDEO promotes an idea that has quickly gained traction across industries, one that Contagious's advisory service uses with many of our clients: How Might We. These three magic words see the objective disqualifier roadblock ahead on the road, and neatly plot a detour to avoid the obstacle. Sure, that might be a reason to say no. But if it weren't, how might we make this idea happen? The further down the road you drive before letting the objective disqualifier get in the way, the more likely you are to produce truly transformational work – to make contagious marketing.

For heretical questions to work, you need to be able to get past no.

'WHAT IF WE JOIN FORCES WITH OUR ARCH RIVAL?'

Leading up to International Peace Day in 2015, Burger King did something unexpected: it took out a full-page ad in *The New York Times* and the *Chicago Tribune*, bearing the title, 'An open letter from Burger King to McDonald's.' The ad proposed a treaty, for one day only, between the at-odds franchises. Here's a snippet of the text:

> *Good morning McDonald's,*
> *We come in peace. In fact, we come in honor of peace. We know we've had our petty differences, but how about we call a ceasefire on these so-called burger wars? Here's what we're thinking . . . The McWhopper. All the tastiest bits of your Big Mac and our Whopper, united in one delicious peace-loving burger. Developed together, cooked together and available in one location for one day only – Peace Day, 21 September, 2015. Talk soon,*
> *Burger King*

The letter was accompanied by a link to McWhopper.com, a website containing the full proposal, including a copy of the letter, information about International Peace Day and Burger King partner non-profit Peace One Day, and a sketch of what the amalgamated burger might look like. Burger King proposed Atlanta as a location – midway between the two brands' Chicago and Miami HQs. The website even included mock-ups of design concepts for the burger's packaging, the pop-up restaurant, employee uniforms, and the burger itself (which included an equal number of ingredients from each restaurant's burger).

Burger King also suggested that, instead of paying with money, customers could receive a McWhopper in exchange for declaring their own truces by filling in the blanks on tray mats with the words 'Today I'll #settlethebeefwith . . .' printed on them.

'Everything in our proposal is up for discussion, from the name right through the packaging. The only thing we can't change is the date. So let's talk soon,' read the site.

To top things off, Burger King bought a few billboards near McDonald's locations, featuring the recognizable hands of the Burger King mascot releasing a white dove, holding up a peace sign, and extending an olive branch.

SAYING NO

The idea wasn't a brand-new one – in fact, Tom Paine, creative director of US ad agency Young & Rubicam's New Zealand operation, had come up with it four years earlier, in response to an open brief for Peace Day. But it hadn't gone anywhere. Jono Key, a planner at Y&R NZ, described the situation:

> Everyone's always loved the idea. No one's ever resisted the idea. But, every time we presented it to anyone, they said, 'The people above us will say no.' It took a little bit of trust to get it to the next stage, but every time we got to that next stage, they would always say, 'Yeah we love it but, the guy above me will say no.'

Finally, Key, Paine, and Y&R New Zealand CEO Josh Moore pushed the idea halfway across the globe to Burger King's Miami headquarters. Moore sent the proposal to future Burger King CMO Fernando Machado, who was the global marketing senior vice-president at the time. When Machado responded, Moore forwarded his message on to the team. Recounts Paine:

> Josh emailed us back later to say, 'Sorry guys I think Fernando's a little lukewarm on the idea.' Jono's reaction was not dissimilar to mine, he was fairly disheartened. I thought, 'Oh, screw it.' I scrolled down to read Fernando's feedback and it was, 'I fucking love this idea.' Josh was just taking the piss. Screw him for that! His words were verbatim: 'I fucking love this idea.'

After four years of marinating internally at Y&R, the idea broke through on the Burger King side and made it to print. There, it reached another no. No doubt after internal discussions that landed on an objective disqualifier, McDonald's declined to take part. In a note posted to Facebook, Steve Easterbrook, CEO of McDonald's, wrote, 'Inspiration for a good cause . . . great idea. We love the intention but think our two brands could do something bigger to make a difference.'

'Plan A was that McDonald's says yes. The campaign that we would have rolled out for plan A would have been fantastic,' Y&R planner Key told Contagious. 'The location for the pop-up restaurant that we chose in Atlanta was specifically chosen because there was a great Burger King and a great McDonald's opposite each other. We tried to take as many barriers away from McDonald's saying yes. It was one place, it was one burger. We're talking about 1,500 burgers that could be assembled between two restaurants. Everything was in place for McDonald's to say yes.'

PLAN B

After the Golden Arches declined, however, Burger King pushed on. Fast food's Denny's, southern chain Krystal, Connecticut-based burger franchise Wayback Burgers, and Brazilian brand Giraffas had all responded to Burger King saying they'd love to be involved. Via another open letter, Burger King proposed the Peace Day Burger, with each restaurant donating a key ingredient from their signature sandwich.

'The strategy grew so that it didn't actually matter if McDonald's responded, whether they said yes, or no, or maybe. If we could get a real groundswell of people making DIY McWhoppers that would be a success for us. We wanted the general public talking about it and sharing it and making it,' says Paine.

Says Key:

> The McWhopper was one newspaper ad, a website and a couple of billboards. The rest of it, the other 99 per cent of the noise, was all people taking the idea and reinterpreting it themselves. The big part of the campaign was giving it over to people. At the end of the day, we did a lot but we did a little. We gave everyone the idea, the recipe, the tools and let them run with it.

They did. More than 10,000 people shared videos of themselves making the McWhopper on their own time and dime, amassing the ingredients from both chains to make the Frankensteinian concoction. One video, titled 'Angry Grandpa Tries the McWhopper', has been viewed more than 2 million times. Meanwhile, in Atlanta, the Peace Day pop-up brought together chefs and ingredients from each participating brand, working together under a Peace Day flag, with proceeds and donations going to the Peace One Day charity.

According to a YouGov BrandIndex report, in the US the campaign increased Burger King's purchase consideration by 25 per cent. Positive brand buzz shot up by 75 per cent, while people's likelihood to recommend the brand jumped by 48 per cent.

Y&R reports that the campaign earned $138 million in media and resulted in 8.9 billion media impressions. And it was the top Twitter and Facebook trending topic in the US, Canada, Brazil, Mexico, Argentina, UK, Italy, Spain, and Turkey. And as icing on the branded cake (or the pickle on top of a branded burger), management consultancy McKinsey and Company found that there was a 16 per cent increase in Peace Day awareness worldwide.

For Key, the success can be directly attributed to asking the right questions. 'One of the reasons why McWhopper worked so well is because we raised more questions than answers at the start. What does a McWhopper taste like? Will McDonald's say yes? What are we going to do if they don't?'

EMPOWERING EVERYONE

In the film *Jurassic Park*, Dr Ian Malcolm (played by Jeff Goldblum) admonishes park creator John Hammond by saying, 'Your scientists were so preoccupied with whether or not they could that they didn't stop to think if they should.' In our ideal company, the scientists would have asked both those questions and a whole lot more. Yes, we're saying heretical questions will save your brand from human-hunting velociraptors. Or, at the very least, will help you keep up with your closest competition.

To make these heretical questions truly powerful, the act of asking them needs to be pervasive. This isn't a once-in-a-while exercise conducted during a senior leadership retreat. It must be an ongoing endeavour by people at all levels of your company. So many marketing missteps make it into the world because people within an organization aren't given the opportunity to feed back on an idea and say 'Is this the best way to send this message?' And business-changing ideas are overlooked (at least, until they're grasped by competitors) because junior employees aren't empowered to speak their minds and question the way things are done.

Asking questions is a tool to see the world through a different lens. To entertain possibilities. To uncover hidden truths or expose opportunities that hadn't previously been considered. Burger King asked a question without knowing what the answer would be, and the result was an impressive and creative campaign that gave it a leg up on its direct competitor. Transavia uncovered fertile selling ground where it could operate without any other airlines even remotely nearby. Domino's wasn't afraid to answer the question of why its sales were slumping and address it head on.

Ask heretical questions – and empower others in your company to do the same – and you'll be much stronger for it.

ASK HERETICAL QUESTIONS / ESPRESSO VERSION

Speaking with *Time* magazine in 2006, Eric Schmidt, at that time the CEO of Google, stated his belief in questions as a tool quite clearly:

> We run the company by questions, not by answers . . . You ask it as a question, rather than a pithy answer, and that stimulates conversation. Out of the conversation comes innovation. Innovation is not something that I just wake up one day and say, 'I want to innovate.' I think you get a better innovative culture if you ask it as a question.

We agree.

Beyond just the obvious, though, we believe difficult, awkward, heretical questions lead to breakthroughs and creative tangents that exploit opportunities and address weaknesses long before they might otherwise be identified.

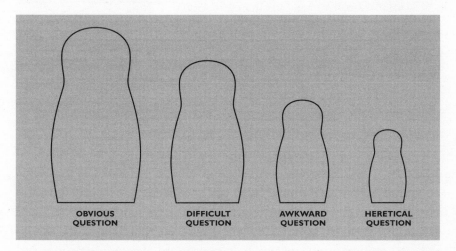

OBVIOUS QUESTION   DIFFICULT QUESTION   AWKWARD QUESTION   HERETICAL QUESTION

Think of questions like a Russian nesting doll. The easiest and most obvious ones are the biggest. Most people are comfortable going one level deeper. They expend so much brain power puzzling over the difficult questions, that this is where they tend to stop. But beyond those difficult questions there are others that are even harder to ask out loud. People stop short of awkward questions, because they know they'll cause inconvenience or even offence. And very rarely do we touch the heretical questions, that solid, inner layer of queries so radical that they question the foundation that a company is built on. These heretical questions can cause schisms. They don't always lead to fun conversations. But they are the interrogations that will truly transform your offering, protect your business, and invigorate your marketing.

Try these on for size:

- // 'What are we doing that is actively undermining our value proposition?'
- // 'How would we put ourselves out of business if we were our competitor?'
- // 'What's the open secret that everyone knows about this company but no one will talk about?'
- // 'Where is there opportunity that requires bold action that we haven't taken? How might we take that action?'
- // 'Do we truly encourage people at all levels of our organization to ask heretical questions?'

The best way to burglar-proof your house is to lose your own keys. Once you need to break in, you interrogate weaknesses in a new light. Lose the keys to your company and ask yourself how to get back inside. As Facebook wrote in its *Little Red Book*: 'If we don't create the thing that kills Facebook, someone else will.' (No surprise, they've spent billions acquiring start-ups aiming to do just that.)

Of course, just asking questions isn't enough – we've all been frustrated by a colleague who only asks questions or identifies problems and never supplies solutions. Once you've voiced the heretical question it's time to get to work on answering it. But we're reminded of the aphorism 'a conclusion is just the place where you got tired of thinking'. Asking heretical questions will help your brain carry on to deeper and more meaningful conclusions.

ALIGN WITH BEHAVIOUR

I n 2015, while doing research to find ways to encourage increased travel to the UK, tourism agency VisitBritain stumbled across a troubling fact. Chinese travellers – an increasingly large portion of international vacationers – found Britain to be unwelcoming. One reason? The Chinese names they used to describe many British attractions were confusing to navigate for non-English speakers.

'As we did some social media listening we found that [Chinese] people give nicknames to everything as a way of having fun but also to have a bit of ownership over something and make them feel more familiar with it. We found that people had already started giving names to places in Britain and to the UK itself,' Jeremy Webb, national director of Social@ Ogilvy for the UK, told Contagious. 'Britain had crap Chinese names for its places, people and things, so we thought "What if Britain could extend an invitation to the Chinese people to name its places, people, food, things?"'

The result was a contest and campaign called 'Great Chinese Names for Great Britain', which invited Chinese visitors to rename 101 famous British places and things. People could submit names to the competition, and whichever suggestions earned the most 'Likes' were added to Google Maps, Wikipedia and the Chinese search engine Baidu. Sherwood Forest, the home of Robin Hood, was renamed the 'Forest of Chivalrous Thieves'; London tailoring district Savile Row became 'Street for the Tall, Rich and Handsome'; and the Highland Games were rebranded as 'Strongman Skirt Party'. Over 13,000 name suggestions were submitted to the microsite and the campaign received international media coverage. What's more, the initiative increased flights to the UK by 27 per cent during the campaign period compared with the previous year.

It's one thing to come up with a left-field idea so compelling that the world lines up to join in. It's another to recognize that the world is already lining up to do something and understand how your aims dovetail with them.

Anyone who wants to conceive an innovative, contagious idea needs to align with behaviour – that is, understand the innate cultural drift in which people are caught. They must understand how people seek specific places or things to supplement that activity – and try to go with that flow instead of fighting against it. Call it consumer-driven innovation. Call it customer-centricity. All it really consists of is paying attention to how people are interacting with the world around them, and then figuring out where you fit in.

Key to success in this area is listening. Marketers need to get to grips with what people are doing or saying in areas adjacent to their idea and then move in that direction, rather than expecting people to change their behaviours and go out of their way to interact with advertising.

IF YOU BUILD IT, YOU MIGHT FAIL

It's a cliché so perfect that it's impossible not to reference: in the film *Field of Dreams*, a young Kevin Costner walks into a cornfield, hears a voice that says, 'If you build it, he will come,' and decides to turn his farmland into a baseball field. Although the field turns out to be a good investment – it brings old baseball players back to life and reunites Costner's character with his deceased father – that voice in the cornfield is dispensing one of the worst pieces of marketing advice you'll ever hear.

Let us state this clearly and without question: marketers; if you build it, they probably will not come. If you build a channel, people will probably not watch it. If you build an app, people will probably not download it. If you create a new event, people will probably not attend. And none of the three will bring back long-dead relatives.

Now, of course there are exceptions to this rule. Some brands are capable of catching lightning in a bottle and creating new behaviours out of thin air. You can read about them in the boxes that follow. But we would argue that those exceptions are outliers – history being written by the winners. The road to that success is littered with the wreckage of failed attempts to get people to adopt completely new routines.

Maybe this pre-wreckage scene is a familiar one: your agency came up with a great idea to make an app. They spent weeks or even months building it, used all the right Pantones, mimicked the best apps around, and tested it to make sure people loved it. Maybe it was a great game where people pop little logos instead of candy gems. You thought it would be a hit and millions of folk would download it, and you'd never have to spend a dime of marketing budget ever again for as long as you live.

Almost without fail, this ends in wasted time, wasted money, and a lot of shaking heads around a conference-room table. Put yourself in the customer's shoes: when was the last time *you* downloaded a branded app? When was the last time you downloaded a branded app that didn't provide a service, like fetching your boarding pass or making it easier to pay for your coffee? And if you downloaded one a long time ago, when was the last time you opened it?

For better or for worse, branded apps just don't get downloaded. In fact, almost *no* apps get downloaded – branded or not. Depending on what data source you trust, the average smartphone owner downloads somewhere between zero and two apps a month. In 2011 Deloitte found that 80 per cent of all apps are downloaded fewer than 1,000 times. In 2016 Muz.li found that 72 per cent of people use six or fewer apps per day, and within thirty days of downloading a new app, only 3 per cent of people are still using it. Don't believe the voice in Kevin's head. If you build it, no one will come.

The misguided push to build standalone apps that dominated the early days of the smartphone era – 'There's an app for that!' – missed out on a few key ideas, none bigger that the fact that apps would soon begin to eat each other. Today in China, WeChat has swallowed other services whole, becoming a sort of operating system within the mobile operating system, with people conducting a huge amount of their mobile activities through the WeChat interface. Elsewhere, Facebook Messenger has similar designs, attempting to bring myriad services under a single app roof, using familiarity and known interaction patterns to get users on board and keep them there.

If we were gamblers, we'd bet that this Great Condensation will continue. People are lazy. We want to accomplish the most tasks with the least effort. And brands need to get on board.

INSTEAD, FIND EXISTING BEHAVIOURS

So what's a brand to do? In the face of this bleak scenario where no one will lift a finger to do anything and people refuse to stray from the well-trodden path, how can you possibly get them to pay attention to your products and services? If you've been paying attention to our commandment titles, you probably know our advice: align with behaviour. Whenever possible, identify what people are *already* doing, and figure out a way to integrate your brand into those routines and processes.

Procter & Gamble hair-care brand Pantene understood this in 2014. After noting that women often searched for weather forecasts before making decisions about their hairstyle for the day, the brand worked with Chicago-based ad agency Arc to develop 'haircasts', which advised women on how to manicure their manes based on the weather in their specific area. Rather than building a standalone app, however, Pantene partnered with the Weather Channel to integrate this content directly into the Weather Channel app, so that the information was served up in the context of an existing behaviour, rather than trying to force new habits (and an additional lookup). A $2 discount coupon at Walgreens, the largest drugstore chain in the US, drove viewers from app to purchase, and resulted in a 28 per cent sales lift for Pantene.

FIGHT THE FRICTION

Now, aligning with behaviour does not simply mean jumping on the coat-tails of existing paradigms. If that were the low bar we were setting, running an advertisement on television *because lots of people watch television* would count as aligning with behaviour. It may technically count, but it's not an exciting tale to tell. The brands that really tickle our fancy are the ones that identify existing behaviour patterns and figure out ways to improve and augment them through products or services.

Take, for example, telecommunications company Vodafone in Egypt. The brand noticed a pervasive behaviour in Egyptian commerce in 2013. Small, independent shops, which dominate the Egyptian retail landscape, will often substitute low-value items for loose change when transacting with customers. Instead of getting a number of small coins back after making a purchase, a shopper might find themselves being presented with a handful of gum or candy, perhaps an onion – small-value items to substitute for loose change.

Realizing that this wasn't necessarily serving the needs of the consumer, Vodafone decided to launch a product aligned with this existing behaviour. Enter Vodafone Fakka. Arabic for 'petty change', Fakka are micro recharge cards for prepaid mobile customers that can sub in for low-value items. Instead of getting a dime's worth of hard candies, shoppers could grab a dime's worth of data or voice time – something more universally valuable. And because Vodafone's customer base in Egypt consisted primarily of low-income, prepay customers (who shop in these types of retail environments), the product was directly aligned with both a cultural behaviour and a customer need. Not only did the name make immediate sense to the target demographic, it gave Vodafone first-mover advantage, and established ownership of the concept in a highly competitive product category.

'This idea is based on the insight that it is a common practice in Egypt that at small shops, stores, kiosks or pharmacies, the shop owners often offer customers products of little value to them in place of the remaining change,' Moataz Abdel-Jalil, head of consumer marketing at Vodafone, explained to Contagious. 'Vodafone Fakka, which is available in these shops, will give customers an alternative they can benefit from instead of wasting change on items that are of little use or relevance to their needs.'

Vodafone and JWT, the agency that worked on the campaign, claimed that Vodafone Fakka revenues exceeded the brand's original target by 510 per cent and increased average revenue per Vodafone user by 7 per cent. Through the introduction of Fakka, Vodafone was able to expand its reach to become the most ubiquitous telco in Egypt, available in more than 46,000 non-traditional outlets.

Another campaign, this time in India, built on a similar behaviour in 2017. In India, 96 per cent of transactions are still made using cash. But often shop owners don't have enough change, and give their customers sweets instead. Payments app Paytm noticed this widespread pain point and worked with McCann Worldwide India in Mumbai to address it with its own brand of confectionery that could be redeemed for money. So-called 'Paytm Sweet Change' was distributed to store owners in four denominations to enable them to give exact change. Customers could then get their lost cash back by downloading the Paytm app and inputting the promo code on the inside of the wrapper. To maul an old phrase, customers could quite literally have their change and eat it too. According to the agency, the app received over 1 million downloads over the course of the campaign, and dropped the cost of customer acquisition for Paytm by a factor of five.

GOOD LUCK, HERE'S SOME CHOCOLATE

One of our favourite examples of aligning with behaviour – and one that's legendary in the advertising world – is Kit Kat's use of the Japanese postal service. Sounds strange, but what Kit Kat did was identify a unique behaviour in Japanese culture and align its product with that exact scenario. And it happened almost by accident.

Turns out, when students in Japan sit for their *juken* exams for entrance to university every February, friends and family wish them *kitto katsu*, a Japanese phrase meaning something along the lines of 'you will certainly win'. And in the past, many parents have cooked up superstitious meals the night before tests with lucky-sounding names like *katsudon* or *tonkatsu*.

As a smart person reading this book, you will no doubt notice that *kitto katsu* sounds a lot like another food product, Kit Kat, which is known as Kitto Katto in Japan. This coincidence explains why Kit Kat saw an unexpected sales surge in Japan every year around the time of the exams.

'We're finding that parents are buying them for their children for exam days, but also some determined pupils are buying Kit Kats for themselves as a sort of reminder that they are really going to give these exams their best shot,' Yuko Iwasaki, a spokesman for Nestlé Japan, told the *Daily Telegraph* in 2005.

Taking this coincidence and running with it, Nestlé worked with agency JWT to launch a campaign in 2009 that put its product at the centre of this behaviour. Partnering with Japan Post, the privatized national postal service, Kit Kat created packaging for its signature chocolate bar that included a space to write good luck messages and could be dropped in the mail and sent to students preparing for the tough exams.

Remember that talk of blue ocean in the third commandment? Beyond simply creating new packaging, Kit Kat created a completely new sales channel, selling its Kit Kat Mail chocolate bars in 22,000 Japan Post locations, far away from any competing products. And what's more, the brand struck a deal to decorate Japan Post offices to highlight the lucky Kit Kat bars.

The campaign was a smash hit, earning a reported $11 million in media coverage while generating hundreds of thousands of sales. It was such a success that the partnership became permanent. To this day, Kit Kat continues to run similar promotions with Japan Post, including the annual custom known as *otoshidama* that involves giving exam good-luck charms and New Years gifts – all sold through Japan Post locations. In 2016 the brand added some extra pizazz to the Kit Kat Mail campaign, working with J. Walter Thompson to create holographic versions. These special-edition packages included a pre-cut clear plastic pattern that could be assembled into a pyramid-like structure and placed upside down on a smartphone. When a certain YouTube video was played on the phone, Japanese boy band Dish appeared on the pyramid walls as a hologram, dancing and singing words of encouragement. The packages sold out in Japan Post locations.

Kit Kat Mail worked because Nestlé didn't create a new behaviour out of whole cloth or run a marketing campaign decreeing that Kit Kats are lucky. Instead, the brand noticed a nascent consumer behaviour within a specific culture, and then nurtured that behaviour by creating values-aligned packaging for its product.

Since the success of Kit Kat Mail, the brand has found other creative ways to align with existing behaviours to deliver value. In 2012, after the devastation caused by the 2011 earthquake and subsequent tsunami in northern Japan, Nestlé learned that people were giving Kit Kat bars to a railway reconstruction team as a form of encouragement. The brand used that as inspiration for a programme that donated ¥20 per bar sold to the railway rebuilding effort. Noticing that travellers often grab a chocolate bar before boarding a train – and acknowledging a semantic similarity between Kitto and the Japanese word for tickets, *kippu*, Kit Kat went a step further in 2014, launching a campaign that allowed travellers to substitute specially marked Kippu Kat bars for train tickets on the Sanriku Railway in northern Japan.

In 2013, hoping to increase its presence in the Chinese market, French sports-apparel brand Domyos blended Eastern and Western cultures to create an all-new fitness activity called Tai-Chip-Hop. Working with agency Fred & Farid in Shanghai, Domyos fused China's most popular form of exercise, tai chi, with hip-hop dance. A launch video featuring the two activities merging together to form a single exercise racked up more than 100 million views.

As Frédéric Raillard, co-founder and executive creative director of Fred & Farid, explained to Contagious,

> You can't just come and start a movement, because that costs too much money. It is easier, cheaper and less time consuming to create an efficient hijack. This is what we implemented for Domyos: instead of creating a new force all about West and East, we needed to interconnect the existing forces. This is

why we identified different disciplines in the two cultures: tai chi for China and hip-hop for Western countries.

The brand invited teams to create their own dance routines, with five schools competing in a live Tai-Chip-Hop contest attended by 15,000 people and broadcast on national TV channels. According to Fred & Farid, on a press and digital media budget of RMB670,000 (£85,000/$115,000) and a production budget of RMB3.5 million (£300,000/$410,000), year-on-year sales in China rose by 80 per cent, ideas for new product development were generated and Tai-Chip-Hop classes started to appear on the schedules of Chinese gyms.

WANT TO FIND BEHAVIOURS TO ALIGN WITH? LOOK AROUND

Much like our second commandment – imploring brands to put relevance on a pedestal – aligning with behaviour is another way to remind marketers to quit navel gazing and pay attention to the world around them and how it is changing. New behaviours develop as people adopt new technologies, creating new opportunities for engagement.

In the past decade, if you've sat in any marketing conference, business conference, technology conference, any conference at all really, you have no doubt heard someone on stage proclaim 'The Era of Mobile' being upon us. Hackneyed though it is, it's true. Mobile devices and the connectivity they bring have fundamentally changed behaviours – and unlocked opportunities.

In Kenya, the mobile behaviour change took place earlier and more profoundly than in more developed areas of the world, where the inertia of established infrastructure forced slower adoption and less instantly pervasive change. While laptop ownership remained low, by 2012 54 per cent of Kenyans owned a mobile phone. And one telecom brand figured out how to align with local behaviours to stand out from the provider pack.

M-PRESSIVE

In 2007 Kenyan telco Safaricom recognized that many of its customers were forced by poverty or pure geography to manoeuvre outside of a traditional banking system (a 2009 World Bank study found that 70 per cent of Africans were unbanked or underbanked), so it created M-PESA, a mobile money transfer system that uses a mobile phone account in place of a bank account, no credit or debit card required. Here's how it works: Safaricom customers can purchase and send electronic funds via one of the 55,000 M-PESA agents across the country, and then retrieve that money in cash from an M-PESA agent near them. Users can withdraw, deposit, or send between 50 and 70,000 Kenyan shillings (KES) (£0.40 / $0.60–£560 / $800) per transaction.

Money can be moved by an individual, sent to friends and relatives, or even used to pay bills. In 2013 M-PESA accounted for nearly a third of Safaricom's profits, with more than 15.2 million active users (Kenya has a population of 41 million). Users transferred an incredible KES 80 billion per month (£650 million / $920 million) across the network – the equivalent of more than 30 per cent of Kenyan GDP. M-PESA has been such a success that it has since spread to Egypt, India, Lesotho, Mozambique, Tanzania, South Africa, Afghanistan, and Romania.

Beyond M-PESA, Safaricom aligned its infrastructure with other needs among its customers. For example, it partnered with mobile-tech company M-KOPA to create a pay-as-you-go solar-power service powered by M-PESA – a useful invention for a country where 70 to 80 per cent of the population has no access to the electricity grid. Also, to provide customers with better access to medical advice, Safaricom teamed up with a medical hotline to create Daktari 1525 (*daktari* is Swahili for doctor). Customers could dial 1525 on their mobile device to place a subsidized call to a doctor. In its first four months the service received 80,000 calls, amounting to 703 conversations a day. It's an invaluable service in a country where there's one doctor for every 10,000-plus patients but more than 70 per cent of people have a mobile phone.

Another service, M-Shwari, even enables Safaricom customers to apply for loans using their mobile phones. Launched in collaboration with the Commercial Bank of Africa, the service accumulated 1 million registered users and deposits of nearly KES 1 billion in its first three months.

'Safaricom is the catalyst that has transformed the country at grassroots level. Although it started as a telecommunications company, it is providing services to each and every sector,' Gaurav Singh, general manager of WPP-affiliated Scangroup told Contagious.

So how did it find this vein of opportunity? Safaricom CEO Bob Collymore credits the company's understanding of its customers with its success in building behaviour-aligned services. 'Because our staff [of around 2,660 people] is almost 100 per cent Kenyan we understand how Kenyans think and behave and what motivates them,' says Collymore, himself a Guyana native. He contrasts this with Safaricom's competitors: Orange (formerly France Télécom) and two Indian-owned companies, Airtel and Essar Telecom. 'They are tempted to take what's worked in other markets and try to bring it here,' says Collymore.

We'd go a step further. Safaricom has succeeded in no small part because of its willingness to go beyond the typical offerings of a mobile-phone company in order to align with existing behaviours among its customer base. Recognizing atypical behaviours as emerging opportunities, and creating services to, quite literally, capitalize, led to considerable success for the brand.

MADDEN MAD MEN

Behaviours don't have to be linked to social infrastructure like financial systems and postal services, of course. Most of the time, the behaviours brands should be paying attention to are just a hop, skip, and a jump from where they're already focused.

In 2014 video game company EA found one such behaviour among American Football fans, when looking to promote its signature game franchise, Madden NFL.

'A game that actually should take an hour to play takes three and a half hours on TV, eleven minutes of which the ball is actually live. So second-screen behaviour for this sport with viewers and fans at home is actually really high,' said Matt Stafford, the Digital Creative Director at agency Heat in 2014. 'During commercial breaks people are either tweeting about that big play that just happened for their team or commenting about how their team is getting beaten really badly. We wanted to try to tap into that.'

So, working with Heat in San Francisco, Grow in Virginia, and Google's Art Copy & Code group, EA created the Madden GIFERATOR, a GIF generator powered by Madden NFL's graphics. (GIF is an acronym of Graphic Interchange Format, a computer file used to send images and short moving sequences and animations on the web.) During the NFL season, fans could choose from a library of Madden GIFs, add their own text, and share them directly to social networks. Dana Marineau, EA's vice-president of advertising and design, told Contagious:

> We just thought, 'Wouldn't it be so much better if Madden was a part of this?' This is a behaviour that people already have, and we thought we could do it way better. And we can: our images, the backgrounds, the way the players look – now Madden is in the conversation.
>
> The younger generation of Madden fans is who this particular part was aimed at, because they're the ones who are using GIFs, second-screen behaviour, talking smack with their friends. That is the culture of Madden, the culture of how you play Madden, the culture of football, how you tweet, how you Facebook. That's how they communicate with their friends now. That is who the target was for this: people who are going to take our Madden assets and use that throughout the season talking about the game – the younger generation of football fans and gamers.

The key: the team thought through the behaviour first, and then built the campaign from that perspective. 'The night before it launched, we were all looking at it and the feeling in the room was "I would use this",' said Drew Ungvarsky, the CEO of Grow. 'Whether or not I cared a lick about advertising, this was something I was going to love. And game one, day one, people were tweeting about this thing at more than one per second. It was pop culture that quickly.'

More than 500,000 GIFs were created through the campaign site, including creative user-generated components like Bible verse GIFs, GIF-ERATOR music videos, and 'analogue gifs' recreating the moving images using action figurines. On average, users spent a stunning nine minutes playing around with the generator. And Madden sales (though likely not tied directly to this single campaign) rose 14 per cent over the previous year.

What's more, the GIFERATOR became the basis for an insightful display campaign. GIFs featuring game updates, created by the campaign team using direct-from-the-source NFL game data, became real-time display ads in banners and social streams.

Mike Glaser, Google's brand lead of creative partnerships, discussed the project with Contagious:

> One thing we like to talk about is 'making companions, not campaigns'. How do you tap into that user behaviour of watching the game and then going into my phone during a time out? None of us want to really click into an ad, but if you can deliver content – in this case a funny GIF with a witty headline, a live score and a clock – you're already delivering information, which is a huge benefit for a lot of folks. And then they can click in and make their own.

GOOD VISUAL

The GIFERATOR built on a behavioural base that has been undeniable for modern marketers: the rise of visual culture. Today, we each carry a powerful computer in our pockets with more processing power than room-sized supercomputers used to run missions to the moon in the early days of black-and-white television. And we use these miracle devices most often to post photos of ourselves to social media.

Behaviours that would have been previously unheard of have become commonplace. Can you imagine replying to a thoughtful note from a friend with a single image summing up how you feel? You wouldn't have done it ten years ago, yet you wouldn't think twice about it today.

As early internet video pioneer Ze Frank puts it, 'Repurposing media not for consumption but for communication is the underpinning of this social age.'

Photos – and increasingly videos – dominate the conversation. 3M found in 2001 that the human brain processes images 60,000 times faster than text. Instagram built a billion-dollar business on simply helping people take better photos and to share them more easily, ushering in a wave of equal parts instant connection and self consciousness, and putting performative photos into the spotlight. And the rise of these visual communications platforms has profoundly impacted the brand ecosystem. Research by Retail Dive found that 72 per cent of Instagram users have made a purchase based on something they saw in their feed.

The rise in visual culture has given birth to fads and phenomena based entirely on how things look in photos. A few examples:

- // The Unicorn Frappuccino. Launched in April of 2017 for a limited time only, this purple, pink and blue Starbucks beverage stormed social media and left a swathe of sparkly destruction in its wake. Multinational investment bank UBS reported that more than 180,000 photos of the drink were posted to Instagram in a single week. As a Starbucks spokesperson told *The Guardian*, 'The look of the beverage was an important part of its creation.'

- // Rainbow Bagels. Similar to the Unicorn Frapp, these technicolour monstrosities have had people queuing round the block at Williamsburg, Brooklyn's Bagel Store. Though the store has been selling the multicolour neon creations for nearly two decades, they have only recently achieved celebrity status, thanks to a 'How Rainbow Bagels Are Made' YouTube video posted in early 2016, followed by a rush of Instagram posts and media coverage.

- // Instagrammable Museums. The Museum of Ice Cream launched as a pastel-coloured pop-up in New York in 2016, with a mission to 'design environments that bring people together and provoke imagination'. In other words, it's a selfie-utopia. In the ultimate self-referential endorsement, the queen of Instagram, Beyoncé, visited a temporary version of the venue in LA on Mother's Day, with her brood and famous hubby in tow. Chock full of photo-friendly environments, including a pool of sprinkles, brightly coloured oversized popsicles, and a room of hanging bananas that looks like an Andy Warhol acid trip, this museum-without-any-historical-artefacts seems explicitly designed to generate shareable images for visitors.

The mobile exhibition sold out a six-month engagement in San Francisco within an hour and a half of putting tickets up for sale. Elsewhere, visual art exhibits such as Random International's Rain Room, James Turrell's light experiments, and the Smithsonian Renwick Gallery's 'Wonder' exhibit have seen similar crowds.

// White Christmas trees. Home-goods retailer Wayfair saw a fourfold increase in sales of white Christmas trees over the period before the holiday compared to the previous year. Spokesperson Julie Cassetina explained the rise to the *Wall Street Journal*, citing the trees' photo-friendly nature. 'Today, everyone is pushing the envelope and thinking about how they can capture a moment through the lens of their smartphone. That plays a huge role when it comes to decorating for the holidays.'

// A Pink Wall. Menswear retailer Paul Smith's flagship location on Melrose Ave in Los Angeles has bright pink walls that have, thanks to visual culture, become a cult destination. Painted in 2005, the walls have recently become a hit, with tens of thousands of photos posted – forcing the store to hire a security guard to manage the mob of people waiting for their chance to pose. The store has also installed a sign with photo rules, preferred hashtags, a geotag, and the brand's Instagram handle. Paul Smith even partnered with Instagram to paint one of the walls rainbow colours in June 2017 to celebrate Pride month.

The list goes on and on. And is brightly coloured.

THE WORLD'S MOST PHOTOGENIC BEER

When visual culture was first starting to boom, agency TBWA\Hakuhodo noticed the emerging behaviour of photographing food and beverages and set out to develop a product aligned with that behaviour for its client, Kirin beer. The resulting product, dubbed 'the Photogenic Beer', deftly exploited young people's unquenchable thirst for social sharing.

The Photogenic Beer utilized specially constructed serving machines to dispense an extra-thick, extra-cold beer foam, shaped like an ice cream whirl, which sat atop each pint of Kirin to provide a perfectly cute photo opportunity. The machines were set up in special Kirin-branded beer gardens and the agency reports that very little actual marketing was used to support the campaign, relying instead on earned media and physical presence to drive awareness, footfall, and purchase.

'We successfully created an experience spiral where the target audience learns about the beer from posts on social media, becomes interested, experiences the product, and then communicates the experience to others,' Mariko Fujimoto, a planner at Hakuhodo, told Contagious.

The machines were trialled in 2012 and within two years could be found in 2,200 locations across Japan and seven other countries. The brand also ran a contest to give away a machine to replicate the beer at home that required entrants to purchase ninety-six cans of Kirin to enter. The agency reports an astonishing 330,000 entries were received. The ice-cream top has since become a hallmark of the Kirin brand around the world. And, most importantly, the campaign generated more than $2 million in earned media and resulted in a 5 per cent year-over-year sales lift for the brand.

Recognizing that its core demographic of young children is locked out of social media networks, toy block brand LEGO found a way to bring social media behaviours to kids under thirteen in a safe and secure way. In 2017 the brand launched LEGO Life, a platform where kids can browse, share, and comment on LEGO creations with complete anonymity. It works like this: youngsters who sign up are given a random three-word username, untraceable to a specific person. Once on the network, kids can post photos of their creations – but only if the photos don't contain any humans in them. Commenting functions on the platform are limited to custom LEGO emojis, meaning the platform is completely safe from abusive language.

'Every piece of social media is, in a sense, a gamified system,' Rob Lowe, senior director of LEGO Life, told Contagious. 'With this one we are just being very open about it and saying the more stuff you build, the more creative you are, then the more kudos you can get inside the experience and the more little rewards you can unlock.'

The platform has been a hit for social-media-starved kids, with more than 3 million users by the end of 2017, less than a year after its launch. Lowe told Contagious in November of 2017 that LEGO Life was adding almost a million new users every month.

TALK LIKE THEY TALK

Alongside visual culture, behaviours have shifted around communications thanks to the rise of messaging apps. And as these new behaviours have emerged and evolved, brands that have quickly aligned themselves have got a head start on the competition. We call it 'talking like they talk'.

Quite simply: mobile *is* messaging. An eMarketer study reports that 87 per cent of teens cite instant messaging as the primary activity on their smartphone or tablet. Messaging apps boast a robust 62 per cent retention rate a full year after download, compared to a measly 11 per cent for non-messaging apps. In 2017 WhatsApp counted a billion daily active users, sending an average of 55 billion messages every twenty-four hours.

We've seen fascinating examples of brands using messaging interfaces to engage with customers. Just a few examples:

// In 2011, after Line (then the leading messaging app in Japan, Thailand, and Taiwan) released emoji-like stickers, brands like KFC, Kit Kat, and Burberry quickly jumped on board to create their own shareable sticker packs.

// In 2014 the Los Angeles County Museum of Art used Snapchat to send amusing snaps juxtaposing modern references and classic works of art (think Rodin sculptures with Beyoncé captions). 'Not only is Snapchat a great way to reach a younger audience, but it also provides us with a platform for play,' LACMA's social media manager Maritza Yoes told culture website Hyperallergic.

// In March 2015 UK footwear brand Clarks launched an interactive documentary, sending messages, photos, and videos from three separate people on WhatsApp in a cascading story that engaged readers through a familiar interface.

// In 2017 South African financial services group Sanlam released a soap opera on WhatsApp to promote its funeral insurance. The show, called *Uk'shona Kwelanga* (which translates both as *The Sunset* and also as *The Death of Langa*), was the brainchild of Cape Town agency King James, and attracted more than 9,000 subscribers and 30 million media impressions. For funeral insurance!

Of course, messaging isn't a new phenomenon. '[Instant messaging] has been around for decades, starting in internet cafes, then moving to computers at home and then onto laptops – now it's available on mobile phones,' Paul Lee, head of telecoms research at Deloitte, told Contagious. 'The behaviour may be jumping device, but it's the same behaviour, it's the same need.'

SOCIAL STORYTELLING

Our core desires might stay the same – we will always seek to find information, communicate with others, express ourselves – but the way we accomplish these desires is undergoing a profound upheaval. Gone are the days where we'd turn to a single source of information for the full story. Instead, we might read about a piece of news on a newspaper website, find up-to-the-minute updates on Twitter, watch clips on YouTube, and talk about it with our friends on Facebook. This weaving together of platforms is a profound behaviour change, and yet many marketers are trapped in a channel-first mindset rather than a story-first one.

An exception to this antiquated linear thinking came in 2013, in the form of a teenage reality show produced by the Chernin Group and agency BBDO for AT&T. Called *@SummerBreak*, the show followed a group of California teenagers in their last summer before college. But rather than playing out in twenty-two-minute, ad-interrupted episodes, the drama unfolded in YouTube videos, Tumblr posts, Instagram photos, and Twitter updates, alongside the rest of the audience's social lives.

Young people, @*SummerBreak* co-creator Billy Parks explained to Contagious,

> use these social platforms as a way to communicate ideas with each other, and it's part of their everyday sharing of entertainment. When you're competing for a teenager's time, whether it's television, Netflix, YouTube, Instagram, Twitter or Tumblr, they are on all of these platforms all of the time. We wanted to create an entertainment experience that could insert itself into the conversation on all of these social platforms in a unique way.

Rather than compete where all the other content lived, the producers took a story-first approach, creating content that targeted the platforms prospective audience members were *already* on, using behaviours that mimicked those platforms' established norms. Said Parks:

> We thought of the show as having its own life on each platform. Each platform has its own core competencies and set of rules, and each platform has its own way that people use it. So we kept every platform consistent with that vernacular. We weren't using it as a marketing tool where we were trying to drive everything from one platform to the other.
>
> If you're going to tell a story about a boy and a girl dating and you want to show pieces of that on each platform, you have to listen to what the audience likes on each of those platforms and be willing to change it based on how you present that information. That doesn't mean the story is different, it just means how you contextualize it is different. We listened. We saw what got the most engagement and went with it. We iterated and changed as we went. We were built to be agile.

The show outpaced expectations, racking up 15 million views on YouTube and 10 million social engagements in its first season. Liz Nixon, AT&T's director of engagement marketing, told Contagious:

We recognized it was a really fresh opportunity as marketers to connect with, and be relevant to, a mobile generation. This is how they live, how they create and how they connect with their peers. We were blown away. The number of video views and engagements were pretty astounding. The value that super fans brought emerged pretty clearly, they have driven engagement. It's not even fair to call them viewers because in a show like this they're participants.

Since the first year, AT&T has continued to produce *@Summer-Break*, evolving the content and delivery based on audience reactions and behaviours. By 2015 the show's videos had amassed 143 million views, including 1.1 billion impressions on overall content from the third season. And content channels continue to evolve. By its fifth season in 2017 *@SummerBreak* material had been published on YouTube, Instagram, Snapchat, Facebook, Tumblr, Twitter, Vine, Periscope, We Heart It, Giphy, and Musical.ly.

BEHAVIOUR-CENTRIC = CUSTOMER-CENTRIC = PLATFORM-AGNOSTIC

Astute readers will notice that *at least* one of the above-mentioned platforms no longer even exists. Which points to perhaps the most important aspect of aligning with behaviour: it allows you to be largely platform agnostic, adapting alongside your audience. The flash-in-the-pan nature of some platforms is further support for the idea that you should align with behaviours rather than trying to create new ones.

We are in the midst of an interface revolution, with consumers quickly moving from computers to mobile devices and now beyond screens to voice-first connected devices like Amazon Alexa and Google Home. Thinking through a platform-first perspective is enough to drive a marketer mad. It's building the foundation of a house on shifting sands. But thinking through a behaviour-first perspective, these changes are much more easily understood and adapted to. Aligning with behaviours allows brands to be agile alongside their consumers, rather than being left holding the bag after a large investment in a single platform fails to perform.

Speaking at a Contagious event in 2017, Anders Hallen and Mattias Ronge from agency Edelman Deportivo talked about the need to be 'culture first, clients second' as an advertising agency. 'We don't get to hold anyone hostage in their living rooms any more,' said Ronge. 'Stay curious. Collect intriguing cultural facts every day, you never know when you'll need them,' the pair advised.

These 'intriguing cultural facts' are often the X-marks-the-spot on the map of behaviour opportunities – something people do in their day-to-day lives that is ripe for exploration and alignment. Find these interesting and unique behaviours and align your products, services, and marketing with them. Consumers won't beat a path to your door. Instead, you'll find your offering overlapping with an already beaten path.

As 'customer-centric' has become a buzzword in the marketing industry, it has lost its meaning. We all say that we're customer-centric. *Of course we serve the needs of our customers!* But in reality, legacy infra-structure and ways of working inside companies often stand between current practices and truly customer-first thinking. Thankfully, approaching problems with a behaviour-centric mindset is a shortcut for actual customer-centricity. It's a concrete way to think about serving customer needs, and will avoid wasted energy trying to lure customers into forming new behaviours that will never take.

ALIGN WITH BEHAVIOUR / ESPRESSO VERSION

No doubt you want your brand to be culturally relevant. It's one of the most overused phrases in the marketing world. Of course every brand wants to be culturally relevant! No one wants to be immaterial.

There's an issue, though: 'culture' is a very difficult word to pin down. In some contexts it means the patterns of a specific society. In others it means music or the arts. In still another context, culture is bacteria growing in a petri dish.

That's why we try to avoid too much talk of culture at Conta-gious. (A favourite slide of ours has a photo of Samuel L. Jackson in *Pulp Fiction* with the words 'Say culture again. I dare you. I double dare you.'). Instead, we speak about behaviour – the manifestation of culture in the way people interact with the world around them. By aligning with behaviours, brands can find entry points into the worlds of their consumers, stay on top of emerging trends, and maintain customer-centricity (and, consequently, platform agnosticism).

It's still daunting to look at everything the term 'behaviour' encompasses and find a place to start. So to help our clients deal with analysis paralysis, we have a tool that breaks behaviour (and consequently culture) into actions, values, and interests.

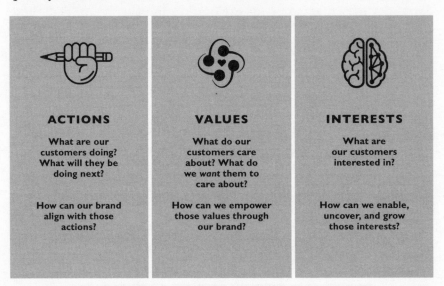

ACTIONS

What are our customers doing? What will they be doing next?

How can our brand align with those actions?

VALUES

What do our customers care about? What do we *want* them to care about?

How can we empower those values through our brand?

INTERESTS

What are our customers interested in?

How can we enable, uncover, and grow those interests?

These columns provide handy starting points for brands looking to align with customer behaviours. Amazon got its start by aligning with actions. Patagonia has aligned with values. Red Bull built its brand on the back of its customers' interests. Pick the column that seems most pertinent to your brand, and start there.

You'll note that the questions above focus on two things: what customers are doing, and how a brand can help them do those things. Above all else, aligning with behaviour is about paying attention to your audience, putting the customers truly at the centre of your mission and your messaging. Rather than creating from whole cloth, catalyse what's already in motion.

BE GENEROUS

Any brand with a bank account can be generous. Financial services firm Goldman Sachs – once described in *Rolling Stone* as a 'vampire squid wrapped around the face of humanity, relentlessly jamming its blood funnel into anything that smells like money' – has donated more than a billion dollars to non-profits around the world through its Goldman Sachs Gives programme. It deserves recognition for that philanthropy. But you won't find us praising the world's top corporate donors here. The generosity we're interested in goes beyond dollar signs.

The key to generosity in marketing is simple: 'Don't ask what's in it for you, ask what's in it for them.' Too often, marketers approach strategic briefs and communications planning the wrong way around. They focus inwards, concentrating on crafting the perfect tagline and promoting a product attribute or competitive difference in a creatively compelling way, and then wonder why their one-way communication efforts are met with indifference after being unleashed into the public domain. It may come as a shock to marketing savants, but sometimes the best advertising *isn't* advertising. It's anthropology. Sometimes the best and most enduring solutions come from being supremely consumer-centric, by studying human society in order to solve the pain points or to facilitate moments of joy in people's lives.

In practical terms, this means thinking and behaving generously. Brands should commit to spending real money in pursuit of real solutions to real problems in the world. We would argue that instead of just donating money to non-profits, brands should aspire to function, where relevant, as quasi-NGOs to solve some of the vital challenges facing society. They should use their clout – their creative communications capabilities, media muscle, operational know-how and organizational assets – to bring about positive change or create value that would otherwise be out of reach or unavailable. They should give, without expectation of reciprocity.

That said, they should welcome reciprocity when it is given (we're not crazy, after all). Generosity can be very good business.

We're reminded of a study, conducted in 2002 and published in the *Journal of Applied Social Psychology*, titled 'Sweetening the Till'. In it, researchers tested the effect of giving a chocolate to diners along with their bill after a meal. What they found aligned with a concept known as the 'reciprocity norm'. That is, we tend to feel obligated to repay kindness, even if that generosity wasn't requested. Diners who received a chocolate after their meal tipped more than those who received no chocolate; diners who received *two* chocolates tipped even more. Perhaps most interestingly, diners who were offered one chocolate and then subsequently offered a second (demonstrating extra generosity on the part of the waiter) tipped the most of anyone.

What we give – and how we give it – would seem to be paid back, plus interest.

GENEROSITY AS A MINDSET

You may recall the tale of the Huichol tribe in Mexico discussed in the introduction to this book. They were the ones who believed that the pain of childbirth should be shared between woman and man – resulting in the tradition of women in labour yanking on strings attached to the testicles of their husbands. Although this may sound surprising, and possibly even vindictive, it was actually regarded as an act of generosity as it enabled the male to share in the spirituality of childbirth. The act was ultimately about empathy and affinity.

While we wouldn't recommend volunteering for extreme physical pain, we would suggest that marketers find ways to be generous around the pain points of their customers. Be present at the birth, so to speak, but don't feel the need to attach the string. By showing that you understand what makes them tick and that you care about making a positive difference in their lives, and by giving freely without expectation, you'll reap great benefits. Generosity leads to dialogue, to great PR. Generosity leads to happy, engaged employees. Generosity leads to better brand reputation. And, best of all, it can lead to a better world.

There are two dimensions to the dictionary definition of generosity: kindness/understanding and scale/value. In both cases, it amounts to giving more than is usual or expected. From a marketing industry perspective, this equates to generosity of purpose, and generosity of creativity. Of course, you can't give everything away. But these need not be vain acts of rash munificence that are likely to bankrupt your business. Instead, a generous, customer-first mindset will spawn creatively pragmatic utilities, shared resources or unexpected experiences that will spark reciprocity and reputation.

If this talk of commercial karma sounds twee and tree-huggy, consider the announcement in February 2018 from Laurence D. Fink, founder and chief executive of the $6-trillion investment firm BlackRock. In a public letter – described by *The New York Times* as a 'firestorm' and 'a watershed moment on Wall Street' – he warned leaders of the world's biggest companies that in future BlackRock will only invest in companies that take their social responsibilities seriously: 'To prosper over time, every company must not only deliver financial performance, but also show how it makes a positive contribution to society.' People are paying attention.

IT'S A FACT: GENEROSITY INCREASES HAPPINESS

According to reputable sources, it was Jesus who coined the adage 'it is more blessed to give than to receive'. Two thousand years later, scientists at the University of Zurich in Switzerland proved him right. They published a neurological study in open-access journal *Nature Communications* in July 2017 titled 'A Neural Link Between Generosity and

Happiness'. Their research established just that – a connection in our brains between being generous and being happy, proving that altruism changes the activity in people's brains, and that the subsequent feelings of happiness serve to motivate further generosity.

In the experiment, fifty adults were asked to complete questionnaires about their current mood, and were then given 25 Swiss francs on a weekly basis for one month. Half were instructed to spend it on themselves, while the other twenty-five were asked to spend it on someone of their choosing each week. The volunteers were then placed inside a functional magnetic resonance imaging (MRI) machine and presented with a screen that flashed up hypothetical scenarios involving spending personal money on other people. Their brain activity was recorded to track how they reacted when assessing the benefits to the other person versus the financial cost to themselves.

According to the study, participants in the experimental group – those who were instructed to spend their allowance on others – made more generous decisions in the independent task inside the MRI machine. What's more, they showed stronger increases in self-reported happiness than the control group. The parts of the brain associated with altruism and reward seemed to be connected.

'Even in a strictly controlled laboratory setting involving decision making in the MRI scanner, commitment induces generosity along with increases in happiness,' wrote the study's authors. By promising to be generous in the future, you increase the likelihood that you will follow through on that promise and get a happiness boost. Hard to say no to that.

What does a happiness MRI have to do with building your business? It could be staring you in the face. Or rather, she or he could. A report on employee activism by PR firm Weber Shandwick found that one out of every five workers is an 'employee influencer' who is deeply engaged with the organization that pays their wages. Its 'Employees Rising' report suggests that these advocates can have a discernible impact on a company's performance, defending it from criticism, acting as an influencer both online and offline, and helping to cultivate a positive and ethical work environment. If corporate generosity can improve their happiness, it could materially impact your company's bottom line.

As Micho Spring, chair of Weber Shandwick's Global Practice, states in the report: 'In today's environment, where there is an alarming lack of trust in all institutions, employees are increasingly the key prism for brand credibility and trust. Engaging them can provide companies the best way to humanize and unify their enterprise voice – a strategic imperative in today's environment.'

A generous, altruistic brand equals happy employees, and happy employees equal happy CFOs. Yes, that may sound glib – but it is an underlying philosophical truth that often gets overlooked by businesses.

In late 2016 luxury chocolatier Godiva launched a special gift box to encourage generosity during the festive season. From the outside, it looked like a normal box of chocolates. Once opened, however, a nested series of progressively smaller boxes was revealed. Each box was, in fact, a pair of boxes, one labelled 'To Keep' and the other 'To Give'. The gifted box contained yet another duo of gift boxes, as did all the smaller boxes, until the last pair of pralines.

Designed by McCann New York, The Box That Keeps Giving was gifted to a hundred lucky customers in twenty stores across America. To launch the project Godiva held a PR event in New York, during the famous Rockefeller Center tree-lighting ceremony.

Godiva's special gift was designed to enable consumers to be generous to someone else, while at the same time enjoying half of the product themselves. As Canadian research psychologist and happiness expert Elizabeth Dunn has proved in a series of experiments, there are tangible health benefits to generosity, and prosocial spending. Participants felt physiologically happier when they were told to get a gift for others rather than buying something for themselves.

COFFEE VS GANGS

Imagine being so emotionally invested in branded generosity, and so determined to bring it to fruition, that you'd be willing to throw out your company's typical processes and endure hundreds of meetings to make it happen. Would you tolerate being the butt of jokes from your colleagues and even risk your job in order to make it a reality?

That's exactly what Emad Nadim and some of his colleagues did. Nadim was a brand manager for Kenco, a coffee brand owned by global snack giant Mondelēz, and he shared his story at the Most Contagious conference in London in 2014. Recounting a Kenco brand-strategy session at the Mondelēz HQ in Zurich, he said:

> I realized that there was something different going on with the people in the room, in that they were genuinely there to affect things in a manner that reflected their own personal values. They had the desire to use the lens of the brand to articulate these values. That's a pretty counterintuitive thing to feel, when you consider these brands have lasted a hundred years. It was powerful. It allowed us to get to a really interesting starting point from which everything flowed.

Empowered to use the prism of personal values to shape business strategy, this group of employees articulated a shared vision of what the brand was about and how it should behave in the future: 'a brand that will fight for fairness in the world'.

A big, hairy, audacious goal. But the group came away feeling excited, liberated, and almost evangelical. So much so that they ripped up the company's usual briefing template and replaced it with the story of how they had sparked their new 'fairness' mission for Kenco. The hope? That generosity would be contagious enough to inspire other people within the organization, as well as the creatives at their agency at the time, JWT London.

The provocation to fight for fairness ultimately led to an initiative called Coffee vs Gangs, in 2014. Part of Mondelēz's Coffee Made Happy programme – a $200-million commitment to building sustainability and entrepreneurship among small-farm suppliers – the programme helped at-risk youth in Honduras avoid gang life by providing better opportunity through education. Specifically, in the fields of a coffee farm.

Launched with a sixty-second TV spot, the eleven-month pilot programme moved twenty vulnerable Honduran youths (chosen in consultation with community leaders) from crime-riddled areas to a coffee farm in the remote town of Yoro, where they learned about growing, harvesting, and selling coffee, as well as being tutored in basic subjects like mathematics and literacy. The goal was to have participants leave the programme with a qualification in coffee production (Honduras is the world's sixth-biggest coffee exporter) and an opportunity to create their own business plan, with advice from a mentor funded by the brand. Kenco teamed up with two organizations who administered the pilot and acted as the brand's eyes and ears: a local NGO called Fundes, and Sogimex, a coffee exporter responsible for the Coffee vs Gangs training element.

Ads encouraged audiences in other countries to follow the project online, where Kenco posted videos and images, introducing the participants in the programme and allowing viewers to follow their journey. Project director Blanca Mejia (a false name given by the brand for her protection) said: 'This is an enormous challenge and won't be easy. But nothing is impossible. You can achieve anything if you have strength, commitment, and passion.'

Companies using education to empower people is a fairly common tactic. AT&T created Nanodegrees alongside Stanford professor Sebastian Thrun to school people in the skills necessary to thrive in an entry-level software job at the company. Bank of America partnered with Khan Academy to design financial-literacy courses. Many others have invested in educating consumers, as a sort of outreach strategy. But for Kenco, the education was happening long before the consumer even entered the picture, far away from the final sale. Rather than viewing the tension between coffee growing and gangs as a marketing opportunity, the team saw it as a chance to invest resources and make a real difference.

It was a brave commitment for a household brand, and fortunately the pilot succeeded. Kenco's generosity was recognized by the end consumer, with an immediate 15 per cent uplift in value share for Q4 2014 compared with Q4 2013. Meanwhile, rival Nescafé suffered a 2 per cent decline in the same period, despite outspending Kenco in media by a ratio of 4:1. Research by Mondelēz found that the perception of Kenco as an 'ethical brand' doubled. The brand helped a violence-scarred region, empowered its employees to be altruistic, and improved its performance in the market, all by thinking differently about what it could accomplish with its marketing budget.

BRAND AS NGO

Brand manager Nadim told Contagious that sustainability credentials universally claimed by coffee brands – such as reduced packaging and green 'badges' like Rainforest Alliance certification – feel quite 'industrial'. Kenco wanted to go deeper. 'We had a real opportunity to push the boundary and to help people understand where their food comes from because in the countries where our product is sourced, a number of social problems exist. We want to be the brand that is bringing those to the fore and allowing people to do their bit.'

Coffee vs Gangs is indicative of a movement that Contagious identified in the early days of our magazine and advisory service: namely, brands behaving as NGOs, filling in some of the societal gaps that governments and institutions lack the wherewithal or resources to solve. Said Nadim:

> We always want to find the next thing that links our consumer with the brand's purpose, which is about creating fairness in the world. If you care for the people who care for the coffee bean you're making a big difference. There's a lot of mistrust and uncertainty globally around governments and corporations, and brands like Kenco that are trying to do something to persuade people to think for a microsecond about the brand they're picking and the choice they're making with a view to triggering an epiphany are more likely to win.

Fast-forward to 2018 and the Coffee vs Gangs initiative means that its students are now building businesses of their own, backed by the brand. From a 'generosity' perspective, Nadim claims that 'the biggest KPI for this project is the success of the participants'.

In the same way that the University of Zurich experiment showed that pledging to be generous primed people to be more giving, the Kenco team's commitment to 'fight for fairness' took them into uncharted territory, far beyond the usual parameters of a job in marketing. The Coffee vs Gangs idea was not only a big shift for the brand but also fraught with legal complexity and logistical headaches, and was a potential short-term threat to sales.

Nadim admitted to a 'huge amount of nervousness' – after all, Honduras is a genuinely dangerous country to operate in. But, he told us:

> By this time, we were deeply invested, wanted to make a difference, and were determined to land this idea. The complexities fuelled our enthusiasm for the project. It became personal. Hundreds of stakeholder meetings later, we were still deeply energized about it . . . We had lived with the idea for a year and a half and had even been a bit of an internal joke. Our sales guys were laughing at us for the constant delays; even our top leadership teased us about whether these gangs were ever going to come out of PowerPoint and into real life.

This deep personal investment, and a collective desire to make a difference in the world turned the Kenco marketing team into a formidable force. Despite extensive link-testing and scenario planning to safeguard the campaign, three days before Coffee vs Gangs was due to go live, Nadim took a call from 'somebody quite important in our organization', asking if it could be delayed. The response? An instinctive fait accompli to protect the idea: 'It looked like a case of cold feet, and that was not good enough,' he declared at our Most Contagious event. 'So we took quite a lot of personal risk by saying, "Do you know what; how about we talk about this on Monday?" knowing full well that Monday was when the TV campaign was booked to go live.' Quite the leap of faith.

Coffee vs Gangs gave Kenco licence to fly a flag for social responsibility. The campaign stood out within a commoditized product category dominated by messages pushing conventional benefits such as aroma and price. The brand's generosity mindset provided a genuine point of differentiation: an important factor, considering a 2017 international study by Unilever revealed that 33 per cent of consumers choose to buy from brands they believe are doing social or environmental good. This equates to a €966 billion opportunity for brands that make their ethical credentials clear.

GIVE WHAT ONLY YOU CAN GIVE

The Kenco project worked because it was clearly close to the brand's heart – a bottled-water brand from Switzerland would have difficulty producing the same campaign with even a shred of authenticity. But because Mondelēz found the centre of the Venn diagram between the Kenco brand world and the Kenco consumer's world, it was able to make something honest and moving, driving employee happiness and customer affinity.

We see this time and time again. Generosity takes a leap forward and becomes a marketing asset when companies give something only they can provide. How is your brand uniquely positioned to share its assets with the wider world?

A prime example of this comes from Japanese car manufacturer Toyota. In Toyota's work environment, innovation and evolution are cherished. It's an idea encapsulated by one of the brand's twelve pillars – the Japanese word *kaizen*, or 'continuous improvement'. Within the *kaizen* approach, all team members associated with the Toyota Production System are invited to think about the process and how it can be improved. At the firm's material handling sites in Europe, around 3,000 proposed changes are made each year. This proactive involvement, according to Toyota's website, 'creates responsibility for the success of the process, increasing both employee morale and quality'.

Recognizing the value and effectiveness of the *kaizen* method, the US arm of Toyota founded the Toyota Production System Support Center in Kentucky in 1992 with the core mission of 'contributing to society' by sharing the company's know-how with other manufacturers, non-profits and community organizations. The thinking behind this 'Toyota effect' is that sharing efficiency ideas helps the car firm's partners and suppliers to stay competitive, preserves jobs, and supports people in need. The company's support centre has worked with a range of companies and causes, including hospitals, schools, and soup kitchens, to increase productivity and improve experiences.

By being generous with its skills and knowledge outside the Toyota brand, the company also highlights its efficiency credentials, amplifies its philosophical values, and enables employees to be generous as well.

In sharing process improvement outside the organization, employees become brand evangelists, excited to give generously of their time and expertise to the wider community in times of urgent social need.

Take, for example, Hurricane Sandy. Eight months after the storm tore through New York in October 2012, the Rockaways area still required food parcels as the community struggled to rebuild itself. Employees from Toyota were deployed to partner with Metro Food Distribution, a relief agency that delivered food boxes to Rockaways families each week. Beyond simply being generous with the time of its employees, however, Toyota also donated its *kaizen* philosophy. The brand willingly shared the secrets of its Toyota Production System – whereby many small improvements are made to a process in order to create a much larger overall impact – and applied these to the challenges facing Metro Food Distribution.

Toyota employees suggested a reduction in the size of boxes used, to minimize unfilled space in each box. This small change resulted in a 45 per cent increase in the amount of food packed into each truck. Toyota volunteers also applied a heavy dose of *kaizen* to the packing line, using a continuous production flow to drop the assembly time for each box from three minutes to just eleven seconds. The overall result? An extra 400 families could be fed in half the time.

Similarly, Airbnb has played a proactive role when calamity strikes, putting purpose before profit and sharing their brand's assets. In the wake of hurricanes Harvey and Irma in 2017, the company activated its disaster relief programme, which leverages Airbnb's network of homes to provide free lodging to those displaced by natural disasters.

In an interview with *The New York Times*, Airbnb's co-founder and CEO, Brian Chesky, said:

> With disasters, we thought about what asset we had that could help the world, and we happen to have 4 million homes. The people that provide those homes are generally kind and generous. We started with Hurricane Sandy when a host contacted us and said that she wanted to host people impacted by the storm [for free]. Since then, our community has donated 11,000 nights for people who have been displaced by disasters.

Between 2012 and 2017 Airbnb's relief programme responded to ninety natural disasters around the world.

It's refreshing to see big brands looking beyond cold hard cash or token gestures as a way of adding value to a social problem. This is the Be Generous commandment in action. Toyota workers and Airbnb hosts are deployed as brand ambassadors who get to share the benefits of generosity in the wider world.

But brand-funded generosity doesn't always have to apply to environmental disasters and social friction. Far from it.

In 2014, as part of appliance brand Whirlpool's 'Everyday, Care' initiative, researchers from marketing and technology agency DigitasLBi in Chicago, were poring over research about the impact of everyday chores like laundry, cooking, and cleaning when they stumbled across a stunning fact: students who don't have clean clothes are more likely to skip classes, miss school, and even drop out of education. 'We found this one little sentence in a news article about how lack of clean clothes contributed to truancy,' Brian Sherwell, DigitasLBi's VP of planning, told Contagious. 'So we started to dig a little deeper and found articles going all the way back to 1917 about how a lack of clean clothes contributed to students missing class. This is an issue that has been around in our nation for at least a hundred years and nobody really speaks about it.'

Motivated by this issue – and its deep connection to the brand's products – Whirlpool sprung into action, working with PR agency Ketchum to conduct the first national survey about the problem. Over 90 per cent of 600 American teachers surveyed highlighted a lack of clean clothes as an issue in their classroom. What's more, administrators began to reach out to the brand about washer and dryer donations.

Whirlpool answered those calls by launching Care Counts, a programme that donated washing machines to schools in areas of high need. Starting with a pilot campaign in 2014, Whirlpool washed 2,300 loads of laundry in seventeen different schools. In those institutions, more than 90 per cent of tracked students increased their school attendance compared to the previous year, with some students attending the equivalent of almost two weeks longer. Teachers also saw increased class participation in 89 per cent of the tracked students. The brand has continued to expand the programme each year since.

What's more, Whirlpool has worked with Brown University and Dr Richard Rende to measure data accurately throughout the programme, turning it into an academic study in addition to a charitable campaign. Rather than being a one-off CSR splash, the Care Counts programme aims to make a long-term positive impact. With generosity baked in as a core philosophy, the Michigan-headquartered company has empowered not just employees, but also partners such as its communications agencies, who know they can dig deeper into wider social issues and help the brand take ownership of a cause that civic institutions have neglected.

'A simple act of care has real meaning in our lives and we wanted to prove that,' says Sherwell. 'That is our brand and that is what Whirlpool has been doing for the last hundred years. People want a brand with a mission they identify with. This was about putting a stake in the ground and saying, this is our mission. It's around everyday care and improving people's lives.'

THE HELICOPTER PARENT

Poop and award-winning experiences don't often share the same sentence, but in the case of Procter & Gamble's Pampers disposable nappies they most certainly do.

In 2016 WPP consultancy Group XP ranked Pampers as the world's leading brand in its *Experience Index*. It's easy to see why, and to recognize a generosity mindset in action. In its citation, Group XP had this to say about Pampers: 'Some brands go beyond expectations by adding value to customers' lives through a succession of small moments of genuine brilliance. They recognize it's the constant striving to improve and enhance people's experience that generates and builds their value.'

Pampers eschewed the product-first route, because a mechanical marketing focus on functional benefits failed to resonate with consumers. In 1997 the brand was low-growth and languishing. However, by 2012 Pampers had ballooned into P&G's best-selling brand; the first to generate $10 billion in annual revenue. As the Group XP report points out: 'Pampers became P&G's best-seller by being a trusted advisor to new mothers in the most important job on earth: raising a happy, healthy child . . . Pampers is the helicopter parent that mothers can call out to when they need assistance.'

Pampers is a textbook example of a brand that constantly asks, 'what's in it for the people who buy our product?' It has acknowledged that new parents need more than just a decent nappy. They crave advice, reassurance, and a healthy dose of empathy. Pampers therefore behaves like a support network, removing friction and adding colour to each step of the journey. The brand's stated mission is to make lives 'easier, more joyful or more interesting', and it achieves this through educational content, practical utilities, handy mobile apps, and community outreach, acting as a trusted advisor for millions of parents around the world.

People who buy Pampers recognize that a little bit of reciprocity generates a whole lot of generosity in return from the brand. We encourage you to go to pampers.com and see for yourself. Every base is covered, brilliantly and generously, in contrast to the hard-sell approaches taken by its competitors. Pampers provides an encyclopaedic array of information and practical tips concerning babies, toddlers, and parents alike, from health and wellbeing information to practical tools and medical advice. Services include a symptoms indicator; pregnancy announcement ideas; a baby shower page; a labour checklist; advice on sleep, feeding, teething, and potty training; exercise regimes; nutrition tips; meditation lessons; games and activities; the psychology of siblings; what to stock in your medicine cabinet; and a collection of real-life stories from recent parents.

Some of our favourites include:

Due Date Calculator / Pampers builds a relationship upstream, before the first purchase. The calculator tracks menstruation cycles and sends personalized updates and advice, long before a prospective parent would have any reason to shell out money for any of the brand's products.

Baby Name Generator / From Areebah to Zacharias, expectant parents can have hours of fun figuring out what to write on the birth certificate, for free.

Credible Expertise / The Pampers Village Parenting Panel corrals up-to-date knowledge from a range of child-development practitioners, offering it to visitors whether they've bought Pampers or not.

A Sympathetic Ear / P&G interviews around 10,000 mothers each year to find out what's on their mind, what's missing in their lives, and what Pampers could do better. Listening creates an intimate knowledge of Pampers' core constituency, enabling the brand to stay honest, innovative, and potentially future-proof.

If you're worried that we've gone all gooey-eyed from looking at cute baby pictures, we'd like to conclude with a cold hard fact. Group XP found that, on average, 'high experience' brands, like baby-pic peddling Pampers, outperform the Standard & Poor's 500 US stock-market index by more than 50 per cent.

GIVE RECKLESSLY

It's tough being a marketer these days. Not too long ago, the arrows in your advertising quiver were television, radio, and print, with a few coupons and direct-mail shots thrown in for heft. As we hurtle through the twenty-first century at lightning speed, however, the armoury of a brand guardian looks more like The Avengers than Robin Hood. Mass-media channels are still part of the mix, but modern marketers need to compete on a 360-degree battlefield that encompasses mobile, social, influencers, immersive retail, e-commerce, artificial intelligence, automation, a data barrage, ad-blocking, short attention spans, personalization, programmatic media, category disruptions, and so on and so forth. It's relentless.

Given that resources are spread so thin, it seems like commercial lunacy to invest the time and energy of some of your best employees and expensive agency folk for six whole weeks to serve 240 people on a single platform. But that's just what Nike did in 2016 with an experiment called Nike on Demand, aimed at millennials in the Adidas heartland of Austria, Germany, and Switzerland. Based around the insight that motivation is a challenge, and it's hard to keep up an exercise regime without the luxury of a personal trainer, Nike provided a bespoke service for 240 people, via a dedicated WhatsApp conversation. These everyday athletes sent their goals to the Nike team via the messaging app and received tailored fitness plans to help achieve them in return.

In an age of automation and mass personalization, we love the fact that this was powered entirely by humans, not bots. The service – created by digital agency R/GA in London – not only sent out professional training plans and advice but also created personal wake-up calls to remind users to get up for their morning run and planned routes tailored to their location. Participants also received playlists, app challenges, coaching tips and access to product trials and VIP bookings, all through the WhatsApp chat.

Over the six-week beta trial, 22,000 messages were exchanged; which equates to 91.7 per person. According to the brand, 83 per cent of the folks involved would recommend Nike on Demand to a friend and 81 per cent would use the service again.

THE PERSONAL TOUCH

From an advertising perspective, this is a high-maintenance campaign with limited reach. From a generosity perspective, though, it was an example of the brand investing in the margins as well as the mainstream, in order to discover, learn, and develop. The objective behind the Nike on Demand initiative was to lure people away from rival brands (especially Adidas) in the hope that, by being immersed in the Nike ecosystem, they would commit to the brand in the long-term. It's a prime example of a brand behaving as a service provider, with only a secondary tie-in to sales. Customer-first.

Contagious asked Simon Wassef, executive strategy director at R/GA London, to explain the brief behind the project: 'The objective was to help young people unlock their potential with Nike, as opposed to with the three stripes [Adidas]. We found there's an audience that is incredibly digitally savvy, quite wary of brands invading their privacy and that's why they're using one-to-one messaging; they like the notion of private conversations.' Wassef explained that the experiment was based around the convergence of three insights: brand, audience, and technology.

Brand / Nike is working at the 'holy grail of personalization, to know athletes so well that it can serve them better'. Therefore, it devotes resources to get to know its customers in greater depth, via data and human interaction.

Audience / People want to be recognized. Whenever someone interacts with any part of the Nike ecosystem, the goal is to greet them by name. Nike is moving away from 'big social things' to focus on one-to-one, organic conversations.

Technology / Personalized interactions with customers, and the data and insights accrued, means that Nike can use technology to create more relevant, nuanced, and hyper-targeted tools, services, advice, discount offers, and creative content than by relying on the traditional assumptions spewed out algorithmically when aggregating someone's purchasing history and their demographic status.

According to Wassef, the magic ingredient in Nike on Demand was Nike's in-house experts, the so-called Ekins (Nike spelled backwards). The equivalent of a Genius at an Apple store, an Ekin knows the brand, the services, and the products inside out. By championing Ekins over algorithms as a service proposition, Nike placed humanity at the heart of the brand experience. As he told Contagious:

We could have created a bot that tells you to run 5K, and then tells you to run it faster, but the magic wouldn't be there. During the pilot, people developed in-jokes, they had certain emoji that they'd send to each other. One of the users was getting ready for her wedding and she sent us photos from her honeymoon doing pad-dleboard yoga, saying 'Here I am with the body that you helped me achieve.' That's the magic. That's what people will give to other people; they won't give that to a machine.

This is where Nike's generosity starts to pay off. The Nike on Demand pilot required a disproportionate amount of resources to reward a tiny group of prospective customers with a hyper-targeted, hyper-contextual, hyper-responsive service free of charge. How-ever, after the six-week trial ended, Nike was able to write a playbook and build specific code in order to scale the idea in the near future, whereby it will then be able to plug in cognitive technologies to make it easier for humans to understand myriad conversations. Was-sef explains:

> Instead of an Ekin having to go through the history of a specific user profile to be able to understand the context, an automated agent could help them. Nike is at the stage where smart technolo-gies, machine learning and artificial intelligence can be adapted, not to replace humans – because then you lose that feeling – but to enable them to scale up without having to hire thousands of people.

In other words, machines can empower humans to maintain an intuitive rather than robotic connection, which from a marketer's per-spective is the definition of personalization. All very happy-clappy. But here's where it gets real: yes, there is emotional value and the pros-pect of deep loyalty and trust being engendered by services such as Nike on Demand, but there's also potential for a big financial uplift. Data from the company reveals that, on average, users of its Nike+ app spend $100 more a year with the brand than non-users. This is attrib-uted to the ability to serve them relevant product offers at contextually relevant times. Fuse the infrastructure of Nike+ and the deep learning that comes from personalized platforms like Nike on Demand, and you can start to imagine the potential impact on sales figures – and brand equity.

In 2017, to tempt incoming tourists to choose Heineken over increasingly popular microbrews, the Dutch beer brand used travel data from airline and hotel partners to target visitors before they'd even arrived.

As soon as someone booked a flight to Amsterdam, Heineken served them a customized pop-up ad offering to brew them a fresh beer for their arrival if they clicked to register. The Heineken brewing process takes twenty-eight days – so, using Facebook Messenger, the brand sent participants updates, photos, and videos of their very own bottle of beer being made, starting twenty-eight days before their arrival in the Dutch party capital. The Messenger chatbot also asked them questions about what they'd like to get up to on their visit and offered relevant suggestions, generally off the beaten track.

When arriving in Amsterdam, participants could pick up their gift from the Heineken Experience, a tourist attraction located inside the brand's original brewery. Each bottle was labelled with the recipient's name and flight data and was wrapped in a personalized map of the city with the locations discussed in their Facebook Messenger chat marked on it.

The campaign was created with agencies DDB & Tribal Amsterdam and delivered 500 personalized beers and unique city trips – maxing out the capacity of the production line. Given that 20 million visitors descend on Amsterdam each year, 500 interactions may seem like a drop in the ocean. However, for Heineken, the value of this experiment lay in the quality of dialogue and the insights gleaned. According to Tribal, 80 per cent of chatbot conversations with this mobile-first audience were sustained for the full twenty-eight days. By positioning itself as the definitive local guide to its home city, the brand pivoted away from the mainstream experience that people expect from Heineken and crafted something quirky and distinctly personal, to beat the microbreweries at their own game.

DATA-FUELLED GENEROSITY

At VentureBeat's Marketing.FWD conference in February 2016 Kristi Argyilan, SVP of media and guest engagement for American retailer Target, talked about how the brand adopts a generous mindset in its use of data to create content that is customer-serving rather than self-serving.

Take, for example, Target's marketing tactics at the Grammys – a music award show that had gradually shifted away from performances in favour of celebrity presenters awkwardly bantering with each other. Data from the brand's social listening tools showed that viewers wanted more music during the event. Target therefore decided to spend some money to create some value. During the 2015 broadcast, the retailer aired a live commercial – a Grammys first – featuring a performance by Las Vegas rock band Imagine Dragons. In a brave move, the perform-ance ran without any visible Target branding.

The following year, building on the positive response to the Imagine Dragons experiment, Target created a pre-edited music video starring singer Gwen Stefani (although this time around they added in some light branding). According to Nielsen, 25 million people watched the 2016 Grammys broadcast, and Stefani's performance was viewed an additional 35 million times online. Target's hashtag, #moremusic, was the top trending hashtag in the United States on the evening of the Grammys, and the second-most popular globally.

'It's risky, of course, to put out commercials like this,' Argyilan admitted at Marketing.FWD, referencing the considerable logistical and financial investment required. 'But we have found that this type of "brand generosity" gives us huge spikes in sentiment, intent to shop, and other emotional responses.' In addition to tracking the sales boost from the Grammys experiments, Target also wanted to gauge the impact on more intangible metrics such as 'brand love'. Argyilan said: 'It's the "love" piece that we're really trying to quantify, because what we see if we have someone that engages with us through, let's say, our social channels, there is just under a 30 per cent chance they will shop at Tar-get within a week.'

This belief in brand generosity is echoed by the corporation's chief creative officer, Todd Waterbury. In an interview with the Ceros blog in November 2016 Waterbury explained that Target uses generous and authentic experiences to break through the walls that 'notoriously fickle audiences' tend to build around themselves in order to keep brands out. 'I don't think anybody wakes up in the morning and *wants* to be disrupted by marketing,' he deadpanned.

To Waterbury, context is king: 'Who is the audience that we're engaging with, and what are their expectations? How do we bring a kind of generosity to it in ways that hopefully leave people feeling like, "Wow, Target showed up there and they brought something to it that made it a little more fun or a little more playful"?' In addition to the Grammys campaigns, experiences engineered by Target include interactive installations at the Art Basel festival, a pop-up Christmas shop in New York City, and a pictorial spread recreating iconic *Vogue* images, using Target products.

'We create meaningful and valuable interactions that lead to sustained transactions,' Waterbury told Ceros. 'ROI, sales per square foot, efficiency, those are important measures, but more and more today . . . choice is infinite. And if choice is infinite, then the one thing that's scarce is attention.'

Interestingly, Waterbury describes the Target brand as 'equal parts warm and cool'. The stores are designed to feel like a 'happy place, both aspirational and inclusive'. In other words, Target wants its customers to feel like they have access to superior products at affordable prices, without the sterile atmosphere associated with discount stores further down the food chain. 'It's a part of what makes us a modern brand,' says Waterbury. 'The balance between warm and cool is critical, and I think these generous experiences exemplify that balance.'

WE'VE GOT YOUR BACK

Generous brands think with their heads and act with their hearts. They are proactive, empathetic, and open. They see marketing as a service, not just a sales tool. They recognize that first impressions build a framework for future interactions.

There's an old Dutch saying that goes: 'Trust comes on foot, but leaves on horseback.' A generous mindset, a strategy of asking 'what's in it for them', can act as a gateway to trust; the most precious consumer commodity of all, and a subject we'll explore later in this book.

In an age of economic uncertainty, fractious politics, and ideological filter bubbles, an opportunity opens up for brands to position themselves as havens of stability and consistency. There's certainly an impetus for brands to behave in a dynamic, three-dimensional way, balancing the weight of commercial imperative with the value of societal expectation. This means that advertising is transitioning into a combination of embedded services (tools, utilities, knowledge hubs) and a fulcrum for change and repair in the wider world.

To paraphrase John Willshire, founder of UK strategic design consultancy Smithery: in the past marketing used to be about making people want things. Increasingly, it's about making things people want, and doing things people need.

BE GENEROUS / ESPRESSO VERSION

What's in it for us? Better question: What's in it for them? In the scramble to hit quarterly sales targets, it's easy for marketers to lose sight of the bigger picture. Contagious believes that brands should aspire to function, where relevant, as quasi-NGOs to solve some of the challenges facing social causes and disadvantaged communities. Take Kenco's Coffee vs Gangs project. Spurred on by a shared vision of 'a brand that fights for fairness in the world', a dedicated team of marketers risked their careers to champion a mentorship programme in a country blighted by gang violence.

What would your big, hairy, audacious goal be? Would you be prepared to lose your job to fight for an idea you believe in?

Generosity starts at home. In its report 'Employees Rising: Seizing the Opportunity in Employee Activism', PR firm Weber Shandwick writes: 'In today's environment, where there is an alarming lack of trust in all institutions, employees are increasingly the key prism for brand credibility and trust. Engaging them can provide companies the best way to humanize and unify their enterprise voice.' When employees are personally invested in an idea, they own all parts of it. And generosity as a marketing asset takes a leap forward when companies give something close to home as well. In Toyota's case, it's the philosophy of *kaizen*, or continuous improvement. The Toyota Production System Support Center shares the company's productivity know-how with non-profits and community organizations. *How can you give what only you can give?*

Don't get caught in the trap of giving away something easy and thinking you're being generous. Generosity amounts to giving more than is usual or expected. From a marketing perspective, this equates to generosity of purpose, and generosity of creativity. A standard bearer is Procter & Gamble's baby-care brand, Pampers. Online, it functions as an expert advisor and life coach; providing a support network for parents, removing friction, and adding colour to their journey. Nike's Nike on Demand experiment provided a bespoke coaching service for a couple of hundred people, via WhatsApp conversations with a team at Nike who provided tailored fitness plans and motivational messages. This takes the brand closer to a future where artificial intelligence and human nuance create one-to-one, organic conversations: the 'holy grail' of personalization.

This isn't pure charity. Just as altruism changes the activity in people's brains, there is a proven link between a generosity mindset and business results. Group XP found that 'high experience' brands that go beyond expectation to provide expert advice and remove friction from people's lives outperform S&P 500 companies by 50 per cent.

For his 2008 book *Buyology*, branding expert Martin Lindstrom conducted a neuroscience experiment that found a correlation between religion and brands. He discovered that the brain activation evident in devout Christians when exposed to faith-related triggers was also evident in fans of 'emotionally powerful brands' such as Apple and Harley-Davidson when familiar iconography from these brands was displayed. For Contagious, the Be Generous commandment bows its head to the four stages of giving celebrated in religious teaching, drawing parallels for brands:

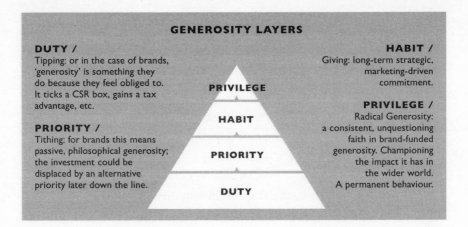

GENEROSITY LAYERS

DUTY /
Tipping: or in the case of brands, 'generosity' is something they do because they feel obliged to. It ticks a CSR box, gains a tax advantage, etc.

PRIORITY /
Tithing: for brands this means passive, philosophical generosity; the investment could be displaced by an alternative priority later down the line.

PRIVILEGE

HABIT

PRIORITY

DUTY

HABIT /
Giving: long-term strategic, marketing-driven commitment.

PRIVILEGE /
Radical Generosity: a consistent, unquestioning faith in brand-funded generosity. Championing the impact it has in the wider world. A permanent behaviour.

To move towards radical generosity, and the benefits that come with it, ask yourself these questions:

- // How does your company's behaviour affect its employees? Do you have a Generosity Agenda?
- // How can you provide a platform for your people to serve as influencers and ambassadors to broaden your brand's appeal?
- // What's your version of the 'Toyota effect'? Does your brand have any unique attributes or working practices that could be deployed to benefit the wider world?
- // What is your brand expert at? Where and how can you share that expertise with people?
- // If you diverted traditional marketing dollars into providing solutions for life's everyday pain points, what would that mean for your brand? What would stop you?

To traditional marketers, these may feel like counterintuitive questions, particularly the last one. If you feel safer deploying standard advertising in the hope that people will notice, we wish you luck. It sure works for some. But, recognize that the feet of corporations paying lip service to making the world a better place are increasingly being held to the fire by consumers, shareholders, investors, and competitors. Walking the walk is easier without scorched toes.

PART TWO
MAKING IT HAPPEN

JOIN THE 5% CLUB

'Join The 5% Club' is perhaps the commandment that best encapsulates the Contagious editorial spirit of optimistic curiosity and a thirst for the kinds of innovations that secure the financial and cultural health of brands. As impartial observers of the marketing maelstrom, ensconced in our metaphorical lighthouse, we were one of the first commentators to urge Madison Avenue to behave more like Silicon Valley. We advocated a culture of 'test and learn', advising organizations to devote a percentage of a brand's media, production, award show – or, hey, even holiday party – budgets into unfettered experimentation and forging unexpected collaborations with start-ups and university labs; to push advertising creativity into uncharted waters.

In its early days, Google famously gave its engineers '20 per cent time', the latitude to spend one day a week pursuing a pet project that didn't relate directly to their main workload. The programme helped spawn innovations like Google Maps, Gmail, and AdSense, although it has become less popular as the company has grown. Ever the pragmatists, and conscious that an additional 20 per cent could well turn your actual workload into 120 per cent and play havoc with a balance sheet, Contagious suggests the more manageable aim of diverting 5 per cent.

We call it The 5% Club – companies that allocate time and resources to exploring ideas at the edges. Ideas that might never be profitable. Ideas that take the company in new directions. It doesn't even have to be 5 per cent specifically. Whatever you can afford, do it! It's vital to stay curious, because complacency is a dead end.

'Failure sucks, but instructs' has become a conference speech cliché now, but The 5% Club is still well worth joining, especially if you're someone intellectually invested in developing the next solution, looking forward to the future and committing to expand your idea of what's possible. Membership of The 5% Club, we would argue, makes you quicker to adapt to today's fast-changing environment. It enables you to research the kernel of an idea as a jumping-off point and it's a smart way for big companies to place small bets before scaling them up if they test positively.

Entry to this club isn't automatic. It takes guts, risk, commitment, and a fundamental belief in the commercial power of creativity. But, we would argue, the advantage of membership is that it helps you to stay ahead, not just to keep up. In this commandment we will look at brands that have done exactly that, whether by investing in experimental labs to drive positive disruption or by playing with pioneering technologies to gain a step on the competition.

LIVING IN A PARADIGM SHIFT

When Contagious opened for business in 2004, students at Harvard were trying out a fledgling 'online directory' called TheFacebook for the first time. Elsewhere, three former PayPal employees had begun mulling the idea of a video-sharing website after struggling to find clips of Janet Jackson's infamous Super Bowl 'wardrobe malfunction' – a terrible state of affairs that would eventually lead them to register the domain name YouTube.com in early 2005. And over in the Mojave Desert, the US Defense Advanced Research Projects Agency had launched its Grand Challenge, offering $1 million to anyone who could build a driverless vehicle capable of navigating 150 miles of unpopulated tracks. Fifteen teams competed in the race, but none completed the course. The most successful vehicle managed a mere 7.4 miles before misjudging a hairpin bend and scudding into an embankment. Many believed the challenge beyond anyone's capabilities.

Six years later, a twelve-year-old company named Google announced that a fleet of its autonomous cars had quietly covered more than 140,000 miles on populated American roads.

Commenting in the book *Race Against the Machine* on the speed with which mankind's technology improved between those two events, MIT scientists Erik Brynjolfsson and Andrew McAfee observed: 'This is the world we live in now. It's one where computers improve so quickly that their capabilities pass from the realm of science fiction into the everyday world not over the course of a human lifetime, or even within the span of a professional's career, but instead in just a few years.'

Like the geek at the back of Ferris Bueller's class trying to quantify just how fast life is moving, renowned computer scientist and futurist Ray Kurzweil reckons that the paradigm-shift rate for technological innovation doubles every decade. By that logic, humans will have witnessed the order of 20,000 years of previous progress by the end of this century.

Just trying to compute the '20,000 years' progress inside a century' thing should be enough to make our heads hurt. And it's not helped by the fact that Kurzweil also told *The Guardian* in 2014 that robots will be making jokes and flirting with us by 2029. But the modern human is a resilient beast. As technology has rapidly improved, people have adopted and accepted it just as swiftly.

Less than two decades ago, the idea of being able to retrieve every song in the world from a small device in our pocket would have felt preposterous. Yet nowadays, the preposterous has become merely the impressive, and whatever is impressive quickly becomes ubiquitous to the point of mundanity. Gesture controls, voice recognition, touchscreen devices, driverless vehicles, drone deliveries, the social web and blockbusters streamed to our TV screens within seconds are now features of everyday life. As editorial director Alex Jenkins put it in the tenth anniversary issue of *Contagious*: 'The hedonic treadmill – the theory that most people revert to a relatively stable level of happiness, regardless of what happens to them – ensures that many of us go from "Wow! That's so cool!" to "Yeah, whatever" within weeks.'

THE MARKETING LAG

While consumer adoption has tended to match the briskness of freshly created tech, brands have largely struggled to keep pace. For decades, most consumers could be reached by spending advertising dollars on a combination of television, radio, print, and billboards. Marketing departments, therefore, built themselves around these proven media channels and tactical processes, with little need to optimize for adaptability. After all, nothing much was likely to change. This status quo (and its healthy margins) sustained a culture of *Mad Men*-esque Martini lunches for nearly half a century. In Contagious's lifespan, however, the need to adapt to change has exploded into an absolute imperative, as new platforms and devices manage to launch and scale seemingly overnight. The ad industry now has to run at full pelt just to keep up.

Take Vine, for example. The short-form video tool was founded in 2012, bought four months later by Twitter for a reported $30 million, and by June 2013 boasted 40 million users – 1 million more than the combined ratings of the United States' two most popular TV broadcasts: *Sunday Night Football* and *The Big Bang Theory*. User numbers rose to 200 million within three years, but Instagram and Snapchat soon usurped Vine, leading to Twitter shutting the platform down in early 2017. This decision no doubt provoked despairing sighs from brands such as Gap, Sephora, Target and VW, which had devoted significant creative energy to honing a smorgasbord of six-second wonders under the false assumption that this new channel would last longer than a military pizza. (Thirty-six months, if you're wondering.)

This is why we advocated aligning with behaviours in commandment four, to insulate your brand from overreliance on a given platform. Brands and their agencies chase consumer attention as it shifts en masse, quickly and often randomly, like atoms in a jar, to nascent platforms and the latest devices. New precedents are being set all the time, which means marketers generally lack the immediate expertise or time to evaluate how appropriate a match these shiny new things may be for the company's commercial objectives.

But at the same time, a decision to 'wait to see what gains traction' can feel like deciding to concede first-mover advantage or, worse still, arriving at the party with your expensive booze just as everyone else is leaving. Given that figuring out where to bet your marketing resources presents a huge strategic and creative challenge, how do you know if you're backing the next Facebook or foolishly chucking cash at another Second Life, the place where avatars go to die? Carving out a slice of budget to experiment without overinvesting can be the difference between being prepped to pounce and scrambling to learn new skills once a behaviour or platform hits the mainstream.

SKUNKS AND SPEEDBOATS

Marketing professionals and the military both love an acronym. For many, the period of disruption described above is best encapsulated by the acronym 'VUCA', a term originally coined by the US Army in reference to the volatility, uncertainty, complexity and ambiguity of the Cold War environment. More recently, the marketing industry has adopted it to prove to the all-important investment community that Adland's fingers are *most definitely not* stuck inside its collective ears while its mouth chants 'la-la-la' very loudly indeed.

In a VUCA world, one of the most successful ways to address the challenges of rapid change has been for organizations to adopt a culture of experimentation. True experimentation has its roots in the rigorous world of science, and a more directed path of exploration. Unless they're in the movies, scientists tend not to follow a philosophy of 'let's sling a bunch of chemicals into a test tube and see what happens'. Rather, they start with a hypothesis, explore it through experimentation and learn from the outcomes.

This approach as a business strategy gained momentum with the release of Eric Ries's 2011 book *The Lean Startup*, in which the software engineer and entrepreneur outlined a philosophy of continuous innovation. Although originally created with tech companies in mind, the concepts have been successfully applied to business in general – notably the importance of a 'build–measure–learn' mentality, an emphasis on minimum viable products and a willingness to accept failure as a necessary part of the learning process. As Ries notes: 'This is one of the most important lessons of the scientific method: if you cannot fail, you cannot learn.' He also stresses the importance of creating an organizational culture that nurtures risk: 'Leadership requires creating conditions that enable employees to do the kinds of experimentation that entrepreneurship requires.'

The cult of 'fail forward' – or, for the time-poor, 'fail forward faster' – may have been destined for the soundbite trashcan if it hadn't had such high-level disciples. One of them is Ed Catmull, president of both Pixar and Disney Animation Studios, who frequently cites the value of failure in his popular 2014 book *Creativity, Inc.*: 'Failure isn't a necessary evil. In fact, it isn't evil at all. It is a necessary consequence of doing something new.' And: 'If you aren't experiencing failure, then you are making a far worse mistake: you are being driven by the desire to avoid it. And for leaders, especially, this strategy – trying to avoid failure by out-thinking it – dooms you to fail.'

In this sense, failure is really a synonym for learning. If organizations can square themselves with the semantics, the logic of experimentation and failure becomes clear. When faced with a VUCA world for which we have no precedents, implementing clear processes for gaining knowledge through experimentation is a smart way to safeguard the future of a business – even though there will be inevitable missteps along the way.

Time and time again with our clients over the years, Contagious has advocated the celebration of useful failure. We've brainstormed ideas, such as giving out internal awards for the most spectacular failures or championing not just the final product but the missteps that led to it. Time and time again these ideas have created a buzz of excitement in their initial stages, as people recognize the mindset shift this could encourage. And time and time again, these ideas have been killed in their final stages by management averse to the word 'failure' and against the idea that anything but success should be put on a pedestal. It would appear that many CEOs and CMOs like to keep a big broom on hand, ready to sweep anything but success under the boardroom rug.

Perhaps as a result of this, as if to save themselves from themselves, we've seen a rise in discrete internal divisions tasked with trying out new ideas, protected from the judging eyes of CEOs or shareholders. This has led to a flurry of PowerPoint slides, Post-It notes and SWOT analysis spreadsheets from ad folk championing the virtue of a 'Skunkworks' culture – a reference to the pseudonym originally applied to the crack unit of scientists, engineers, and designers at Lockheed Martin's Advanced Development Projects who were flung together in a secret building during the Second World War and ordered to come up with a better fighter jet than the Germans in record time. (They did, in just 143 days.) 'Skunkworks' is now widely used in business circles to refer to an autonomous group of people inside an organization who have been tasked with cracking a gnarly problem or inventing a whizz-bang new solution, unencumbered by bureaucracy.

These ring-fenced hothouses – also given labels like innovation labs, brand-innovation centres, garages, foundries, kitchens, or hangars – allow businesses to explore new platforms and technologies in a safe, creative environment, immune from the usual corporate constraints. In issue 27 of *Contagious* (2011 / Q2), then director of strategy at Google Creative Labs and former co-founder of BBH Labs, Ben Malbon, used the analogy of a lab being a speedboat compared to the supertanker that is the main company: 'Scouting into the future, feeding back knowledge, opportunities, talent; literally, operating over the horizon . . . To survive, agencies must effectively become innovation companies, moving at least as fast as culture, quickly triaging new technologies, formats and opportunities both on behalf of their clients as well as their own business.'

While the role of a dedicated lab has been the subject of debate (if you have an innovation department, then by extension the rest of the company is stagnating), the importance of an R&D mindset outside the traditionally product-focused R&D department has found widespread acceptance. Companies in traditional sectors, such as AB InBev, American Express, British Gas, Delta Air Lines, Fidelity Investments, Ford, Marriott, Mondelēz and Verizon have all at various times committed to innovation labs in a bid to keep pace with the changing environment. Similarly, company 'hack days' are becoming commonplace, indicating just how deeply Silicon Valley working practices are impacting on the wider world.

COMMUNICATE WITH THE MASS,
NEGOTIATE WITH THE NICHE

Contagious first began talking about The 5% Club back in 2009, within the context of something we labelled 'two-track branding'. By that, we meant the art of combining mass-market advertising with experimentation in the niches – those emerging channels and behaviours where brands had the opportunity to engage on a more personal level with the more proactive members of their audience.

One of our favourite examples of this two-track branding was billed as a 'Durexperiment', the name being taken from a well-known condom brand. Durex partnered with wearable technology pioneers Snepo in Sydney and designer Billie Whitehouse to prototype Fundawear: interactive undergarments that used haptic (tactile) feedback and an internet connection to enable long-distance lovers to virtually create physical contact when they were apart. It worked via a dedicated mobile app which, when one person touched their phone screen, sent a wireless signal via a real-time server to their partner's handset. The signal instantaneously connected to touch-actuators woven into the fabric of the Fundawear, transferring the sensation of touch directly to their skin. A YouTube film showcasing Fundawear was viewed 4 million times in five days, generating 4,000 blog posts and widespread media coverage – the point being that niche ideas can generate mass attention, offering an instant return on an experimental investment.

Another branded prototype from the Billie Whitehouse stable was the Alert Shirt, for Australian subscription TV service Foxtel. Like Fundawear for sports, this tech-enhanced jersey allowed users to 'feel' the emotions of professional players, in real time. By connecting the shirt to a smartphone app, a football fan could receive haptic sensations, created by turning data collected live from players on the field into mimicked sensations of pressure, impact, adrenaline or exhaustion. Ad agency CHE Proximity commissioned 4,000 of these shirts to promote Foxtel's subscription channel Fox Footy. Some were gifted to loyal subscribers, with the rest being made available for sale.

In some cases, a niche experiment can even grow to be a pillar of a brand's messaging strategy. In 2013, after losing sponsorship of the NHL to rival Molson, Budweiser used some 5 per cent thinking to re-establish its hockey bona fides in Canada. Working with Anomaly in Toronto, the brand created the Budweiser Red Light – a connected light that looks like the sirens mounted behind hockey nets that blare and flash whenever a goal is scored. For $149, Bud drinkers could buy one of these Wi-Fi-enabled replicas, and they were so popular that the brand struggled to keep them in stock. When asked what the main challenge in the campaign was, brand director Kyle Norrington told us simply: 'Keeping up with demand!'

Given that Budweiser was not an official NHL sponsor, this acted as a neat little slice of guerrilla marketing, helping to generate 25 million media impressions. But, more importantly, the experiment has become an ongoing marketing platform for Budweiser Canada. More than 1.5 million Red Light products are in circulation: not bad for a country of 36 million! Later in 2013 Bud introduced flashing helmets for fans at a Calgary Flames game, and in 2014 the brand flew a 70ft dirigible that lit up the skies whenever the Canadian team scored during the Sochi Winter Olympics. The brand continues to build on the red light messaging, including a stunt in 2016 around pulling a giant light 'to the North Pole' and a nationwide rollout of connected glasses with light-up bases that are synced with hockey goals or momentous events in other sports. All told, the campaign has generated hundreds of millions of impressions, solidified Budweiser's connection to Canada's favourite sport, and given the brand a consistent platform to stand on – all because of a single, small, off-the-wall experiment.

In 2017 grocer Tesco surprisingly ticked a 5% Club criterion by venturing into the world of nanotechnology. Chinese shoppers feared that pesticides associated with fresh fruit and vegetables would put them at risk of brain damage, neurological problems and even cancer – quite logical concerns based on a Greenpeace study which had found that 90 per cent of all fresh fruit and vegetables sold in Chinese supermarkets contained harmful toxins. A number of additional scandals, including contaminated baby formula and cooking oil that had been reclaimed from gutters, meant that consumer trust in food was at an all-time low: 71 per cent of Chinese consumers considered food safety to be the country's number-one problem, ahead of corruption and pollution.

Tesco took a leadership position to help solve the crisis. The firm's ad agency, Cheil Worldwide, partnered with a leading photocatalysis laboratory in Hong Kong to develop Safety Bags, to be distributed in Tesco supermarkets. The project took a year from ideation to execution. The science works like this: the bags are coated with an inner layer of titanium dioxide, a highly refractive pigment. A process of nanophotocatalysis – the breaking down of compounds using light – is triggered when the bags are exposed to light for a few hours. This works to break down any toxic residues found on the fruit or vegetables, dispersing them into the air. All shoppers then need to do is rinse the produce with water, and it is safe to eat. The ingenious simplicity of Safety Bags matches Tesco's local brand positioning: 'shopping made easy'.

During the test phase of this FDA-approved and patent-pending idea, nine out of ten shoppers opted for the Safety Bags. Given that China is the world's second largest economy, the financial upside of a successful beta programme is huge. Tesco will also have the option to roll the idea out globally.

TO LAB OR NOT TO LAB

For every corporate lab, skunkworks or innovation centre that opens, another seems to close down. Recent demises include Adecco's Ignite Lab, British Airways' Ungrounded, Coca-Cola's Founders Initiative, Disney's research lab, *The New York Times'* R&D Ventures, Ogilvy Labs, Target's Food + Future lab, and Turner's Media Camp. A 2016 report from consultants Capgemini found that, while corporate innovation labs may be opening at a rate of ten per week, up to 90 per cent fail due to insufficient results.

So, what are the pros and cons?

NAY

Critics argue that innovation labs are a distraction: a marketing smoke-screen; a sop to shareholders; hipster money-pits that sap resources and provoke schisms within companies. They are not magic buttons. Driven by genuine constraints, start-ups are a much more productive model than labs because there's no safety blanket. In a VentureBeat article, Anderee Berengian, the co-founder of Cie Digital Labs, claimed that genuine experimentation doesn't fit inside a neat box: 'If such labs work, why do Google and others spend billions on start-ups? Because innovation is hard to recreate in house. It's alchemy, not science.' He cited the examples of two large retailers: Whole Foods, which bought the fledgling delivery service Instacart; and Walmart, which spent a whopping $3.3 billion to acquire – or, rather, to 'outsource its innovation' – to the two-year-old low-cost shopping site Jet. com, despite having its own innovation lab. 'Executives need to wake up to the fact that real innovation comes from outside your company,' he says.

For innovation centres to be sustainable in the long term, they need the active support of the company CEO. Too often, though, the leader delegates downwards, which leads to a lack of integration between an outpost lab and the core company. Because labs tend to focus on existing business models and view technology through such a lens, the result is often tweaks, not transformation. Therefore, there is a lack of commercial viability, which ultimately leads to innovation fatigue among those senior executives who signed off on the investment in the first place.

YAY

Innovation labs prove that a company is committed to the future by funding game-changing ideas and lean ways of working that can enhance or transform the business. This can serve to retain top staff and to attract high-calibre recruits, who may be more likely to inject original, entrepreneurial thinking. Provided there is a clearly defined link to a specific business strategy or goal, innovation labs can breathe new purpose into an otherwise cautious culture. They should be seen as protected spaces, with a remit to explore radical, ambiguous ideas and to ask the kind of heretical questions explored in the third commandment. If given sufficient scope, labs enable companies to focus on moon shots, not incremental steps. They democratize innovation within the organization.

Start-ups often get carried away with tech for tech's sake, whereas established companies already have a deep understanding of consumer behaviour and the nuances of a product category, making them more attuned to spotting gaps and solving pain points through innovation that caters to genuine needs.

Collaboration is a powerful tool. In a LinkedIn post in November 2017, Village of Useful co-founder Andy Howard referenced the success of Procter & Gamble's 'Connect and Develop' innovation model: 'designed to bring outside thinking together with P&G's own teams, [it] is attributed with helping to double the P&G share price within five years. When the share price had doubled, 45 per cent of P&G's product development portfolio had key elements developed externally.'

Over half of the companies in the Fortune 500 share index have either merged, been acquired or filed for bankruptcy since 2000. With start-ups chomping at their heels, standing still is not an option for incumbents; prototyping is a vital way of navigating the immediate future. If labs are ring-fenced from normal business activities and challenged with a clear commercial forecast, the team is focused and incentivized. Every Daimler innovation project, for example, requires a commercial forecast, mapping out how the proposed new venture could ultimately generate at least €100 million in annual revenue.

As a father of three, Paul can testify that grouchy babies do indeed fall asleep more quickly in cars, probably because of the soothing movements of the ride. Automaker Ford used this insight to increase consumer interest in its family-oriented Max range by designing a crib that replicates the sensations infants experience while on a drive. The Max Motor Dreams cot, developed by WPP's GTB agency, Ogilvy & Mather in Madrid, and creative studio Espada y Santa Cruz, mimics a car's lulling movements, restrained engine noise and the blur of passing street lights. Parents can control these using a dedicated app, which lets them record their baby's favourite outside noises and then play them back when their little darlings need to nod off.

To discover the product, people initially had to visit the brand's website and schedule a test drive in a Ford dealership. The Max Motor Dreams now features on Ford's main site, and people who configure a family car online have the option to purchase the smart crib as an add-on. As the product will be manufactured on demand, the price will depend on the number of requests. The agency reported that the campaign resulted in a 93 per cent boost in the number of visitors to Ford's website, with 83 per cent of those scheduling a test drive: a textbook example of a 5% Club idea crossing over into the mainstream.

PROJECT FLY

What works for your company will not necessarily work for the company next door. For some of our Contagious clients, innovation labs have been a catalyst for new thinking in the organization. We've advised others to break down silos within a company and task all employees with experimentation rather than making it the purview of a single team.

As it happened, Contagious was able to gain first-hand experience of building a lab, in 2012. After being commissioned by Maria Mujica, Mondelēz International's Latin American director of gum and candy, to write a report on innovation culture within the marketing industry, we were invited to be a founding partner of the Fly Garage, working alongside Argentinean innovation agency +Castro. This was Mondelēz's bold experiment, designed to ignite 'big bang engagements' for its brands by liberating traditional internal processes and ways of working.

As Mujica recalls, the purpose behind Project Fly was 'to create unmatched digital connections with consumers, offer them brand experiences that would delight them, in a way that would drive higher engagement that converted into growth'. This strategic initiative was a response to Mondele⁻z's assessment that Latin American consumers were rapidly embracing new behaviours, spurred on by the acceleration of digital media. 'Our leading brands had an opportunity to unleash more engagement if we could just leap forward and embrace that fast pace with consumers,' Mujica told us. 'As shapers, we wanted to push ourselves to keep innovating as to how we connected with consumers. We were clear that we had to have a radically different approach if we wanted to leap. We had to open up a space to experiment and do things differently.'

PARK YOUR EGO

The company took a three-year lease on a space in the creative district of Palermo, Buenos Aires. For each session, a combination of Mondelēz employees and external experts collaborated over an intense two-week period. These contributors were sourced from a diverse range of professions, and included ad-agency creatives, architects, designers, musicians, psychologists, strategists, students, and technologists. 'Now, this diverse blend of talent is the new normal, but in 2012, it was most unusual,' says Mujica, who believes that a fusion of divergent mindsets creates 'a fertile context for co-creation'.

This collective spirit broke entirely new ground for the Mondelēz participants, whose traditional roles as marketers would never usually plunge them so deep into the creative process. Mujica described the atmosphere of co-creation as feeling like a science fair. The first rule was: no hierarchy; candid conversation was king. Egos and job titles were left at the door. The second rule was: no paper briefs; another decision likely to shove most marketers outside of their comfort zone. Instead, the brief was a slogan on a T-shirt, handed to all participants. The rationale behind this was to reduce complexity, and to synthesize the brand's creative opportunity into a few simple words. 'The power to create that we already have inside the teams; it is released when you free people from job titles, roles and power-based processes,' states Mujica. 'Ego is a big value destroyer. For us a key element in the Fly Garage was about not exactly knowing the job description of the rest of the team, and focusing on what each person was bringing to the party to contribute. You had to "earn" your space on the team.'

A special characteristic of the Fly Garage was that teams would rotate every three hours, so that no single individual could take ownership of an idea. After a rigorous interrogation process, the strongest concepts were quickly prototyped before being shared with an invited target audience, who were encouraged to share their feedback first hand. 'That is amazing, because you have these inventors presenting the ideas,' Mujica told *Fast Company* magazine. 'We get to look at the faces of the real people and ask what they like and what they'd change.'

JUMP AND GROW WINGS

Once an idea had been approved at the Fly Garage, Mujica then played the role of an internal venture capitalist, identifying 'intrapraneurs' (in-house entrepreneurs) within local business units who could commit to taking ownership of the prototype. Her role would then be to facilitate the investment required so that the idea could be fast-tracked into the real world.

The first fruit was Random Fest for gum brand Beldent, which took only ten months from concept to execution. The brief on the T-shirt had been 'Kill Boredom', tapping into millennials' love of serendipity. The live festival featured four stages around a 'lighthouse', which randomly illuminated a stage, where one of four bands then played. The 10,000-strong audience – who had signed up via social media and special on-pack promotions – could vote via a mobile app for their favourite band to play an encore, and watch live on big digital screens to see which band was getting the most votes. Additionally, 250,000 fans watched a live stream of the event online.

Speaking to Contagious in 2012, Mujica used a Ray Bradbury quote to describe Fly Garage's entrepreneurial spirit: 'It's jumping off the cliff and growing your wings on your way down. We're investing in things which we don't really know will work but we know this is the way to learn and produce real innovation.' Fast forward to 2018, and Mujica remains a proud exponent of the Fly spirit:

> The key is to have patience, resilience and be ready to fail when you experiment. It's also important to have leaders strong enough to support teams at times when things don't work, recognizing that making mistakes as part of the official process unleashes the possibilities. A crucial personal learning for me has been to learn to be comfortable in chaos first, leading without having all the clarity and abilities I felt were needed and ultimately understanding that the new way of working had to be developed and iterated versus expecting to receive any 'THIS WILL WORK' assurances.

The Fly Garage not only made a lasting impact on Mujica (she claims she now lives her life 'in beta mode') but has also built a living legacy within Mondelēz. The fact that the company closed the physical space it rented in Palermo between 2012 and 2014 was evidence of its success.

> Having a space out of Kraft Foods/Mondelēz International at the start was important to generate a playground to experiment, to free us up from established processes while we learned new ways of creating. But for us it was always clear that success was scaling the learnings and making them part of how everybody unleashed creativity for their brands. In this regard, it succeeded. Fly Garage evolved into continuous versions that leveraged learnings at the service of our business strategies. It mutated, iterated always, keeping the Fly essence but taking different formats.

These new iterations include Fly Camps (pop-up Fly Garages in Buenos Aires, helping teams from Brazil, Colombia, Mexico, and the US to develop innovation projects for local use), and digital accelerators that adopted Fly's 'hyper-collaboration/fast orientation' model to collaborate with start-ups and digital platforms. Out of twenty betas, four had been scaled to activation at the time of going to press, encouraging Mondelēz to accelerate its digital marketing spend from 7 per cent to 40 per cent of overall brand investment. In 2018 Mondelēz marketers in the Latin America region frequently use 'Fly scaling' tactics to work with their creative part-ners. 'We often have compressed sessions with external agitators, fast prototyping, and even detox exercises embedded in the development pro-cess of our creative work. It is increasingly part of the culture, and I expect to see this scaling gaining traction as teams see how much it impacts the business,' confirms Mujica. She points to 'ambassador' cases such as the *#deciloconMilka* project for Milka Chocolate in Argentina, which applied the Fly model to develop an interactive packaging app that enables people to create customized messages for their loved ones on Milka wrappers.

Setting money aside to test new forms of advertising creativity has obvious advantages, but the notion of The 5% Club takes on a more fundamental dimension when applied to the founding of innovation labs. Investing in a longer-term commitment requires both a cultural and a strategic shift, and can come into conflict with a corporation's short-term needs. There has to be a clear purpose (or, ahem, organiz-ing principle) and a recognition that new rules may need to be written. New frontiers tend not to come with handy maps.

The Mondelēz story also shows that labs don't need to be permanent. They can be limited-lifespan divisions that help a company evolve to the next level, then get closed until they're needed again. But whether you do it in a lab or elsewhere, The 5% Club is a mindset that can be transforma-tive within an organization. It allows you to maintain the long-term agility we discussed in the first commandment, staying on your toes and ready to react to the next big technology, behaviour, or business-model upheaval.

YOUR BRAND IS YOUR NEMESIS

Many businesses believe that their brand is their biggest asset, but Linda Bernardi, IBM's former chief innovation officer, believes it could be their greatest enemy. In her book *The Inversion Factor: How to Thrive in the IoT Economy* (co-written by Sanjay Sarma and Kenneth Traub) she outlines a new business model called 'inversion'. This, according to Bernardi, is when 'a business's mission and core competencies are defined as "needs first" rather than "products first"'. In other words, the driver of change is the customer, not the company.

Traditionally, businesses have worked the other way around, creating products or services that were deemed to fit certain needs, and updating them incrementally. But that system no longer cuts it. In an interview with *Contagious* magazine in 2017, Bernardi said: 'An inverted company begins by asking what the market needs before building things to exceed people's expectations.' She cited the examples of car-sharing company Zipcar and electric-automobile pioneer Tesla. Rather than building and selling a branded car, Zipcar instead developed an efficient way for people to get from A to B in cars that already existed. And prior to selling or even showcasing their electric vehicles, Tesla installed charging stations in Seattle and San Francisco, thereby directing the public dialogue towards alternative forms of energy.

The rise of Internet-of-Things technology has made identifying and meeting customer needs much easier, as the technology enables people to be connected to products in real time, encouraging transparent dialogue and instant feedback loops with manufacturers. However, the companies taking advantage of this trend tend to be rookie start-ups, not established players. Big brands need to adapt to people's evolving expectations, and to do that they must rewire their perspective: 'if you don't invert, you won't be relevant,' warns Bernardi. 'Consumer needs will end up creating something that your company may have been totally unaware of.'

This is where a 5% Club mentality presents a competitive advantage. Traditional companies that have been around for decades tend to have a large customer base using their products. It would be commercial suicide to abandon what they're doing and rush headlong into a new business vertical based on the advice they'd read in a Silicon Valley book; after all, people still need to fly on a plane, rent a car, keep their money safe, and so on. Committing to an innovation lab or a culture of experimentation is a smart way to initiate a gradual transition into the inverted world, to open up new opportunities.

ROOM SERVICE

Take the global rise of Airbnb. Bernardi points out that 'hotels won't go away tomorrow, but over time the needs and experience preferences of the consumer are driving them towards Airbnb, so the business model of hotels will need to change. Often the biggest obstacle to companies inverting is exactly the thing that makes them powerful: their brand. Their brand becomes their nemesis, but to protect themselves they hang onto it.'

There are definite signs of a fightback from hoteliers against the likes of Airbnb. In France, for example, the AccorHotel group – owners of brands ranging from Ibis at the budget end to Sofitel in the luxury space – decided to pilot AccorLocal, a radical app-based service and alternative business model that not only connects guests with local suppliers but also enables nearby residents to use the hotels' facilities and services without having to stay there. We spoke to Scott Gordon, CEO of AccorLocal, and he admitted that 'in our fifty years of existence we've focused purely on the traveller, but we've completely forgotten about a target that's four to five times superior, that surrounds all our hotels: the local residents.'

The idea behind AccorLocal is to sweat the assets – the company owns 4,200 hotels globally, all of which are open twenty-four hours a day – and to break the 'taboo' of entering a hotel when you're not staying in it. The app offers basic facilities to locals, such as hiring meeting rooms or using the gym. Next are the 'hybrid services', which sees AccorLocal aggregate the 'non-utilized space' in their hotels and pair it up at short notice with a local supplier. For example, a yoga teacher could be invited to run a class in an unused conference room. Above that is a curated 'digital integration' platform whereby hotel managers handpick local merchants and artists, offering them the chance to sell their products and services directly to guests and local residents, who can use the hotel as a convenient pickup point. By encouraging greater levels of interaction with neighbours, Gordon hopes the brand will enhance people's lives on a daily basis by providing them with frictionless convenience: 'With AccorLocal you can go and pick up your laundry when you're coming out of a nightclub or drop it off before taking your kids to school. Our doors are open.'

All well and good, but in business terms it's a reactive response from an industry that allowed itself to be blindsided by online travel agents, aggregators and home-rental services. True inversion would have been an insurance company beating Airbnb to the private letting game. After all, insurers have existing contracts with people who already trust the brand's reputation. What was lacking was the lateral thinking to identify the opportunity.

AIRBNB ON WHEELS

One company that has grasped inversion and joined The 5% Club is Daimler, owners of the Mercedes-Benz and Smart brands. Against a backdrop of increasing urbanization and environmental pressures, car manufacturers have acknowledged that their future lies beyond sheet metal. Instead, they need to start thinking more broadly about mass-mobility solutions and the advantages – from a consumer perspective at least – of access rather than ownership.

In December 2016 Daimler tested a car-sharing service, Croove, that encouraged residents in the German city of Munich to rent their cars to fellow citizens. Such services are not new: Ford, Volvo, and Nissan have all launched variations on the car-sharing theme, from joint leasing programmes to shareable digital keys. Indeed, Daimler's innovation team initiated the Car2Go car-sharing service, now the largest of its kind worldwide. However, what made the Croove experiment so bold is the neutrality behind the business model, and the fact that the pilot launched under a discrete brand name, with no obvious association to Daimler as the parent company. The Croove service – described at the 2016 Paris Motor Show by Daimler CEO Dieter Zetsche as 'Airbnb on wheels' – allows an owner of *any brand of car* to rent it out during periods when it would otherwise be sitting idle on a driveway or in an office car park. Research by Daimler showed that, on average, workers in German cities use their cars for between thirty minutes and an hour a day. The business opportunity lies in those hours of idleness.

To join Croove, car owners simply needed to create a profile and specify their vehicle's availability and the app suggested an appropriate rental price to charge. Renters located nearby cars through the app. Once the owner confirmed the renter's request, they could either meet in person to exchange the keys or the renter could pay a valet service to deliver the car. Payment was taken from the renter before they picked up the car, and received by the owner at the end of the rental period. Renters were automatically insured through Daimler's strategic partnership with Allianz. By April 2017 Croove moved past the six-week pilot phase and was being rolled out to other German cities, including Berlin.

1 + 1 = 3

We like this concept for a number of reasons. Daimler's strategic alliance with an adjacent partner (in this case the well-known insurer Allianz) is what we refer to at Contagious as a '1 + 1 = 3' (a business analogy made popular by British ad legend Dave Trott and his book of the same name). For us, it means two brands combining forces to create a consumer-friendly product or service that neither could easily build on their own is a smart way to accelerate innovation. The Croove service is based around the three customer pillars of convenience, security, and price. Convenience comes in the shape of the digital experience: everything happens through the app. Security is assured by the presence of Allianz, which provides insurance protection and trust, thereby breaking down an obvious barrier to entry. And the price of the service is optimized by limiting it to a digital experience, with low overheads and the physical inventory (the cars) being owned by the users.

This scheme shows that Daimler is attuned to shifting consumption patterns and new consumer behaviours. For example, a January 2016 report by management consultants McKinsey and Company on the auto industry showed that car sharing in North America and Germany grew by 30 per cent annually over the previous five years – and predicted that one in every ten cars sold in 2030 will be a shared vehicle. In January 2017 Croove CEO Daniel Rohrhirsch told Contagious:

> We recognize that mobility has been changing, and will continue to, especially in the next few years. So, we decided to participate in that change, jump on the wave, rather than be left behind . . . It might seem a bit strange for Daimler to open a sharing platform, but our main goal is to learn from it, and gain that experience as quickly as possible. We decided to start Croove as an open brand to have the chance to gain enough traffic and enough information to find out how sharing could develop, what the customer likes and what's important to them.

Rohrhirsch echoed one of the fundamental tenets behind The 5% Club philosophy: 'The most important target for us is to gain experience. These six weeks in the market haven't been about making money.' For

Contagious, this is one of the key drivers behind experimentation: anyone investing in a 'test-and-learn' approach should see that the value is in the learning, rather than chasing revenue: an opportunity to seek the truth behind the hunches in order to shape viable strategies. It's about the bigger picture; finding solid ground from which to step into the immediate future.

Another example of $1 + 1 = 3$ in practice is UK-based alcoholic drinks conglomerate Diageo, which has adopted a strategy of turning the competition into collaborators. 'Start-ups can get a strong foothold in the marketplace and take market share, sometimes before large corporations have noticed who they are or what they're doing.' So said Syl Saller, the Diageo CMO, speaking about the threats of entrepreneurs to big corporations at London's Media360 conference in May 2017. She described how Diageo is mitigating against disruption by partnering with smaller businesses. 'Big will not beat small any more,' she said. 'It will be the fast beating the slow.'

This is why Diageo runs Distill Ventures, its accelerator for small spirits businesses. The company provides cash investment, mentoring and in-market expertise in exchange for an equity stake. Brands in its portfolio include Stauning, a Danish whisky, and Seedlip, the world's first distilled non-alcoholic spirit. For Saller, the value of such partnerships lies in the objectivity that external collaborators bring: 'When you raise category-disruption ideas internally, they face a lot of hurdles because you are up against your own paradigms.' Tongue firmly in cheek, she painted the unlikely scenario of a product like Seedlip ever getting off the ground internally: 'I imagine speaking to Ivan [Menezes, the Diageo CEO] and saying, "Let's get into the non-alcoholic business, even though we're in alcohol; let's distil a spirit without alcohol, and let's charge £28 for it, even though there's no duty." I don't think he would have believed me. Better to let somebody who has that idea show us what's possible. They have no constraints.'

Another multinational adopting an 'if you can't beat them, join them' approach to start-ups is L'Oréal. It has created a beauty tech accelerator programme with Founders Factory, an incubator based in London. Investments include Canadian product-sampling experts Sampler, and New York start-up Riviter, whose patented AI technology powers a search engine that recognizes products in images and matches them to products online. 'We love beauty start-ups,' L'Oréal's chief digital officer, Lubomira Rochet, told Contagious in March 2018.

'Firstly, because we buy some of them and secondly because we reverse engineer their tactics for our bigger brands.'

MAKE YOUR 5 PER CENT EITHER FIRST OR FAST

There's an old phrase that says it's easy to spot the pioneers: they're the ones with arrows in their backs. So, from a business perspective, is it better to be a first mover or a fast follower? The answer is: it depends. *The Economist* found that innovators capture only 7 per cent of the market for their product over time. Apple is a classic example of a company that has profited by biding its time. It certainly wasn't the first mover in the digital music, tablet computer or smartphone categories, yet it managed to steal the momentum in all three spaces by waiting until a consumer need had been established and then ensuring that Apple's products were better, thanks to a relentless focus on human simplicity of design.

Speaking at the All Things Digital: D8 conference in California in 2010, Apple co-founder Steve Jobs explained the firm's rationale:

> The way we've succeeded is by choosing what horses to ride really carefully. We try to look for these technical vectors that have a future, and that are headed up. Different pieces of technology kind of go in cycles. They have their springs and summers, and autumns and then they go to the graveyard of technology. And so we try to pick the things that are in their springs. If you choose wisely, you can save yourself an enormous amount of work versus trying to do everything. And you can really put energy into making those emerging technologies be great on your platform, rather than just OK because you're spreading yourself too thin.

Yet for every Apple there's an Amazon, whose early move into electronic books and cloud computing gave it a competitive edge that it has exploited ruthlessly ever since. Writing on the *Harvard Business Review* site in 2012, Scott Anthony of the consulting firm Innosight pointed out that in a 'high-velocity organization that is always learning and improving, there are real benefits to moving first. After all, when someone copies what you have in the market, they are copying the artifact of your past effort. As you keep innovating, you create further space between you and the competition.' The flipside of that, however, is that companies who are not so quick off the mark 'have the benefit of learning from [their] rival's in-market experiments [and] can potentially avoid some of their mistakes and leap-frog over their solution'.

But, as Google executive chairman Eric Schmidt tweeted in September 2014: 'When tech's cheap and experimentation's easy, over-worrying about risk is a great way to fall behind.' Within this context, being a member of The 5% Club seems a small price to pay for future-proofing your brand.

Martin Weigel, the head of planning at Wieden+Kennedy, echoed this sentiment in his 'Case for Chaos' speech, presented in Amsterdam in January 2018 at an event hosted by the membership organization for strategists in the communications industry, the Account Planning Group. He told his audience:

> The economist E. F. Schumacher was right: 'Without order, planning, predictability, central control ... obedience, discipline ... nothing fruitful can happen, because everything disintegrates.' But he also said: 'yet without the magnanimity of disorder, the happy abandon, the entrepreneurship venturing into the unknown and incalculable, without the risk and the gamble, the creative imagination rushing in where bureaucratic angels fear to tread – without this, life is a mockery and a disgrace'. The modern corporation cannot afford not to stay flexible, fluid and willing to try new things.

CLUB TOGETHER

Given the relentless pace of technological change, Contagious will argue till the cows come home that a 5% Club mindset should be a mandatory part of the marketer's toolkit.

Taking the American market as an example, the average lifespan of an S&P 500 company has fallen from sixty-seven years in the 1920s to around fifteen years now. Logic would suggest that two-thirds of current companies may be gone or vulnerable by 2028. With ennui at one end of this equation, and voracious start-ups at the other, established brands *must* experiment in order to stay relevant.

Competing against the number crunchers (or 'Math Men', as the trade press often calls them) at management consultancies who believe that brands are built on end-to-end customer experience rather than just advertising, agencies *must* find the budget to take risks and to beef up their expertise. Gut instinct and an innate under-standing of human behaviour are what makes agencies special; they need to have the freedom to experiment with fringe ideas that they can then hit the mainstream with in no time. Creative leaps are their currency.

CEOs and senior leaders *must* get comfortable with the notion that safe ideas are often the ideas that ensure a slow frog-in-boiling-water demise instead of growth and diversification. It's natural to hide behind statistics that suggest mass-media penetration is the most predictable way to sustain market share. But think back to our first commandment, where we explored the advantages of agile long-termism. This means keeping your eyes on the prize, but being adaptive and flexible in the short term. Investing in The 5% Club, we would suggest, is a means of discovering, incubating and then accelerating tomorrow's long-term solution.

Mondelēz's Maria Mujica agrees with this perspective: 'The more "lab DNA" a company has in its cultural veins and ways of working, the fitter it will be to flex, adapt, shape the landscape and win.'

Whether it's 0.5 per cent, 5 per cent, or 50 per cent, if you do not have time, energy, and resources explicitly committed to experimenta-tion, developing new ideas, and going beyond the status quo, you will be left behind by those who do. Amazon is now so used to roadkill, it doesn't even look in its rear-view mirror to see what it hit. Innovation is risky and demands commitment, but in a fast-paced environment it boils down to one simple question: do you want to be the rabbit or the headlights?

JOIN THE 5% CLUB / ESPRESSO VERSION

The futurist Ray Kurzweil reckons that humans will have witnessed 20,000 years' worth of progress by the end of this century. Living inside a paradigm shift means brands need to innovate or die.

That's why Contagious has always championed the continuous innovation culture of Silicon Valley, and its 'build, measure, and learn' mentality. Our advice to marketers is to devote a percentage of a brand's media or production budget to unfettered experimentation and collaborations. Whether by building a lab, investing in start-ups or briefing for innovation across the entire organization, membership of The 5% Club makes you quicker to adapt to volatility. It allows you to test your hunches and then scale up if they prove positive. Trial and error teaches you how to judge new precedents; to gauge how appropriate they are against your company's commercial objectives.

You'll make mistakes, of course. If you don't, you're probably not doing it right. Pixar's Ed Catmull believes failure is a necessary consequence of testing something new: 'trying to avoid failure by out-thinking it . . . dooms you to fail.' Yet so many organizations are hardwired to treat mistakes like pariahs. An entrepreneurial culture is a culture of transparency, perseverance, and feedback loops.

The membership code for gaining access to the The 5% Club is 'EEEE'. Set aside some funds to Experiment; foster a climate of frank and honest Evaluation to uncover the best ideas; have the bravery to let them Evolve creatively, into the hands of your consumers; if the reaction is positive, Expand them, fight for them, build a business strategy around them and watch them fly. Then repeat.

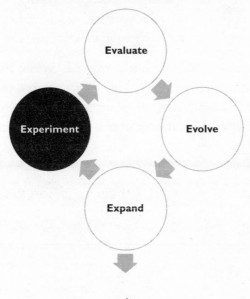

If you don't experiment and evolve, it's easy to get trapped by the past. Most businesses believe that their brand is their biggest asset, but it could be their biggest enemy if they protect it at the expense of new opportunities. See your customer as the driver of change. Make it your mission to have a needs-first agility rather than only looking at the world through the narrow lens of your own product. A smart way to invert business models and accelerate innovation is for two brands to combine forces to create a consumer-friendly product or service that neither could easily build on their own. In a case of $1 + 1 = 3$, car-maker Daimler teamed up with Allianz Insurance to create Croove, an 'Airbnb on wheels' service that allows people to rent their cars (any marque) to fellow citizens.

Once you've signed up to join The 5% Club, use these questions to get started:

- // What are the goals you have when you're experimenting? How are they linked with your broader purpose?
- // What's the unmet consumer need or gnarly business problem that means you need to 'jump and grow wings on the way down' in order to help your company fly?
- // Does your organization give out internal awards for the most spectacular failures? If not, why not?
- // Do you champion not just the final product but the missteps that led to it? What is your leadership afraid of?
- // Write a list of the experts, visionaries or mentors you'd like to collaborate with. What's stopping you making the call?

As Google's Eric Schmidt once tweeted: 'When tech's cheap and experimentation's easy, over-worrying about risk is a great way to fall behind.' Whether it's 0.5 per cent, 5 per cent, or 50 per cent, if you do not commit to experimentation you risk being left behind.

PRIORITIZE EXPERIENCE OVER INNOVATION

A collective groan rumbled through Contagious Towers a few years back when one of the day's crop of press releases heralded yet another 'world first'. This time it was from an ad agency in Australia: 'Cummins&Partners change the game forever with the release of "The World's First Crowd-Sourced 3D Printed QR Code, Live Streamed Via GoPro to a Smart Phone or Tablet Device, Drone Delivery Ticket System Project."'

Upon closer inspection, the editorial team sussed out that the 'project' was in fact a sardonic jibe at an industry eager to chase shiny new objects and to jump on the latest bandwagon. It turned out simply to be a video promoting a good old-fashioned advertising awards show. But the joke had a strong lesson at its heart: even though 3D printing and drones and other highfalutin tech are full of wonder and promise, they are not an end in themselves.

If you are reading this book and you don't work in advertising, you may find yourself scoffing at the likelihood that any industry professional worth their salt could have been fooled by such a preposterous claim. Well, we're afraid you're very much mistaken. At the

Cannes Lions International Festival of Creativity in 2016 – the ad industry's equivalent of the Oscars – a German entry for a sun-cream brand featured a remote-controlled robotic seagull drone equipped with UV sensors that was designed to squirt sunscreen onto unprotected children at the beach. Yes, that's right: a branded seagull that defecates on minors. The incredulous jury president, industry legend and co-founder of BBH, Sir John Hegarty, had this to say at a press conference attended by Contagious: 'It's the most stupid thing I think I've seen in my whole life. I actually thought the Monty Python team had got together and entered it, to see if we would vote for it.' Suddenly the parody from Cummins&Partners doesn't sound so far-fetched.

Whenever a technological breakthrough or new media platform emerges, the advertising industry does have a compulsion to rush headlong towards it, presumably under the assumption that novelty attracts attention. However, such attention is insubstantial – a cheap currency – if it is not underpinned by meaningful utility or an obvious bridge between the tech and the brand. Experience should always triumph over empty innovation. Deploying the latest gadget may deliver a fleeting PR spike, but unless it delivers a superior customer experience, it won't help your brand in the long run. The German agency's incontinent avian was a silly gimmick that deserved the scorn that flocked its way.

We are living in a complex, cluttered world where billions of people have developed a cognitive immunity to unoriginal marketing messages. Consumers have an abundance of choice, and the democratization of technology means that product parity is rapidly assured. Whether delivering convenience or captivation, experiences therefore wield a disproportionately high value, especially if they are unique. In an age where photos and videos play a key role in not just recording memories but also building social currency, brands that provide people with compelling experiences to treasure and transmit stand a better chance of differentiating themselves amid the din. From a Contagious perspective, this means that innovation must always be viewed through a human lens. The priority must be: *How can this enhance the experience of people's everyday lives?*

DON'T BUILD BARRIERS

Innovations live or die based on whether the rewards outweigh the effort. Take QR codes, those little pixelated squares that started popping up like chickenpox across magazine ads and outdoor sites in 2011. Short for Quick Response codes, they were heralded as the link between offline and online marketing, a nifty means for consumers to scratch an immediate itch should their imagination be captured by a branded message. Fantastic in principle but clunky in practice, these codes required people to download an app onto their smartphone before they were able to scan one. Then, having fired up the app and managed to get their camera to focus on this small piece of creative real estate, they would have to wait – sometimes a considerable number of seconds – for the app to recognize the code and retrieve the correct online link back to the brand's content.

Given that a 2016 study from Google's DoubleClick found that 53 per cent of mobile site visits were abandoned if pages took longer than three seconds to load, it's easy to see why consumers didn't warm to this new technology. Yet, despite this momentum-killing barrier, hordes of brands ploughed time and money into the QR code 'revolution'. In principle, the allure of being able to capitalize on consumer attention held obvious commercial promise.

In many cases, though, advertisers fell into the trap explored in the fifth commandment: they were so focused on what was in it for them that they neglected to consider what was in it for an end user who went through the hassle of snapping the code. In many cases, the rewards for consumers were low-value sales coupons or merely arriving at the same landing page they'd have found by typing the brand's name into a search bar. Meagre, to say the least.

Nevertheless, many advertisers and their agencies felt so compelled to ride the wave that they ignored two of the basic tenets of marketing communications: context and call to action. QR codes depend upon close proximity between phone camera and code – yet Contagious came across countless tales of small QR codes placed on billboards fifty feet in the air, in areas without mobile service, or – astonishingly – on trackside posters in London Underground stations that would have required passengers to step over a live electric rail to get close enough to scan the ad! No wonder that research carried out by Inc in 2012 suggested that 97 per cent of American consumers didn't even know what a QR code was. That same year, an anonymous Tumblr user created, wryly, a completely empty page entitled 'Pictures of People Scanning QR Codes'. There's nothing contagious about an underwhelming experience.

RESPECT THE PLATFORM

Fast forward to 2018 and, amazingly, QR codes are thriving – predominantly in China. That's thanks to the massive adoption of WeChat (now close to 1 billion active monthly users), which has inbuilt QR functionality, enabling citizens to interact seamlessly with the codes. They can even pay for goods and services by simply pointing at a similar photographable, digitized symbol. Similarly, Snapchat hopped on board the now-user-friendly bandwagon by introducing Snapcodes, which give users their own unique QR-like identifiers. Taking a picture of a Snapcode automatically adds that person to your friend list, saving the effort of hunting them down through search.

Brands, predictably, were quick to jump aboard, but this time the balance of power had shifted. We'd like to think that advertisers were chastened by previous consumer indifference, and sensed that they needed to provide intuitive, entertaining, and value-driven experiences that rewarded people for taking the trouble to interact. But the second wave probably had more to do with the fact that the usability of the technology had evolved, making it easier for marketers to deliver better experiences on the back of it.

One of the first brands to pioneer a more sympathetic approach was Coca-Cola-owned soft drink Sprite. The RFRSH Na Lata (RFRSH on the Can) campaign, by São Paulo agency CUBOCC, saw Sprite print the Snapcodes of sixteen carefully selected social influencers on a limited run of cans. Young adults looking for interesting content could scan a can and see up-to-the-minute posts from YouTube stars, skaters, graffiti artists, singers, and Sprite's own Snapchat account. The brand also invited people to submit their personal Snapcodes for a chance to have them printed on the side of cans, available at retail.

The idea of using Sprite as a gateway to access content (or 'product as entertainment portal' in marketing lingo) resonated with the demographic, precisely because experience and discovery were baked in. This was advertising that didn't feel like advertising. Felipe Simi, the chief strategy officer at CUBOCC, told Contagious: '40 per cent of the target doesn't pay attention to advertising. They are looking for authenticity and for them, advertising is not authentic at all. They have a really low attention span for branded content. They are the skip generation.'

Television viewership in Brazil is high, including among millennials. Primetime ratings on the largest network, Globo, often nudge beyond 65 per cent of the nation's homes, which means that most advertisers still flock there. CUBOCC's strategy ran counter to this herd mentality, instead treating Sprite's product as if it were a broadcast medium. 'We exchanged TV for packaging,' Simi told us:

> Sprite is present in 82 per cent of all beverage retailers in Brazil. When we think about the impact that this packaging generates at point-of-sale crossed with the frequency of people there, it will probably generate more Gross Rating Points than a TV commercial and it's also direct to our target. Our research showed us that 60 per cent of the target only communicate with each other using messaging apps, and their favourite social network was Snapchat, because it's quick content, their parents are not there, they can't be tracked, so they feel more free to be themselves. By printing the Snapcodes on the packaging, we instantly created a connected product, and also made a mobile campaign without any mobile ads.

When customer experience becomes the bedrock of a new technology, it is much more likely to soar. In their first iteration, QR codes were largely about one-way, transactional conversations, which is why consumer adoption rates were meagre. Once they became more user-friendly and unlocked richer content, they began to boom.

Putting Snapchat's QR tech into the hands of 178 million people per day certainly served to boost wider adoption, and now platforms like Facebook Messenger, Pinterest, Shazam, and Spotify have also incorporated their own QR code functionality. Amazon has added its own twist by introducing SmileCodes to magazine content. In a tie-up with the publisher Hearst, readers are able to use the Amazon app's camera to scan codes positioned alongside editorial content, opening a dedicated *Cosmopolitan* or *Seventeen Magazine* Amazon page where they can automatically buy products featured in the magazine. Elsewhere, the Bank of Thailand announced in 2017 that, as part of its agenda to increase the volume of cashless payments in the country, it had persuaded MasterCard and Visa to introduce a standardized, interoperable QR code payment platform, allowing consumers to easily make secure transactions with their mobile devices.

If technology is subservient, and designed to enrich and expedite the consumer experience, then people will willingly flock to it. The fall and rise of QR codes is an interesting example of how a technology managed to evolve from gimmick to useful tool, buoyed by the improved quality of the experience it unlocked and of the process of unlocking it.

UNEXPECTED ITEM IN THE BAGGING AREA

In marketing terms, Contagious defines an 'experience' as the interaction a person has – anytime, anywhere or anyhow – with a company. Today there are many places and opportunities for these interactions to happen, presenting a clear strategic challenge. Do companies break into little pieces in order to spread themselves across all the touchpoints now available (media channels, retail experiences, social networks, emerging technologies, customer service centres and so on) or do they think about 'experience' more holistically and cumulatively?

The management-consultant brainboxes at McKinsey & Company would argue for the latter. The problem they have identified is that most companies are wired for transactions, whereas they should be wired for the journeys their customers take, across multiple channels over time. In March 2016 McKinsey principals Nicolas Maechler, Kevin Neher, and Robert Park argued that firms should resist the logical temptation to fixate on discrete touchpoints, no matter how well optimized they may be. In an article posted on McKinsey.com, they wrote: 'This siloed focus on individual touchpoints misses the bigger – and more important – picture: the customer's end-to-end experience. Only by looking at the customer's experience through his or her own eyes – along the entire journey taken – can you really begin to understand how to meaningfully improve performance.' McKinsey's cross-industry research found that performance on journeys is more strongly corre- lated with customer satisfaction than performance on touchpoints. The clear conclusion was that 'delivering a distinctive journey experience makes it more likely that customers repeat a purchase, spend more, recommend to their friends, and stay with your company'.

These findings corroborate a 2013 *Harvard Business Review* study which found that focusing on the entire customer journey is 30–40 per cent more strongly correlated with customer satisfaction than one touch- point. And it's 20–30 per cent more strongly correlated with business out- comes, like high revenue, repeat purchase, and low customer churn.

Think back to the first commandment, where we encouraged you to establish an organizing principle; a central belief that drives every- thing your company does, from internal policies to external communi- cations. Things tend to fragment when organizations lose sight of this core promise and its impact on the entire customer journey.

Take, for example, UK supermarket Tesco. If your advertising slo- gan is 'Every Little Helps', yet your stores appear to prioritize auto- mated self-service checkouts that alienate elderly people or parents of young children who may appreciate a helping hand, it risks feeling like an empty slogan rather than the dynamic, customer-focused organizing principle that it could be.

Tesco is certainly not alone in this (and, to be fair, the company has now rejigged its operational structure to place more staff on the shop floor). Most of its metropolitan rivals in the UK have adopted simi- lar tactics. Sure, some shoppers prefer the anonymity and convenience of being able to scan a few items themselves before whizzing back to their busy lives. But when the scales tip towards the nakedly obvious cash-saving benefits at the expense of the inclusive embrace of cus- tomer experience, the brand starts to lose some of its sheen.

A more elegant solution to the same problem, crafted from a con- sumer experience perspective, are so-called 'grab-and-go' stores like Amazon Go and BingoBox (see the second commandment), which elim- inate waiting time and require less staffing by creating fluid customer interactions without any need to master a new interface. It's a model that uses technology to enhance experience, rather than needlessly cluttering what was previously a better interaction in the name of cost savings.

Think of your own brand, no matter what sector you are in, and ask yourself: *what is our unexpected item in the bagging area – that glitch in the customer journey – and what steps can we take to reduce or resolve it?*

GOOD TECHNOLOGY IS NO EXCUSE FOR A BAD IDEA

From a Contagious perspective, we certainly don't have an issue with technological innovation within the retail space, as you will see over the next few pages. However, innovation needs to be geared towards human experience if it is not going to suffer rejection or even ridicule.

This probably explains why Google Glass proved to be such a damp squib, stumbling from launch to withdrawal inside two years. The futuristic spectacles, housing a miniature monitor, a camera, microphone, accelerometer, voice command, Wi-Fi antennas, and lots of other geeky stuff, undoubtedly made sense inside the hermetically sealed optimism of Silicon Valley. They could, after all, augment a human's life by placing the equivalent of a tiny computer with access to the World Wide Web directly over your eyeball. However, what its inventors failed to account for was impact in the real world. Normal people, by and large, thought that the early adopters, those inhabitants of technology's filter bubble who paid $1,500 for Google Glass, looked weird wearing them. The very presence of these geeky glasses automatically excluded those who were not part of the gang.

This was the killer problem: the devices gave people the creeps. Writing in *The Guardian*, John Naughton, author of *From Gutenberg to Zuckerberg*, stated: 'Glass made everyone around you feel uneasy. They thought the technology was intrusive and privacy-destroying. Bouncers wouldn't let wearers – whom they called "Glassholes" – into clubs. The maître d' would discover that the table you thought you had booked was suddenly unavailable. And so on.' Technology columnist and consultant Tim Bajarin echoed that thought, recounting his personal experience of Google Glass in an article on the Techpinions website shortly after the product was withdrawn in 2015: 'It was the worst $1,500 I have ever spent in my life. On the other hand, as a researcher, it was a great tool to help me understand what not to do when creating a product for the consumer.'

The net result was that Google lost millions of dollars by placing innovation on a pedestal, at the expense of user experience. But, much like QR codes, once the experience side of things caught up, the innovation began to make sense. A few years later Google Glass returned to the headlines, this time as an enterprise tool, better suited to functional settings such as factories and industrial-design labs. Conveniently hands-free and now embedded with tech that enables real-time image search and language translation, the glasses are capable of unlocking superior experiences – and are suddenly (albeit in niche-use cases) relevant again.

In a brilliant fusion of experience and innovation, Nike created a digital stadium in Manila to promote the launch of its top-of-the-range LunarEpic trainers. The brand worked with agencies BBH Asia, Party/New York and Jack Morton Worldwide to create the Unlimited Stadium, which was open for two weeks to coincide with the 2016 Olympic Games in Rio de Janeiro. The 200-metre running track was shaped like the sole of a LunarEpic shoe and was lined with vertical LED screens. Runners set the pace with their first lap and then raced against a digital avatar of themselves, which matched the speed of their first effort. Participants could then progress onto a series of time and distance challenges. Up to thirty runners could use the track at any one time.

Nike chose to open the Unlimited Stadium experience during the Rio Games to capitalize on the habitual spike in people's interest in athletics and to provide a synergistic backdrop for the brand's core message of urging people to push themselves. Usually when runners try to beat their personal best, the battle takes place inside their head. But in Nike's Unlimited Stadium runners were able to race a visible avatar, making the contest more tangible. Visually competing against yourself is a unique experience for any runner, of any standard, and this is one of those out-of-the-ordinary encounters that is likely to be offered freely only by a brand. A city council wouldn't make Unlimited Stadium and a gym or a theme park would charge cold hard cash. Here, Nike – which was not an official Olympic sponsor – was clearly on a mission to link experiential marketing dollars to word of mouth, sparking a saboteur-style PR drive at a time in the media cycle when sport is top of mind.

IT'S THE EXPERIENCE ECONOMY, STUPID

When a senior spokesperson at the world's largest furniture retailer declares that the West has probably hit 'peak stuff', it's time to start placing your bets on memories rather than mattresses. Speaking at a *Guardian* Sustainable Business debate in January 2016, Ikea's head of sustainability, Steve Howard, implied that the appetite for the mass consumption of material goods, including home furnishings, had reached an apex moment: 'We talk about peak oil. I'd say we've hit peak red meat, peak sugar, peak stuff.'

Now, before we all start thinking it's curtains for consumerism – good luck brewing an aromatic cup of Bai Han Oolong Tea or making a phone call with an experience – there has undeniably been a collective shift in mindset that now sees people placing a greater value on doing stuff than buying stuff.

The term 'Experience Economy' has its roots in a 1998 book by management advisors Joseph Pine and James Gilmore: *Welcome to the Experience Economy*. They argued that in an advanced economy where most products and services have become commoditized or undifferentiated, the most effective way to gain a competitive advantage is by investing in extraordinary customer experience. Their assertion was that people place a disproportionately high value on the experience surrounding a purchase, service or event. Creating notable experiences, therefore, becomes a primary differentiator. Indeed, in an Eventbrite poll conducted by Harris Interactive in 2014, 72 per cent of millennials said they intended to increase their spending on experiences rather than physical things and 77 per cent revealed that their best memories are from an event or live experience, largely because attending live events and experiences make them feel more connected to other people, the community, and (thanks to the broadcast power of social media) the wider world.

A 2015 study, 'We'll Always Have Paris: The Hedonic Payoff from Experiential and Material Investments' by Cornell University psychologists Thomas Gilovich and Amit Kumar, builds on this. It posited that experiential purchases tend to bring more enduring happiness – known to boffins as 'hedonic return' – than material purchases. In simple terms, this means that money spent on *doing* delivers a bigger bang for your buck than money spent on *having*. Their argument is that experiences provide enduring satisfaction, build social capital, and foster an enhanced sense of self 'by becoming a more meaningful part of one's identity'.

Interestingly, the Cornell research indicates that 'the hedonic benefits extend to anticipation as well'. In other words, in addition to creating the emotional value of wellbeing through lasting memories, experiences also deliver a psychological benefit in advance: people enjoy getting excited in the build-up. Just ask Santa Claus. Or Science, if you'd prefer. Writing in the *Journal of Experimental Psychology* in 2007, American researchers Leaf Van Boven and Laurence Ashworth reported on a series of experiments conducted to explore whether anticipation arouses greater levels of emotion than retrospection. Participants in the study were asked to contemplate past or future events. Their emotional reactions showed that they experienced a greater intensity of feelings *before* rather than *after* an event. For example, feeling more excited about a future skiing holiday than one in the past, both hypothetical and real.

But why such a downer on material goods? 'Part of the reason we seem to get such little enduring satisfaction from our possessions,' conclude the Cornell researchers, 'is that we quickly habituate to them. Once we get used to them, they provide very little in terms of lasting happiness, causing us to want more and more, a phenomenon that has been dubbed the "hedonic treadmill".' The power and enduring value of experiences ('from prospect to retrospect') lies not just in the treasure trove of memory, but in the stories they allow us to tell. This is primal stuff. Humans are hardwired to talk about our experiences and to keep our stories alive. In contrast, 'our possessions often just sit there, collecting dust, becoming obsolete, and being all but forgotten'.

ALL THE WORLD'S A STAGE

There is an obvious symbiosis between the growing number of people who crave unique, memorable experiences and brands that want to explore alternative, deeper ways of connecting with audiences. Unsurprisingly, many advertisers have turned to immersive theatre groups and experience designers in the hope of creating moments of magic to drive richer engagement with loyal and prospective fans alike.

The acclaimed British theatre company Punchdrunk has enjoyed a number of successful collaborations with brands, including Absolut, Louis Vuitton, Samsung, Stella Artois, and W Hotels. Back in 2011 they dragged gamers from the sanctuary of their sofas to participate in a live theatrical experience, entitled 'And Darkness Descended', to promote the PlayStation video game *Resistance 3*. Participants were placed inside a simulation of a ravaged London and were challenged to find the last pocket of human resistance in the aftermath of a brutal Chimeran invasion. Lighting, sounds, and smells were all specifically inspired by the game, with players required to work together, echoing *Resistance 3*'s collaborative multiplayer elements. Punchdrunk's artistic director, Felix Barrett, told Contagious that the 'visceral fusion' of the project transcended theatre and gaming: 'The emotional and experiential potential of finding yourself within a video game is huge – you are your own avatar.'

In 2013 alcohol giant Diageo invested in the Singleton Sensorium: a sensory experiment that proved a change of environment can enhance the experience of enjoying whisky by up to 20 per cent. Led by Professor Charles Spence, head of crossmodal research at the Department of Experimental Science at Oxford University, it was the world's first scientific study exploring the senses in relation to whisky. The professor ran tests conducted by sensory architects Condiment Junkie at a specially constructed bar in London that featured three rooms with contrasting atmospheres. A 'grassy' room complete with turf and birdsong was designed to accentuate the nose of the Singleton Single Malt

Scotch Whisky. A room with red fruits, curved shapes, and chiming bells brought out the dark berry and dried fruit flavour of the whisky. A room replete with double-bass notes, a cedar scent, and a crackling fire represented the lingering taste of age and wood in the drink. The study was followed by in-lab testing and under both conditions participants reported significant variations in their ratings of the taste, scent, and flavour when drinking Singleton Single Malt in different environments. The results inspired Diageo to extend the concept into curated retail activities, including tasting rooms at Asian airports.

But it's not just fancy whiskies and multibillion-dollar videogames that get the experiential treatment. Even something as prosaic as baked beans can have its moment in the sensory limelight. Developed in 2013 by London experience-design studio Bompas & Parr, the Heinz Beanz Flavour Experiences were a collection of spoons and bowls that synced up with various Heinz products to supposedly enhance the eating experience. The spoons came equipped with an MP3 player embedded in the handle. The magic happened only when the spoon was inside someone's mouth. People enjoying the Fiery Chilli flavour, for example, listened to samba music, while those eating the Curry variant heard a Punjabi Bhangra composition.

Bompas & Parr's bespoke bowls matched each of the flavours. The bowl for the Garlic and Herb beans was moulded out of laser-cut paper to resemble a garlic bulb, and the Cheddar Cheese bowl was crafted out of wax to look like a cheese round. They proved so popular they were even sold in the high-end food emporium Fortnum & Mason, adding a curiously luxurious experience to humble beans. By bringing enhancements directly to products themselves, traditional marketing distractions are stripped away to leave the product at the centre of the user experience.

Dutch start-up Sensiks has developed a sensory reality pod that combines audio-visual recordings with scent, temperature, air flow, vibration, taste, and light to create immersive experiences. The pods can create a range of encounters, from stress-reducing strolls through the countryside to 'sensified' films (featuring less appealing smells such as sewers or car exhaust fumes). Participants wear a VR headset while sitting inside a pod that is fitted with vents, lights and heat lamps. Biometric sensors monitor heart rate, skin conduction, and respiration, which enables Sensiks to track how participants are reacting to the experience. Then, using that data, the artificial intelligence system built into the pod can give suggestions for future content.

'People want a world where brands no longer tell them about products, but invite them to "feel and live" the service or product,' says Debbie Ellison, head of digital at Geometry Global UK, one of Sensiks' agency partners. 'Brands are looking to tap into sensory to connect more closely with people.'

In 2014 Eventbrite reported that 66 per cent of millennials said they felt more fulfilled by live experiences than purchasing an item of the same value. More recently, the Harris Group found that 57 per cent of consumers crave experiences that stimulate their senses, a figure that rises to 78 per cent for millennials. For brands that sell physical products, this fixation on experiences can have a negative impact; retailers including Next and Ikea have blamed the experience economy for sales dips. Technology such as Sensiks' sensory reality could give bricks-and-mortar retailers a future-facing solution for creating experiences around their products that can only be realized in a physical setting, thus attracting footfall.

TRANSFERENCE OF EXPERIENCE EXPECTATION

So, from reading *The Contagious Commandments* thus far, you know that people value experiences, resent pain points and are prepared to reward brands that provide one and solve the other. This explains why user-centric services like Amazon, Spotify, and Uber have flourished, thanks to effortless experience and wallet-friendly pricing. The challenge for marketers – who are increasingly responsible for the entire customer experience – is that people are becoming ever more demanding and judgemental in the real world, precisely because they are routinely exposed to superlative treatment from firms rooted in the digital.

Adam Morgan, founder of UK-based marketing consultancy eat-bigfish, has a brilliant term for this. He dubs the phenomenon 'Uber's Children' – a new generation of 'unreasonable consumers' who, after experiencing the benefit of a chauffeur for the price of a taxi with just two clicks on an app, no longer expect the trade-offs of old. If Wi-Fi is free at Starbucks, it should be free on planes. (It increasingly is.) Why can't I order pizza by sending an emoji? (You now can.) If Spotify knows me better than myself, why the hell is the receptionist at the hotel I'm staying at for the seventh time this year asking me if it's my first visit? It's natural nowadays to expect services in seemingly unrelated industries to offer the same level of personalization and frictionless experience that we get from the brands we have come to love the most.

Contagious refers to this as the transference of experience expectation. People automatically expect the experience they receive from every brand – irrespective of the category it's in – to be consistent, compelling and convenient. The role of the marketer becomes much more demanding, but ultimately more rewarding. From data analytics, in-store activity, customer service chatbots, mobile, social, voice, traditional advertising channels, immersive retail experiences and beyond, the marketer's professional reward lies in the efficient administration of a multitude of experiences that build an enduringly positive and coherent image of a brand in the memories of its audience. Memories fuel mental availability, which influences consumers' decision-making at the point of purchase. As John Kearon, founder and CEO of market research agency System1 Group, told us: 'If you make people *feel* more, they are more likely to buy more.' And therein lies the power of immersive theatrical events and beautifully constructed commercials that either tickle the funny bone or tug at the heartstrings.

FEEL THE DIFFERENCE

An obvious benefit of living in the age of the unreasonable consumer is that standards have risen accordingly. The customer-centricity of Amazon (personalized recommendations, free shipping, same day delivery, or even a 120-minute shipping window with Prime Now) has ensured a 'rising tide lifts all boats' scenario in e-commerce and digital. Few brands are incapable of putting their product inventory onto a website and getting your chosen items to you pretty quickly in a relatively convenient manner.

Equally, technology is fundamentally a democratic beast. In purely scientific terms, there's barely a few molecules difference between an Adidas, Asics, Nike or New Balance running shoe. They're all made of more or less the same materials and perform the same function. The winner in the race to innovate, it would seem, is parity. The essence of branding has always been about creating the differentiating factor between undifferentiated products, but now experience adds another dimension. Certainly in the retail environment, experience is a curated way to bring the brand to life and to express its defining nuances, attitude, and philosophical principles.

Take Asics as an example. The Japanese footwear brand is transforming its retail environments into 3D marketing exercises, using bespoke experiences and expert human guidance to differentiate itself. For its communications platform, the brand has adopted a 'Sound Mind, Sound Body' philosophy, with a mission to educate and inspire people around the physical and mental benefits of exercise. In Europe, it operates concept stores in cities including Amsterdam, Berlin, Brussels, London and Vienna, all of which are focused on people's overall well-being. Asics' marketing efforts reach a crescendo in these places. The concept stores feature both workshops, from yoga to high-intensity interval training, and complimentary services provided by personal trainers and physicians with no affiliation to Asics. They function as hubs where the company's goals and its audience's needs intersect.

The flagship store on London's Regent Street features a robotic product-delivery system and kinetic coloured lighting display that pulsates at the same pace as the heart rate of a 100-metre runner. Alongside this are four Asics proprietary Motion ID areas, using sensors to capture the consumer's natural posture and style of movement when running in order to select the most appropriate shoe. This is immersive, multisensory retail that uses experience to channel innovation, acting as a driver of competitive advantage, and builder of positive memories.

Consumer electronics giant Samsung brought its virtual reality technology to UK festival goers as a way to transform the traditional music experience. The brand partnered with Scottish band Biffy Clyro to create a dynamic VR encounter that plunged music lovers into the heart of the video for the group's song 'Flammable'. Samsung's giant experiential structure, the Hypercube, used the latest in VR technology, 360-degree cameras and the Samsung Galaxy S7 smartphone to create a unique experience. Up to fifty festival goers could enter at a time, don a headset and find themselves directly immersed inside the video's pyrotechnics. The experience was developed by London agency Iris.

Other VR collaborations between Samsung and music artists include a campaign by electropop group Years & Years that gave fans a preview of their European tour using the Samsung Galaxy S7 Edge and Gear VR headsets. Immersive, exclusive experiences like these serve to position Samsung as more than an electronics company in the minds of music fans. Marc Mathieu, chief marketing officer at Samsung Electronics America, told us that the brand deploys innovative technology to trigger an emotional response from people. 'We aspire to be a brand at the intersection of technology, humanity and culture,' he said. Heightened experiences are more likely to live longer in the memory, be seen as a valuable social currency, and therefore boost affinity for the brand.

By building something as ambitious and communal as the Hypercube, Samsung overcame the usually solitary experience of wearing a VR headset and created a shared experience at scale; as well as placing both the phone and VR headsets into the hands of an influential target group. The number of active virtual-reality users is forecast to have reached 171 million by the end of 2018, according to market researchers Opinium. This is why brands like Samsung are responding to the fact that, for many consumers, the virtual world has started to blur with the physical one, breaking down geographical barriers, boosting education, enhancing entertainment experiences and adding a new dimension to socializing.

EXPERIENCE IN MOTION

For some brands, the ambition to create heightened experiences extends beyond redefining the conventional retail environment. Car-maker Buick, for example, conjured a striking visual metaphor to represent its design chops and technical know-how. Blending cutting-edge innovation and theatrical stage design, it built a futuristic eco-home to tempt Chinese drivers to test its Velite 5 hybrid car. This battery-shaped smart home was christened 'Lifezone'. It incorporated the same kinds of technologies used in the Velite 5 and was constructed using recyclable materials. Solar-power panels, rainwater collection and a waste purification system provided energy. Guests could drive a Velite 5 directly into the living room and use voice commands to control household appliances, play music and adjust lighting levels.

The pop-up was only available for a month in Shanghai, and prospective visitors had to apply via Buick's WeChat account. In terms of lead generation, it certainly delivered: 13,300 people signed up, despite only twenty-four spaces being available. Those selected could test drive a Velite 5 during their visit. The Lifezone was then taken to numerous Chinese cities.

Cheelip Ong, chief creative officer of Buick's ad agency, Mullen-Lowe China, said: 'We want to create unforgettable brand experiences that deeply engage with our consumers. Instead of a traditional print ad or television commercial that tells drivers what Velite 5 is about, Velite 5 Lifezone allows them and their friends to live out the design philosophy behind it.'

Buick's activity reflects an increasing trend in the automotive and general retail sectors: deploying experiential marketing tactics to drive sales and advocacy. The aim here is to create a bond between consumer and brand by immersing them in a memorable experience. This is especially important for automakers as the bulk of consumers (67 per cent, according to a US survey by digital marketing company Netsertive) now visit only one or two dealerships before making a purchase, and car brands often have little control over how people experience their brand online. The trade-off is that experiential campaigns can usually reach only a limited number of consumers directly. This explains why MullenLowe worked hard to ensure maximum ROI, knowing that images of the lavish, futuristic Lifezone would attract extensive social media coverage by tapping into the popularity of so-called 'property porn'. The result was 1.64 billion media impressions and 25,504 purchase inquiries for Buick.

Another automotive brand that places a high value on experiential tactics is Land Rover. The SUV market is booming: global sales have risen by 87 per cent since 2013, according to industry consultants LMC Automotive. The consensus within the category is that this popularity is largely down to people wanting to do more with their lives, Tony O'Toole, the head of auto strategy at Imagination, Land Rover's experiential agency, told Contagious in 2014: 'We've reached product saturation in many ways. People don't want more stuff, they want an experience they can feel and talk about in an interesting way. SUVs are a natural partner to the growth of this experience lifestyle.' (In other words, 'Buy our thing, because we know you don't want to buy things from other brands.')

Taking advantage of this behavioural shift is, unsurprisingly, a crucial business objective for the brand. Land Rover's advertising reminds people that these vehicles let you do more, see more, and, ultimately, achieve more with your life. Underpinning this is a strategy that stresses the superiority of the Land Rover experience: 'Demonstrating the engineering that goes into these products in an experiential way is the key differentiator for us,' said Mark Cameron, head of experience at Jaguar Land Rover.

To bring this proposition to life, the brand audaciously succeeded in crossing the Empty Quarter: the world's largest and most inhospitable sand desert, situated on the Arabian peninsula. Rally driver Moi Torrallardona drove an All-New Range Rover Sport across 528 miles of epic dunes and canyons, setting a new record time of ten hours and twenty-two minutes. The car had received only one modification – a plate to protect the underbody from sand. The brand shot a documentary of the escapade, capturing authentic, adrenaline-fuelled footage live in the moment.

Adaptations of this content then percolated through Land Rover's marketing channels – involving fans vicariously in the experience and bolstering Land Rover's capabilities at the same time. 'As well as being a documentary, the Empty Quarter was an actual event, a TV ad, a print ad, and provided real-time PR and social content,' David Murray, the global strategy director at agency RKCR/Y&R, told us. Nowhere does this content work harder than on social channels. Land Rover has three key audiences – fans, prospects, and owners. These live events tick each box: fans love the vehicle imagery, prospective owners are impressed by the technical capabilities, and owners feel proud to be part of the Land Rover family.

FEEL MORE, DRIVE MORE

Bolstering mass-marketing initiatives such as the Empty Quarter are more targeted, one-to-one product demonstrations that let consumers feel exactly what it's like to be behind the wheel of a Land Rover. The brand has three levels of live experience, each with a specific business objective in mind. The first of these takes place in city-centre locations. Land Rover sets up an off-road course using Terrapod equipment – essentially portable slopes and cross axle ramps that mimic extreme off-road conditions – and then uses the ten-minute mini test drives to raise awareness and maximize reach in urban areas.

Second are Land Rover Experience centres, where people are taught how to drive the vehicles on demanding terrain, like steep inclines and deep fords. 'These centres can be used as loyalty programmes or con-quest tools,' noted Cameron. Showroom visitors who are interested in purchasing a vehicle (but not yet 100 per cent convinced) are given a voucher to attend one of the centres where they can drive the SUV in a genuine off-road environment. In the UK, soon after taking delivery of their SUV, every new customer is invited to take part in one of these days. 'The insight here is that most people don't know what they've bought, in terms of technology, so why not turn them into advocates by showing them what their car can do,' Cameron told us.

The upper experiential tier, called the Global Expedition Pro-gramme, is for serious Land Rover fans with serious wallets. They pay upwards of £10,000 to be guided across an area of outstanding natural beauty, such as the Serengeti National Park in Tanzania, in a convoy of Range Rovers or Land Rover Discoveries. Participants gain access to sections of the park usually closed to the public. Here, a physical experi-ence is essential in communicating both inherent product innovation and intangible brand values.

The brand's experiential investment (20 per cent of the global marketing budget) plays a major part in social conversations, by giving people distinctive experiences to share across their networks. This, effectively, creates an adjacent stream of communications whereby vehicles and terrains are captured and shared by fans, for fans – placing experience at the centre of marketing communications and actively supporting the rest of the brand's advertising. Here, innovation is being used to enhance consumers' interactions with the brand, driving affinity by building memorable experiences.

PIONEER AROUND PEOPLE

One strategic approach is to lead with innovation to build experience; the other is to lead with customer experience to build innovation. But what happens when a company links innovation to experience by adopting an anthropological relationship with its customer base, helping it to transform the category it competes in?

In the spring of 1991 an employee at the Turkish bank Garanti risked his career by sending an extraordinarily candid letter to the bank's owner. The handwritten document, sent by the then executive vice-president of marketing, Akin Öngör, outlined his proposal for a radical shake-up of the company – one that involved halving the number of bank staff in order to invest in technologists instead. His vision was simple: reinvent the company around the customer, and apply innovation to change the concept of banking by aligning with new consumer behaviours. Two weeks later, Garanti's owner accepted the plan and Öngör was promoted to chief executive.

Being the first Garanti leader from a marketing background, he was intent on using his expertise to understand customers' needs and to design experiences around them. For Öngör, this meant repositioning the bank as a pioneer. And so, throughout his nine-year tenure, Garanti became a company of technological, experience-driven 'firsts'. In 1997 it became the first private Turkish company to launch digital banking services, at a time when national bandwidth was so slow that Garanti removed text from its webpage so transactions could process.

Two years later, the bank created the first virtual point-of-sale system, enabling merchants to process purchases made over the web.

Even after his retirement in 2000, Öngör's legacy of technological milestones lived on. In 2005 the bank offered SMS-based money transfers, and a year later enabled people to personalize credit cards by choosing the interest rates and rewards programmes that suited them – both world firsts. In May 2013 the bank released iGaranti, a suite of twenty-three different banking services contained within a central smartphone app, affectionately billed as 'the smart friend in your pocket'. The app – developed by service design specialists Fjord – gets to know the customer, their spending habits and their wider interests. It can forecast how much money they will spend, using an algorithm that crunches personal spending habits over the past six months. If things look rosy, iGaranti advises customers to divert some cash into a savings account. If things look tight, the app offers a micro-loan until payday. Crucially, these contextual, personalized services take the worry out of banking, inspired by the company's mantra of 'helpful simplicity'.

At the centre of Garanti's vision is a platform agnostic, omnichannel strategy – a commitment to provide a seamless, personalized and connected customer experience across all available touchpoints. The strategy succeeds because it mimics the habits of one of the most digitally demanding populations on the planet. Even as far back as 2012, 80 per cent of transactions took place through the bank's digital platforms. When targeting consumers, conventional banks tend to use segmentation models based on demographics. In contrast, Garanti creates its own distinct model centred on behaviours. This is based around the idea of 'Generation C: the connected customers', who are fast adopters of technology, whether eighteen or eighty years old.

TO TECH IS TO SERVE

Underpinning the bank's trailblazing prowess is Garanti Technology, a subsidiary responsible for maintaining Garanti's status as a global leader on digital platforms, and for keeping up with technological advances in the wider world. The firm employs 1,000 IT experts, sector analysts, and software developers. In order to encourage agility and objectivity, the facility – in true 5% Club fashion – is located apart from Garanti's headquarters.

One of Garanti Technology's biggest technical accomplishments came in 2016, when it unveiled a Turkish natural-language equivalent of Apple's Siri, capable of interpreting financial questions. Called Mia (Mobile Interactive Assistant), the technology took eighteen months to develop. Using voice commands, customers can perform tasks such as paying rent, requesting foreign exchange conversions and locating the nearest ATM. Why did the bank go to such lengths to achieve this hands-free, linguistic extravaganza? Because it knows that its mobile-first customer base finds it faster to talk to their devices, rather than type.

Keeping close to your consumers gets to the heart of what Contagious means by 'experience over innovation'. We're not saying innovation isn't important, but any new means of interacting with people needs to start from the right place. Innovations are adopted only if the needs and behaviours of real people are prioritized.

Building successful experiences requires an almost obsessive devotion to listening to customers, acknowledging preferred behaviours, and adapting your services to match the needs of the people you would like to engage with. No wonder that, for Garanti, every innovation starts with a clear instruction: *This has to be useful, simple and instantly understandable.* Rather than falling into a trap of tech for tech's sake, the brand's innovations are born out of a commitment to improve the banking experience. Humans must always win.

OBSESS ABOUT EXPERIENCE

'Experience' as a marketing strategy is so sprawling and crosses so many disciplines that it often falls between stools inside organizations. At a Contagious conference in 2015 that explored the theme of 'Obsessing Experience', Tom Raith of service-design company IDEO identified this as a 'back-of-the-deck' problem. Less-progressive clients are used to buying 'conventional' advertising but find it tougher to commit to experiences, because they require discrete budgets and shared responsibility across teams. However, by prioritizing the customer and the role the brand can play in their lives, many of these back-of-the-deck ideas can be brought front and centre – especially those that drive loyalty, recruit new users and amplify awareness. The most effective way to embed experiential thinking, Raith suggested, is to work iteratively and maintain a relentless focus on people's everyday needs and ambitions.

The new paradigm – innovating around the consumer – is heavily influenced by service design, a discipline that rose to prominence around the time Contagious was founded. Unlike traditional design practices, service designers create experiences around the needs of the customer. Close attention is paid to reducing friction in the customer journey and speeding up processes so that there's a consistent, intuitive flow. Every touchpoint – from call centres to distribution, marketing and point of sale – is an equal hero, because all leave an equal impression with the customer. Optimized brilliantly – and engineered as the cumulative, end-to-end journey advocated by McKinsey that we mentioned earlier in this commandment – this experience-centric approach can transform a business.

'Experience' is central to the future of marketing, because of the two-way communication channel it opens between a brand and its audience, and the subsequent scope for word of mouth – the most effective medium of all. Experience, executed well, becomes the bridge between the promises made by a brand's marketing and the reality encountered by those real people formerly known as 'targets'.

PRIORITIZE EXPERIENCE OVER INNOVATION / ESPRESSO VERSION

What is an 'experience', anyway? Contagious defines it as the interaction a person has – anytime, anywhere or anyhow – with a company. Given that organizations need to spread themselves across new technologies, media platforms, retail experiences, and social networks, it is more important than ever to nail exactly what promise (or organizing principle) your brand is making, and ensure that this is consistently and elegantly manifested across every single touchpoint, as part of a cumulative, end-to-end customer journey. Keep close to your customers. Observe their behaviours and anticipate the gaps.

Don't fall into the trap of 'tech for tech's sake'. Innovations are adopted faster and used more deeply if the needs and behaviours of real people are prioritized. And utilities will always beat gimmicks. Remember: just because you can, doesn't mean you should.

Whenever a technological breakthrough or new media platform emerges, the ad industry has a tendency to rush towards it. Yes, novelty can attract attention. But attention is a cheap currency if it is not underpinned by meaningful utility or an obvious bridge between the tech and the brand. As well as getting the basics right, marketers need to behave as scientists, cultural curators, and service designers: experimenting with technological change, creating memorable stories and experiences, and

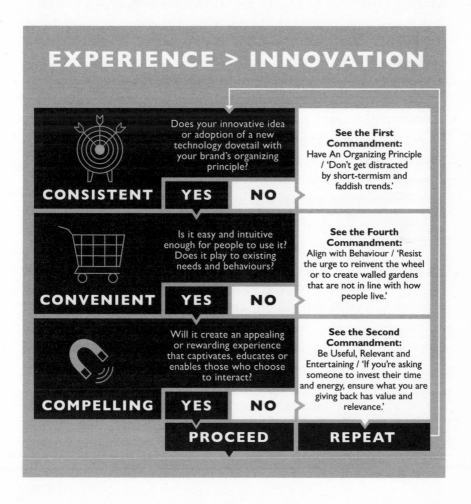

working iteratively on the needs of real people in order to add benefit and remove friction. Being an advertiser is all well and good, but is it better to be seen as the smart friend or helper? Enable, don't distract.

Experience must come first when thinking about innovation. If an innovation doesn't serve the key points of experience – compelling, consistent and convenient – it's probably not worth the effort. Consult the flowchart shown on the previous page to make sure your idea is ticking the boxes.

By focusing on experiences, you'll unlock a dirty secret the advertising industry has always known: stories are better than stuff. It's widely acknowledged that we have reached 'peak possessions'; that people place a greater value on doing stuff than buying stuff; and that extraordinary, intangible experiences have become the prime differentiator in a landscape of commoditized products and services. This environment enables brands to treat customers as co-producers of value, encouraging a two-way dialogue to improve quality and sense-check new technologies. It also places greater emphasis on experiential creativity as a way to connect with consumers. The enduring value of experiences lies not just in the treasure trove of memory, but also in the stories they allow us to tell. Humans are hardwired to talk about experiences and to keep our stories alive.

Some essential questions to start you on your journey:

// Think of your favourite products and services that you use in your personal life. What makes the experience distinctive or useful enough for you to remain loyal? Will your brand pass this 'transference of experience expectation' test? In other words: how does it stack up against the best experiences in any product category, not just your own?

// What kind of heightened experiences can you create that will appeal to people's senses?

// How can you invite people to feel or 'live' your product or service? What kind of memories do you want your brand to be associated with?

WEAPONIZE YOUR AUDIENCE

Y ou know what's cooler than paying for advertising? *Not* paying for advertising. One hundred per cent of marketers – even the bad ones – would rather get something for free than pay for it out of their marketing budget. (We know from experience.)

It's a fact: organic reach, where people share content and campaign ideas of their own volition, is better than paid reach, wherein a brand buys media to ensure wide distribution of its collateral. The two work together, of course. Paid distribution is critical to reaching consumers, and thus critical to creating organic reach. But paid reach is magnified once ideas take hold among real people and they begin sharing content voluntarily. Every customer who advertises on your behalf increases the effectiveness of your marketing by an incremental amount.

Creative effectiveness researchers Les Binet and Peter Field, in their renowned Institute of Practitioners in Advertising publication *The Long and the Short of It*, call this ability of creative campaigns to drive earned media 'fame'. And they cite fame as the best method to drive brand success in the medium term. 'Fame campaigns outperform on all metrics,' they write: sales, market share, price sensitivity, loyalty, penetration, and profit. If you can create work that drives people to share it online and offline, you're on the road to success.

This should come as no surprise to you – marketers have spent more than a decade talking about the power of consumer-driven advertising practices. In early 2007, for example, *Ad Age* named 'The Consumer' its Agency of the Year for the previous year, citing viral videos of people dropping Mentos mints into Diet Coke as driving a 15 per cent sales spike for Mentos. Wrote *Ad Age*: 'The key question that gnaws – or should be gnawing – at just about anybody who wants to sell their product to consumers in the twenty-first century: Should I try to get my consumers to do something like this?'

It's a question that led the marketing industry down dark paths. The chase for virality was on, to the extent that being asked to make a viral video by a client became a punchline in pub conversations. Grace Helbig, creator of YouTube hit channel Daily Grace, herself a successful viral star, made a video in 2013 sending up the question by outlining a fifty-step process for making a viral video: 'Step 1: You can't. Step 2: Don't try it. Step 3: No. Step 4: No. Step 5: Just, you can't . . .' You get the point.

There are, of course, some hints for how to 'go viral'. Speaking with Contagious in 2015, Karen Nelson-Field, senior researcher at the esteemed Ehrenberg-Bass Institute for Marketing Science at the University of South Australia, outlined which ads work best in the earned-media world:

> What you put in your ad makes a difference in terms of how much earned media you'll gain. Anything that's highly emotional, i.e. high arousal, will get shared more. And that's even found to be consistent around emails and memes too. We found that not only do high arousal videos share more, but they cut through. They help you be remembered.

In the same interview, Nelson-Field underlined the need for brands to distribute their content widely in order to find that organic reach:

> Brands look at all these big famous videos – Dove Sketches, Volvo Epic Split – and think: 'Those guys can do it, we can do it.' But the

reality is that those brands have put huge amounts of money behind the distribution of the ad. I've spoken to a lot of those brand owners and they said: 'We were smart, that's why it got big and famous. We paid for a lot of people to see it.'

High-arousal ads with paid media reach tend to spread better than the competition. But of course, virality for virality's sake is a fool's errand. Your well-spread message needs to have some connection to the brand you're trying to promote. As Ezgi Akpinar and Jonah Berger (author of an inconveniently named book, *Contagious*) point out in their 2017 paper 'Valuable Virality': 'Campaigns need to create value for the brands being advertised. Millions of consumers might share an advertisement, but if watching it does not increase sales, then shares will not really benefit the brand.' They talk about 'emotional, brand-integral ads' as the key to widely shared content that makes an impact on the bottom line.

TURNING PEOPLE INTO MEDIA

In the decade since 'The Consumer' earned the honour of Agency of the Year, understanding of contagious content and the role people play in spreading said content has evolved. Smart marketers have moved beyond chasing free virality and instead invest time and money wisely to create campaigns that will spur earned media on top of paid. Rather than waiting to catch lightning in a bottle with a piece of content that sparks wild organic sharing, they are creating assets that are designed to spread. We call this 'weaponizing your audience' – using audience members as a mouthpiece for your brand, the distribution network of your ideas, or the omnipresent reminder of your very existence.

This rarely happens by accident. Instead, brands accomplish weaponization by planning carefully, paying attention to their audience, creating engaging content, investing in distribution, and embedding mechanisms that encourage sharing.

Even surprise 'viral' hits, like the ALS Ice Bucket Challenge have mechanisms baked in to spur their spread. Early on, the Ice Bucket

Challenge achieved wide reach via professional golfers and a PR initiative, sharing the message across their extensive networks. From there, the campaign utilized individuals as mouthpieces, leveraging their personal connections to spread the word. Even the structure of each video (that is, dumping a bucket of ice water on one's head and then nominating three connections to do the same) engineered a level of interest and obligation that spread the phenomenon like wildfire.

In 2014 Contagious worked with brand consultancy Flamingo to carry out qualitative research gauging consumers' perspectives on privacy. One striking observation was the way respondents spoke about concentric circles of trust, with themselves in the centre, close friends and relatives in the next ring, acquaintances and colleagues in the third ring, and strangers and brands in the outer ring. The goal for marketers should be to move a concentric circle or two closer to their prospective buyer by activating other people in that individual's network to persuade the buyer to give greater consideration to a product or (gasp!) even purchase it.

When athletic-apparel brand Under Armour first started, for example, founder Kevin Plank famously sent three shirts to his athletic friends in the National Football League, telling them to wear one and give the other two to the players with neighbouring lockers. Plank realized that the recommendation would mean more coming from a trusted teammate than an unknown brand, so he gave away branded assets to friends and asked them to directly share the shirts with their closest network. He essentially weaponized his friends, turning them into a marketing channel.

Tobias Nordström, head planner at Swedish agency Forsman & Bodenfors, refers to this strategy as 'turning as many people as possible into media'. Forsman & Bodenfors grasped this idea and used it when promoting Volvo Trucks in 2014 with its Live Test Series campaign.

The campaign consists of a series of daredevil videos showing various technological details of Volvo's new line of tractor-trailer trucks. In one, Volvo Trucks president Claes Nilsson stands on the cab of a truck suspended from a crane high above Gothenburg Port, held only by the truck's towing hook to demonstrate its strength. In another, Volvo Trucks technician Roland Svensson is buried up to his neck in sand while a truck drives over him, demonstrating the vehicle's ground clearance. And in the most famous of the Live Test videos (mentioned earlier by Karen Nelson-Field), action star Jean-Claude Van Damme does an 'epic split' between two trucks as they drive down the road with Enya's 'Who Can Say' playing in the background, demonstrating Volvo Trucks' dynamic steering.

The videos racked up more than 100 million views and 8 million shares for Volvo, worth an estimated $171 million in earned-media value for the brand. And according to the agency, visits to the Volvo Trucks website in Europe nearly doubled, from 175,000 to 300,000 per month. Sales in the final quarter of 2013 jumped 23 per cent.

In essence, these ads are like Pixar Films, which appeal on different levels to adults and children simultaneously. Similarly in the Volvo campaign, a portion of the audience is attracted to one aspect of the ads while another portion keys in on different details. Laymen watching the ads are entertained. Truck drivers, on the other hand, are informed. Both are compelled to share the videos with friends – and since the brand paid for distribution to a wide network, that sharing effect snowballed into an impactful viral spread.

As Olle Victorin, managing partner at Forsman & Bodenfors, told Contagious, 'Reaching people outside of the target group and getting them to talk about the brand is an effective way of impacting the primary target.'

Rather than target its niche-buyer demographic of truck fleet owners, Forsman & Bodenfors realized Volvo Trucks could push for widespread sharing among the population at large to eventually impact a smaller audience. Understanding that purchase decisions are influenced by many people in different contexts, they turned people into media, and weaponized them to reach their prospective buyers.

THE POWER OF WORD OF MOUTH

Beyond simply being cheap, this sort of authentic word-of-mouth spread is a powerful lever for brands to pull. In the concentric circles of our relationships, the closer the connection, the more trust there is. According to

Nielsen, 83 per cent of global consumers trust recommendations from friends and family, while 66 per cent trust opinions proactively posted online by strangers. Consultancy BCG maintains that direct word-of-mouth recommendations from friends and family are four to five times more influential than so-called 'indirect recommendations' by print media or TV.

Here's a fascinating fact: according to Deloitte's 2009 Brand Advocacy and Social Media report, brands retain customers referred by other customers at a 37 per cent higher rate. So not only is weaponizing your audience a way to spur advocacy and create new customers, but those customers are more likely to stick around than customers courted through other channels. Word of mouth not only improves acquisition but also reduces churn.

In a 2009 paper published in *Marketing Science*, authors David Godes and Dina Mayzlin talk about 'engineered' or 'firm-created' word of mouth (WOM). 'We can think of firm-created WOM as a hybrid between traditional advertising and consumer word of mouth,' they write. 'The former is firm initiated and firm implemented, whereas the latter is customer initiated and customer implemented. WOM marketing, on the other hand, may be characterized as being firm initiated but customer implemented.'

The paper shows that so-called 'firm-created word of mouth' can drive real sales – that is, word of mouth doesn't have to be completely organic in order to impact a brand's bottom line. 'From a managerial perspective, this result gives credence to the evolving notion that not only is WOM important, but it is actually something that is under the firm's control,' write Godes and Mayzlin. Hopefully, this doesn't come as a big shock to you. Advertising, after all, is just a close cousin of word of mouth; the job of marketers is to get people to talk about, and then buy, their products and services.

ASSEMBLING AN AFFILIATE ARMY

At its most basic form, firm-created word of mouth can be seen in affiliate programmes and refer-a-friend schemes, which reward customers for spreading the word about a company or its offerings.

Take Amazon. Rather than relying entirely on its own marketing, Amazon realized early on that it could mobilize its shoppers to proselytize on behalf of the brand. By signing up as an 'Amazon Associate', customers can earn up to 10 per cent commission (although typically lower) on purchases made directly through links they provide, essentially monetizing their own word of mouth. Posting about a book you read on Facebook? Why not toss an Amazon link in there, in case anyone is inspired to pick it up, netting you a buck or two. Affiliate links became a money-making strategy for everything from personal blogs to respected publications, and Amazon managed to worm its way into conversations that would have otherwise been brandless. In 2008 a job posting from the brand reportedly touted that Amazon had more than 2 million people participating in the programme.

Increasingly, brands are building these sorts of rewards-driven programmes to spur word of mouth among their consumers. Domino's in Australia, for example, launched a campaign called Pizza Mogul, wherein fans could design their own pizzas, promote them to their networks, and earn commission on each pizza sold. The campaign's top participant reportedly earned nearly US$6,000 weekly through the Pizza Mogul programme. Said Allan Collins, CMO of Domino's Australia, 'We now have a whole army of people selling pizzas, engaging with Domino's and spreading the word about the pizza they created . . . It's a fundamental shift in how you market a brand.'

Elsewhere, sites like Dropbox offer more storage space to people who refer friends. Myriad brands utilize loyalty-programme bonuses for referrals and other forms of social advocacy. No matter what form they take, the fact of the matter is that sweetening the pot and giving back to consumers when they spread the word about your brand can pay dividends in both the short and long term.

THE POWER OF A CHILD'S GUILT

In 2015 McCann Melbourne found a power even stronger than the power of word of mouth. Patrick Baron, executive creative director at the agency, told Contagious: 'Guilt from a mother is one of the most powerful forces on earth.'

McCann Melbourne created a campaign called Guilt Trips, based on this inescapable force, for Australian train operator V/Line, which runs services between Melbourne and towns throughout the state of Victoria. The brand wanted to boost leisure travel and increase the number of trips made by people visiting friends and relatives, with a particular focus on young people who had headed for the city and left their parents at home in the country.

Here's how it worked: parents were encouraged to visit a website where they could create, send, and book a so-called 'Guilt Trip' ticket to bring their child home. Then, to increase the pressure on the children to actually use the ticket, instructional guidebooks were issued to help parents hone their guilt-trip messages to encourage them to travel. A series of films on YouTube provided tips on how to persuade a child to come home (one key scene shows a mum practising the line 'Sometimes I get quite lonely'). Meanwhile, traditional multimedia elements such as out-of-home ads featured copy like 'Don't feel bad, we'll just do the family portrait without you.'

'We quickly realized that if we were going to leverage guilt, we would need people to do a lot of the work for us. An advertising message from V/Line could never possess the power to move our target, but a "guilt" message from home is another story,' McCann account director Alec Hussain told Contagious.

'We understand that advertising doesn't work like it used to where clients would have to be on air most of the year to buy people's attention,' adds McCann Melbourne planning director Danish Chan. 'If we're going to create something that actually works, it has to be a PR idea or a brand experience idea, something that people want to participate in. It's that simple. We're finding that across many of our clients, the day has gone where they can pay and spray.'

The campaign was a success. V/Line figures show that off-peak ticket sales increased by 15 per cent and 123,000 tickets were bought as a result of the initiative, generating $4 million in additional revenue. All told, Guilt Trips delivered a return on investment of 1,047 per cent on a budget of $500,000. And no doubt inspired some people to call home.

'Remember mixtapes?' asked Netflix in 2016. Harking back to days of yore when people would record cassette tapes of their favourite songs to give to friends and crushes, the streaming video giant launched Flixtape, a service that updates that exchange for the modern era. Developed with Los Angeles agency Stink Digital, Flixtape enables Netflix subscribers to create a playlist of up to six movies or TV shows that can be shared directly with friends or posted online for the world to see. Creators can name their mixes, create cover art, and craft thematic blends of their favourite Netflix offerings. Love horror films? Share your top six with friends on Halloween. Looking to 'Netflix & chill' with that special someone? Toss some romantic flicks into a Flixtape, name it after them, and hit send. Or, if you're feeling completely devoid of ambition, Netflix provides prefabricated Flixtapes, each centred on a theme like 'Summertime', 'Kiss & Tell' or 'Besties'.

Essentially, Flixtapes enable cultural exchange while positioning Netflix as the purveyor of that culture. The opportunity to publish a playlist on social media or share directly with friends and family plays into people's tendency to use their tastes to signal their identity. And in doing so, Flixtapes encourage people to advertise Netflix's service on behalf of the brand. After all, which are you more likely to respond to: an advertisement about a new film or your best friend sending you their must-watch movies directly? Plus, for non-Netflix subscribers receiving a Flixtape, it's not only a peek at what content they're missing out on, but also a personalized recommendation for content to watch if they choose to sign up.

BEYOND INFLUENCERS

When you think about it, V/Line's Guilt Trips campaign is an influencer campaign taken to the utmost degree. It's one or two key people encouraged to talk to a very targeted audience over whom they have influence about a service in exchange for a reward. Just like in the afore-mentioned affiliate programmes, the referrer has something to gain if the person getting the referral accepts or converts.

More typically, influencer marketing works like this: a brand gives someone real money in exchange for an Instagram photo or a gauche tweet mentioning its product or service. Followers of the influencers, despite understanding that this is a paid relationship in which said influencer is being compensated for pushing a brand, then flock to that product or service. Everyone lives happily ever after. It's really just the centuries-old concept of hiring a spokesperson, dressed in shiny new clothes.

This relationship between brand and messenger recalls an old Dave Chappelle stand-up routine: 'I've done commercials for Coke and Pepsi,' he reveals. 'If you want to know the truth, can't even taste the difference. Surprise! All I know is Pepsi paid me most recently so: tastes better. That's pretty much how the game goes.'

But increasingly, people see through this game. In a paper titled 'Customers or Sellers? The Role of Persuasion Knowledge in Customer Referral', researchers at Erasmus University Rotterdam identify two factors that affect the efficacy of both influencer marketing and affiliate programmes: social connection and ulterior motive. On the plus side, the closer your social connection to the person making a recommendation, the more likely you are to trust the referral. But on the flip side, when you can sense an ulterior motive, you're less likely to trust the referring party. In the words of the authors, 'increased accessibility of ulterior motives decreases the impact of word-of-mouth recommendations, and has a negative impact on the perceived sincerity of the recommending peer'.

For this reason, true audience weaponization is *not* an affiliate programme and it is *not* influencer marketing. In fact, it's nearly the opposite. Weaponization is opt-in and based on authentic affinity. It's an opportunity to increase social connection *without* ulterior motive. Brands create assets, channels, and opportunities and make them available to their audience. Then, it can only be judged a success if real people decide it's worth their while to actively use those assets, channels, and opportunities.

Weaponization requires true belief that a brand (or something it has created) is beneficial in the consumer's life. Call it advocacy. And brand advocacy on the part of a real person inherently involves risk, as they are putting their own reputation on the line by proactively aligning with a given brand – even if it's only for a few seconds. Where influencers create awareness (and perhaps acceptance) of a product, advocates create trust, belief, intent, and, ideally, action.

In the marketing world, we often talk about 'tapping into' and 'targeting' specific audiences and passionate fan bases. In order to weaponize their audience and provoke advocacy, however, brands must often go beyond this pop-in, pop-out mindset to become true allies to people in these subcultures.

Cosmetics retailer Sephora, for example, understood in 2014 that the online beauty community was a burgeoning bastion of potential brand converts, with YouTube tutorials and Instagram accounts racking up millions of views from people hoping to replicate the looks they contained. Rather than simply placing ads against these posts or hiring influencers to replicate their content, though, Sephora went several steps further to nurture, enable, and weaponize members of the community. The brand launched Beauty Boards, a Pinterest-style social platform integrated into its e-commerce site, where members could post images of their looks, advice, reviews, comments, and information about which products they used to create the look. Since then, Sephora has built on the platform's success, creating personalized make-up tutorial apps, emoji keyboards to enable its fans to communicate more effectively, and artificial intelligence tools that help shoppers find the right shade of make-up for their skin tone.

The brand has given its consumers tools to express themselves, rather than simply exploiting their attention, and has nurtured a passionate group of brand advocates in the process.

TURNING PEOPLE INTO MEDIA MAKERS

We'll add another wrinkle to the viral idea of turning people into media. These days, brands should also aspire to turn people into media *makers*, by giving them the resources and assets they need to spread the word. Beyond simply hoping people act in response to good content, brands can put assets and products in the hands of people in new and interesting ways that will catalyse advocacy.

Get your content and platforms right, and you can turn people into media, willing to spontaneously spread your brand's gospel far and wide. Provide them with a platform to participate in your products and services, and you have the chance to embed people directly into the narrative or fabric of your brand. Build a marketing concept based on audience insights, and then hand the responsibility of spreading the product over to the audience.

Hotel chain Marriott did this in 2015 with a programme called #TravelBrilliantly. Anyone staying at one of the chain's seventeen Caribbean and Latin American hotels and resorts was given a GoPro video camera upon checking in for use throughout the duration of their stay. Guests were encouraged to upload their photos and videos on social media, using the hashtags #GoPro, #travelbrilliantly, and #viajegenial ('great trip'), with the best content featured on Marriott's own social feeds as well as the resorts' in-room entertainment system.

By incentivizing its guests to take photos/videos and upload them onto social networks, Marriott encouraged user-generated content. Enabling guests to record the most adrenaline-fuelled, exciting parts of the holiday (scuba diving, surfing, para-sailing etc.) increased the hotels' organic presence on sites like Instagram and Facebook, while lending excitement and diversity to its own feeds – and perhaps sparking a few more bookings with the snorkelling instructors.

The campaign reportedly reached more than 13.5 million people on social media, and resulted in $11 million in earned media for the brand. 'It's low-hanging fruit,' Daniel Kelsay, GoPro's resort and camp marketing manager, told *Outside Magazine*. 'Marriott's guests have always taken videos, and they love to share them, but Marriott could never harness it. It's basically free marketing.'

Similarly, in 2015, beauty brand Benefit Cosmetics seized on the power of weaponizing an audience by partnering with *Elle* magazine in the UK to distribute its Roller Lash mascara before the product was even in stores, along with a simple 'selfie frame' reflective card. Recipients, excited to get their hands on the product, took 7,000 selfies and tweeted

38,000 times about the mascara – and Benefit's premium mascara market share subsequently grew from 25 per cent to 38 per cent in the following two quarters, without any additional advertising.

'If you are thinking about [the customer] as much as possible, you build naturally robust plans to drive word-of-mouth recommendations that take the place of advertising,' Benefit Cosmetics' UK marketing director Hannah Webley-Smith told *Marketing Week*. '[We] add value to their agenda and gain value back in a more genuine, authentic way.'

In the right circumstances, weaponizing your audience can take the place of traditional product demonstrations. And perhaps no sector understands this power better than the automotive. Rather than waiting for a customer to wander into a showroom asking for a test drive, auto makers have begun weaponizing their existing customers to talk to prospective buyers about their cars.

In Sweden in 2015, Audi worked with Stockholm agency Åkestam Holst to develop Svenska Snöräddare – the Swedish Snow Rescuers. The app, created to promote the Audi Quattro, enlisted Quattro owners to assist travellers unable to navigate through snow due to their inferior vehicles. People stuck in adverse weather conditions could simply open the app, log the location of their breakdown, and be connected to a nearby member of Audi's Snow Rescue force via phone or message. Quattro drivers could show up like a heroic Saint Bernard, saving the stranded drivers, reinforcing their purchase decision, and spreading the Audi gospel at the same time.

Nearby, in Norway in 2013, Toyota leveraged its network of drivers in a similar way. Working with Saatchi & Saatchi, Oslo, the brand let its existing customers act as brand ambassadors as part of its Try My Hybrid campaign. Toyota launched a platform whereby hybrid owners could volunteer to let friends and neighbours test drive their cars, with selected Toyota hybrid owners featured in outdoor and print ads as well. Over 1,100 people registered for a test drive, the campaign was covered by local media, and a popular Radio Norge show even broadcast from a hybrid car. Saatchi & Saatchi reported that videos of the test drives were viewed a total of 1.9 million times and one in three Norwegians can 'remember the campaign'.

We've seen the trend of car-makers weaponizing their audience continue to grow. In France in 2017, Honda and agency Sid Lee transformed the garages of ten brand fans into pop-up dealerships, rather than spending millions of dollars building actual dealerships in underserved areas. The campaign reached a million people in three weeks, and more than a thousand of them booked test drives at the pop-up forecourts. Honda plans to expand the concept to Belgium next.

And in 2016 in Germany, Smart baked some audience weaponization into the very leasing model of its Fortwo and Forfour models. Together with BBDO Group, Smart devised Social Leasing, wherein it leased its cars free of charge to people for six months, on the condition that those people let ten friends drive the car every month. The campaign received 455 applications for the five available cars. Just like that old saying: 'Give a man a car, he'll drive for six months. Teach his friends about the car, they may drive it for a lifetime.'

DARK SOCIAL

In recent years, a particular behaviour has emerged that makes weaponizing your audience more necessity than luxury: dark social. Coined by journalist Alexis Madrigal in 2012, the term dark social refers to closed platforms like email and messaging apps such as WhatsApp, WeChat, and Facebook Messenger, where conversations and links can't be easily tracked. As open platforms have become more established and marketers more prolific in using those platforms, people are retreating into the shadows where their conversations can't be interrupted by brands.

Data experts RadiumOne examined people's online habits in 2016 by analysing data from nearly 1 billion unique users. The resulting paper, 'The Dark Side of Social Sharing', found that 84 per cent of content sharing happened via dark social channels, with the majority (62 per cent) of actions, or 'clickbacks', taking place on mobile devices rather than desktops.

These cold, hard statistics show that marketers need to create solutions that are mutually beneficial to their brand and the consumers they choose to target. As 'The Dark Side of Social Sharing' points out, there is an 'investment disconnect in the sharing economy'. In 2016 marketers and their agencies spent over $1 billion per month on mobile advertising with Facebook, 'despite the fact that just 11 per cent of site-originated mobile shares and 21 per cent of mobile clickbacks happened via Facebook worldwide'. In other words, the bulk of sharing is happening outside Facebook, yet a significant chunk of marketing spend goes straight to that social network. That's a pretty big disconnect.

It's common sense that marketers can't ignore a domain where people spend a significant amount of time and share copious amounts of content, especially since the data above suggests that people are increasingly less inclined to broadcast on open social networks. Brands face two challenges: one practical and one philosophical. Deciphering dark social can engage people in a more intimate space, creating opportunity. But in doing so, brands run the risk of invading a private space where people neither expect nor appreciate being dragged into a conversation with a car-maker, cosmetics company or cereal brand.

Good news: weaponizing your audience can bridge this gap.

PEPPERONI.GIF

In 2016 Domino's wanted to find an entry point into conversations among its mobile-first, internet-native audience who spent a ton of time in the shadows of dark social. So they worked with London agency Iris Worldwide to analyse more than a year's worth of Domino's (and competitors') social interactions on Facebook, Twitter, Instagram, blogs and forums, and 60,000 Domino's feedback surveys to unearth the language and emotions used by their target of so-called 'social snackers'.

As part of the brand's So Tasty The Mouth Boggles campaign, Iris then created GIFEELINGS, a collection of GIFs to help consumers express these emotions in their private conversations. 'The outputs allowed us to understand how our customers felt about the taste of Domino's pizza, discover the emotional opportunity in the market, and identify just how and where our audience communicates with their peers,' Iris senior planner David Austin told Contagious.

Added Domino's senior marketing manager, Hayley Tillson: 'We wanted to arm them with content that they could participate with and share with their mates. We provided the right tools to allow our market to do the marketing. Using our fans as the ultimate media channel, and GIFs as the fun, tasty advertising, we broke into internet culture.'

Hosted on GIF search engine Giphy, the collection consisted of sixty-seven GIFs, each lightly branded with a Domino's logo in the corner. Some GIFs were quirky illustrations, like a cartoon head exploding into kittens and pizza slices. Others took snippets from Domino's ads and overlaid animated elements. A group of GIFs even enlisted classic art figures like the 'Mona Lisa' and Vermeer's 'Girl with a Pearl Earring' to endorse the brand. In addition to hosting the GIFs on Giphy, Domino's partnered with GIF keyboard brand Tenor to become the first brand to have GIFs on WhatsApp.

The response to the campaign proves that when pertinent assets are created and released into the world, fans of a brand will respond. One year after the campaign's launch, the GIFs had been viewed more than 145 million times. One GIF, of an animated heart hugging a piece of pizza, routinely showed up in the top five Google results for a search on the term 'GIF' and racked up 33 million views. The agency and brand, using Domino's 2016 Econometric Study and Facebook's average cost per thousand impressions (i.e. the cost to reach 1,000 potential consumers, or CPM), claim the campaign produced a return on investment of 93:1. And although its success can't be traced entirely to pizza GIFs, the brand saw a year-on-year growth of 26.6 per cent in e-commerce sales during the campaign period.

Whether or not those sales can be tied to an animated GIF in a private chat, Domino's undeniably found a way to get customers talking about the brand on their own accord, simply by paying attention to how their audience communicated and giving them a helping hand. Says Iris planner Austin: 'The beauty of dark social is that it's private, it's a space where brands can't disturb or interrupt, they can only be invited in.'

IMITATION AND ITERATION

Domino's isn't the only one playing the GIF game. Console-maker Play-Station teamed up with London youth-marketing agency Livity in 2017 to create its own branded Giphy page. Rather than making their own assets, however, PlayStation weaponized its audience to even create the content. They populated the channel with GIFs created by popular gaming vloggers, and crowdsourced captions among a hand-picked WhatsApp group of young gamers. The GIFs, mostly clips from Play-Station games or snippets that featured the vloggers, were marked with small logos, and Livity worked to ensure the clips had a unifying feel that meant they could be easily identified as belonging to the brand. According to the agency, the PlayStation GIFs were downloaded 245 million times and the campaign generated 777,000 organic engagements on social media.

Indeed, we've seen this sort of thing time and time again. Step one: brands create an asset that enables people to talk about them in a fun way. Step two: people flock to it. Step three: other brands imitate and iterate. Think of Snapchat's filters and lenses, which took the world by storm in 2016. Like the Gatorade lens released on Super Bowl weekend that allowed people to pour a (branded) virtual cooler over their heads, which, according to Kenny Mitchell, senior director of consumer engagement at Gatorade, received more than 165 million views. The branded asset generated a 30.2 per cent lift in ad awareness, and an 8.3 per cent lift in purchase intent, and drove a 4.3 per cent lift in brand favourability. Of consumers who engaged, 88 per cent either liked or loved the lens. Give an audience the right weapon, and they will use it.

Just a few months later, a Taco Bell Snapchat lens that allowed people to turn their heads into a talking taco was used 224 million times in twenty-four hours on Cinco de Mayo – a day that celebrates Mexican culture, predominantly observed in the US. 'We wanted to find a fun way to celebrate Cinco de Mayo, capitalize on the festive mood and give fans something to interact with throughout the day. This was really about giving the Snapchat community a very infectious thing to play with,' Taco Bell's senior manager of social strategy, Ryan Rimsnider, told Contagious. 'The brief was about finding something that's contagious, something that drives playtime and makes people use it not just once, but multiple times. Ultimately, we were hoping this would be something they'd want to share and talk about.'

We've seen brands work their way into dark social worlds with all sorts of different assets, as well. In 2016 cosmetics brand Sephora created a sticker keyboard for messaging apps called Sephojis, allowing users to create custom emojis using its Color IQ service, which uses Pantone colours to match anyone's skin tone perfectly. And, as we mentioned in the fourth commandment, brands like Burberry and KFC have found success with branded sticker packs in messaging app Line.

Indeed, aligning with behaviour and weaponizing your audience are commandment cousins – each represents an understanding of how and why people communicate with each other, while offering an entry point for brands to get involved by invitation instead of invasion. And once brands have armed their army, they have a very powerful force indeed.

Way back in 2011, Contagious wrote about a local Australian campaign from Coca-Cola and ad agency Ogilvy that 'plays on people's narcissism, getting them to go out and find cans with their name on it, and encourage word of mouth and social network sharing'. The campaign launched 150 variations of Coke cans with forenames on them, inviting Australians to 'Share a Coke' with one another.

The rest is marketing history. Share a Coke – with its audience weaponization core – took off like a rocket, succeeding first in

Australia, where the brand saw a 4 per cent increase in volume and a 7 per cent uptick among young consumers. Taking the local campaign global, Coke expanded the personalized packages to more than eighty countries. In the US, the campaign was credited with a 2.5 per cent increase in sales, representing the first period of growth after more than a decade of declining volumes.

When asked about the initial campaign in an interview published by Coca-Cola itself, Coke creative excellence lead Jeremy Rudge talked about the power of handing an idea over to consumers. 'Share a Coke showed that this new landscape was here. There is still a belief in the marketing world that you need to spend big on media to make sure people see your ideas, but Share a Coke proved that you can focus your resources on building ideas people want,' said Rudge. And when asked what he would change if he did it over again: 'We'd probably spend a fraction of what we spent on TV.'

IT TAKES TWO TO TANGO

In the best situations, audience weaponization goes a step further and crosses into co-creation. We've discussed examples where brands like EA's Madden NFL and PlayStation have enlisted their audience in creating what essentially become marketing assets. But, in certain situations, brands are giving their fans tools to impact the very products themselves.

Now, co-creation has taken on buzzword status in the marketing world, overhyped and overused to the point of being unrecognizable. But occasionally, true co-creation does take place. Take, for example, the Adidas football boot called Glitch, a shoe comprised of an inner core and swappable outer skins.

To develop and launch the Glitch, Adidas tapped into one of its so-called Tango Squads – groups of well-connected and influential young football fans living in key cities around the world. Marc Makowski, Adidas

Football's director of business development and leader of the Glitch project, invited London Tango Squad members, and some other football influencers living in the city, to join an Adidas-owned messaging group, interact with prototypes of the shoe, give feedback, and talk about how they saw the new boot. 'It's normal to make sure that you integrate consumer feedback into your product development process, but we took it further,' he told Contagious. 'I think it resonates with this teenage mindset of wanting to be involved in something and be empowered to make decisions, not just be told to do something by someone else.'

The Tango Squad process was a fruitful back-and-forth, with the customers sharing ideas of how they might use the shoe, which triggered design changes, which sparked more thoughts from the young footballers. 'We really went through a process of developing the whole concept with them,' says Makowski.

Inspired by the development process, Adidas also saw an opportunity to launch the Glitch in a new way – by further weaponizing their passionate Tango Squad. So the brand involved this core group of fans in the actual rollout of the product. There was, says Makowski, a 'clear commitment from us that once we opened it up to the public they would be the first ones to go out and be the messengers of Glitch, not us'.

When the shoe launched, Adidas weaponized the initial 250 participants as proselytizers, giving them the new boot, an app, and sharing codes they could pass around to interested parties. Anyone who received a code could buy the shoe and get a few codes of their own to share, radiating outward like ripples from a stone tossed in a pond. Participants were encouraged to share codes in order to earn things like free skins – interchangeable covers for the shoe – by referring people who purchased. Says Makowski:

It's been super interesting to observe the way people's behaviour changes because of the exclusivity. People were looking for codes, people were offering codes; we essentially gave people a reason to connect with each other. You could follow someone looking for a code on Instagram, getting a code and then thanking the guy who gave him the code in an almost posed advertisement of their purchase.

A lot of people talk about this eye-to-eye kind of relationship, and I think we created that by building the concept based on audience insights, and handing the responsibility of spreading the product over to our audience.

Don't forget, this was the global launch of a new football product; a vital sector for Adidas. To devolve the responsibility to 250 people rather than investing in a mass-media campaign aimed at 250 million was a brave move indeed, and indicates the shift in power in favour of the audience. According to Possible and Iris, the agencies that worked on the Glitch initiative, more than 60,000 people downloaded the Glitch app in its first six months and codes seeded by 'first influencers' resulted in a 75 per cent sale conversion rate. In late 2017 Adidas expanded the Glitch rollout to Berlin and Paris.

By involving its audience upstream, in the development of products as well as the marketing of the resulting output, Adidas cultivated a passionate core of engaged consumers, ready and willing to spread the word as soon as they were given licence to do so. The brand weaponized its audience by giving them access and control – a risk, to be sure – and reaped rewards as a result.

BUILDING COMMUNITY

Perhaps no brand understands the powerful synergy of co-creation better than LEGO. Indeed, this sort of thinking is baked into the very core of how LEGO operates: it constantly gives its audience the tools to reimagine what can be done with the brand – toy construction, product development, and even marketing.

This mindset is even voiced by Emmet, the hero of 2014's *The LEGO Movie*, a hit feature film with characters and sets made almost entirely out of the iconic toy blocks. 'Look at all these things that people built. You might see a mess,' says Emmet, voiced by Chris Pratt. 'What I see are people inspired by each other and by you. People taking what you made and making something new out of it.' It's as if LEGO is riffing on its organizing principle via a branded avatar. Fittingly, as that line is voiced in the film, screens behind Emmet show five movies created by LEGO users, submitted via a competition on the brand's social media platform ReBrick.

Peter Espersen, the former head of community co-creation and one of the brains behind ReBrick, estimated in 2014 that there were between 15 and 20 million pieces of LEGO-inspired, user-generated content spread across the web. And although ReBrick, which attempts to tie those fan creations together, was made by LEGO, everything on it is fan-driven – from content moderation to the name itself, chosen in collaboration with the community.

LEGO is audience weaponization taken to the utmost degree, turning over all but the master key to your fans and letting them drive your brand into new spaces. Inundated with thousands of ideas without any way to process them, LEGO has instead given the process to their fans, with a platform called LEGO Ideas. Users can submit designs to the site, which are then voted on by the LEGO community. Ideas that receive 10,000 votes are reviewed by LEGO to see whether they will go into production, and people whose ideas are selected for production are rewarded with 1 per cent of the total net sales of the product.

In some cases, the co-creation goes even further. For the LEGO Exo Suit, a kind of homage to the original LEGO Classic Space theme with a bit of Tony Stark thrown in, LEGO involved the community not only in the design of the product, but also its marketing. Together with LEGO, a crack team of fans hand-picked by Exo Suit creator Peter Reid workshopped the suit's backstory, the artwork for the box and the launch campaign itself, including teaser images, blog posts and videos.

This kind of collaborative effort is a clear win–win. LEGO is exposed to new ideas and talent; users, meanwhile, get to influence new product development and earn money off the back of their creations. When people praised him for LEGO's collaborative smarts, Espersen came back with a response worthy of Emmet himself: 'I would like to say, when people say, "Oh my goodness, you do some great things," no, actually our users do some great things, with the things we provide for them.'

Activating an audience like LEGO's is really high-grade community-building. They found the specific things people congregating around the brand wanted to accomplish and gave them the tools to do those things. In other words, back to weaponization square one: turning people into media. Find people willing to spread your brand's gospel far and wide. Embed them directly into the narrative or fabric of your brand. In the case of LEGO, all their army of builders needed were a few different kinds of bricks and a bit of a challenge.

YOU'RE NOT IN THIS FIGHT ALONE

As we noted in the intro to this book, advertising is riddled with the terminology of warfare. We target our prospective customers with guerrilla campaigns and ad blitzes, carpet-bombing them with tactical messages. We tell tales of the Cola Wars in the 1980s. But rarely do we leverage the foot soldiers in our branded battalions – the people buying the products and services we sell.

As advertising shifts, and consumers gain insight into its inner working as well as control over many of the levers it has historically pulled, brands will need to incorporate people into their processes more than ever. Arming people with tools to communicate – by creating passive-aggressive notes to send along with a train ticket home, by making emojis that match real skin tones, or by building a platform for people to share ideas – inspires word-of-mouth advocacy that makes a long-term impact on customer acquisition, customer satisfaction, and customer retention alike. It allows brands to step back from the microphone and give someone else a chance to speak on their behalf, moving closer to the inner circle of trust. As you'll read in the ninth commandment, cultivating that trust is a whole other story.

WEAPONIZE YOUR AUDIENCE / ESPRESSO VERSION

Getting people to advocate on your behalf is hardly new. Proselytizing on behalf of someone else has been encouraged at least since, well, biblical times. In fact, cavemen probably paid fewer mammoth furs for a spear if they brought a fellow caveman to the spearsmith. You get the idea.

But more than ever before, successful brands are activating

advocacy through marketing, building sharing mechanisms into creative campaigns and creating content designed to empower consumers to spread the word – or at least keep the brand close to top of mind. We call this weaponizing your audience: arming people with tools, platforms, and opportunities to spread the word about a product or service on their own account, rather than relying on traditional paid marketing to carry the message. Instead of focusing on the pursuit of customers and consequently seeing them as an end, brands should focus on the empowerment of customers and see them as a means.

In the most basic sense, this happens through affiliate programmes, wherein customers are paid for their so-called loyalty (insofar as a mercenary can ever be considered loyal). Think of it as influencer marketing where the terms of payment vary depending on how successful the influencing is. These sorts of referral programmes work to an extent, especially in building an audience for a new start-up or product, but fall short of true weaponization.

At a more advanced level, weaponizing is a hub-and-spoke model, with the spokes leading to another hub (whose spokes hopefully lead to yet another hub, and so on and so forth). Each member of the audience becomes their own personal hub, broadcasting to the spokes that comprise their network. Brands transmit to those hubs and (assuming whatever is transmitted is compelling) the audience then pass it along in the form of word-of-mouth (WOM) mentions to their nearest and dearest.

If you're paying attention to how your audience behaves (and we assume you are, since you've already read the second commandment) you probably already know where to start. What types of conversations are your customers having? What sort of content do they react to? The next step is to build on that knowledge by arming your audience with content that's designed to spread. Ask yourself:

// How is my idea amplified by those who come into contact with it?

// Can we turn people into media? Or empower them to make media on our behalf?

// How do we reward people for engaging with our marketing?

// How can we make it easier and more compelling to share?

You'll notice that the brand doesn't stand alone in this model. Weaponization is informed by the actions, values, and interests of a brand's audience, increasing the likelihood that people will want to engage and pay it forward. And similarly, brands can tune in to the hubbub of the resulting distribution, and decipher signals that in turn influence future product design, creative content, new media channels, and more. Brands weaponize their audience and replenish their own arsenal at the same time.

When brands listen well enough on the left, and act with agility to respond to sharing patterns on the right, it creates a cycle of audience feeding into brand feeding into audience. It's a cycle that can look almost indistinguishable from co-creation – and indeed can lead to brands understanding the power of co-creation to form invested brand communities. Once you've mastered messaging that turns people into media and leverages their existing behaviours on behalf of your brand, ask a couple of questions to deepen that relationship over the long term:

// How can we include people in the creation process?

// How can we use our marketing to foster community?

Weaponize your audience and encourage the distribution of your message, and you might find yourself with a willing army of customers ready to go into battle for your ideas.

MAKE TRUST SACRED

'D o you trust me?' asks Aladdin, before whooshing Jasmine away on a magic carpet. 'Do you trust me?' asks Jack before teaching Rose to fly on the prow of the *Titanic*. 'How can you trust a man that wears both a belt and suspenders?' asks Frank in *Once Upon a Time in the West*, before noting, 'The man can't even trust his own pants.'

OK, maybe the last quote is less relevant. But brands play the role of Aladdin and Jack every single day. Whether consciously or not, brands ask consumers to trust them every time they make a purchase. Can I trust that this product or service will work as promised? Can I trust that I'm paying fair value for it? Can I trust that it's created the way the brand says it is? Every purchase, large or small, is the condensation of an internal question we ask ourselves: is this brand trustworthy?

As a result, when brands talk about building trust among prospective customers, they need to start with the same question. Not 'How can we build trust?' but 'Is our brand trustworthy?' Don't look for strategies to trick consumers into believing what you tell them. Instead, honestly interrogate whether you deserve trust, and if the answer is no, skip the rest of this commandment, rectify whatever ails your company, and come back when you feel your actions merit trust.

Trust is sacred. Rachel Botsman has written a book on the subject:

Who Can You Trust? She told Contagious, 'I think some buying decisions are purely about cost/convenience and in these instances money is the currency of transactions. But trust is the currency of interactions. And if a brand wants to transcend to a place where there is meaningful human or lasting connection, they absolutely need trust.'

TWILIGHT OF BRANDS

In a 2014 essay in the *New Yorker* titled 'Twilight of the Brands', business journalist James Surowiecki spelled out a bleak future for brands as we know them. Thanks to the universal availability of consumer reviews, he argued, brand history would cease to matter and a company would become only as good as its latest product. He writes:

> Today, consumers can read reams of research about whatever they want to buy. This started back with Consumer Reports [a product-testing publication that advises buyers], which did object-ive studies of products, and with J. D. Power's quality rankings, which revealed what ordinary customers thought of the cars they'd bought. But what's really weakened the power of brands is the Internet, which has given ordinary consumers easy access to expert reviews, user reviews, and detailed product data, in an array of categories. In the old days, you might buy a Sony televi-sion set because you'd owned one before, or because you trusted the brand. Today, such considerations matter much less than reviews on Amazon and Engadget and CNET.

While much of what Surowiecki says is accurate, we'd argue that his takeaway isn't entirely correct. True trust enables consumers to bypass the information collection stage. As Roderick M. Kramer wrote in his paper 'Trust and Distrust in Organizations', published in the *Annual Review of Psychology* in 1999, 'From a psychological perspective, one way in which trust can function to reduce transaction costs is by operating as a social deci-sion heuristic.' Translated into plain English, trust allows people to make assumptions about a transaction when they buy from a company – this is a fair exchange, I don't need to inspect the product for flaws, if I have an issue it will be addressed. Consequently, the mental load of doing business with that company is much lower than with a competitor.

In fact, we believe that trust is more important than ever before. In 2017 Contagious conducted research with agency J. Walter Thompson and found that 58 per cent of people in the US believe trust has become more important in their decisions over the past three years. What's more, 77 per cent of people say they buy products only from trusted brands.

Of course, people have different propensities for trust. Some people will never truly trust a brand. But our job is to create companies that are *worthy* of trust. And the hope is that the rest will follow.

HOW TRUST IS BUILT

Reading smart opinions about how trust is built is like listening to a musical fugue – variations on a similar theme are repeated, with slight modifications, in different voices. (Forgive us for adding to the cacophony.) Research by David DeSteno and Piercarlo Valdesolo showed that we trust people who mirror our behaviours (synchrony), even to the extent that just seeing someone tapping the same rhythm as the music we're listening to can make us trust them more. Author and marketing consultant Simon Sinek talks about a similar sort of synchrony: we trust people who are from where we're from and believe what we believe.

Philosopher Onora O'Neill, speaking at a TEDXHousesofParliament in 2013, boils trust down to three main components: competence, honesty, and reliability. 'If we find that a person is competent in the relevant matters, and reliable and honest, we'll have a pretty good reason to trust them,' she says. Miss one, though, and you lose that trustworthiness. 'I have friends who are competent and honest, but I would not trust them to post a letter, because they're forgetful,' continues O'Neill. 'I have friends who are very confident they can do certain things, but I realize that they overestimate their own competence.'

In another TEDX talk Jim Davis, professor of strategic management at Utah State University, riffs on the same components when talking about what motivates people to take a risk by placing trust in someone else. In place of O'Neill's 'competence' he uses 'ability'. Reliability and honesty combine to form 'integrity'. And he adds an additional wrinkle: benevolence. 'If all I have is ability, without benevolence, I'm an assassin,' says Davis.

For brands, we believe trust is made up of all of these things and more. In helping our clients think about this new era of trust and how brands can play an active role in building that bridge with customers, Contagious breaks the concept into five components that we feel are integral to building trust:

II Expertise / *How good are you at doing what you say you do?*
II Reliability / *How consistently can you do what you do?*
II Organizing Principle / *Why do you do what you do?*
II Transparency / *How do you do what you do?*
II Honesty / *How do you talk about what you do?*

For the most part, Expertise and Reliability are table stakes for any successful brand. What's more, they probably are held outside the marketing discipline. No matter how good your branding, marketing, advertising or communications are, if the product sucks (or even just *sometimes* sucks) it probably won't succeed. In fact, as Mad Man Jerry Della Femina wrote in his book *From Those Wonderful Folks Who Gave You Pearl Harbor*: 'There is a great deal of advertising that is much better than the product. When that happens, all that will do is put you out of business faster.'

Organizing Principle, Transparency, and Honesty, on the other hand, are firmly within the job descriptions of marketers. We talked about organizing principle at length in the first commandment, so we'll focus on transparency and honesty here. If you have nothing to hide, you should be able to knock both out of the park.

The stakes for building and maintaining trust have risen in recent years for a key reason we haven't yet addressed: data. Marketers have more access to personal information about their customers than ever before. In some ways, that enables companies to serve people better. But simultaneously it opens up the possibility of privacy violations and abused trust that is nearly impossible to repair.

The last few years have seen a series of high-profile privacy breaches, whether Yahoo account info or Ashley Madison profiles (one headline: 'Site for People Who Can't be Trusted Can't be Trusted'). A few hours, or even minutes, of a black-hat hacker's attention and all of a sudden personal information, financial details and whatever data has been stored by a site are available on the dark web to the highest bidder. Data breaches have made even the least tech-savvy very sensitive about what data they are generating and where it is going.

According to Contagious's research, 81 per cent of people in the UK have considered no longer using a product or service owing to concerns about how it was using their personal data, and 54 per cent of people aged eighteen to thirty-four have already switched. And this was before the Cambridge Analytica–Facebook scandal. (Of course, we also tend toward being mercenaries when it comes to data. A 2013 study by retail software provider Swirl found that 47 per cent of women would share their location with a retailer in exchange for a $5 credit; 83 per cent would do so for $25. Shoppers and their data are soon parted?)

Never forget: data is a manifestation of the lives of living, breathing people. Pledge not to violate their trust. With great data comes great responsibility.

DIRECT TO CONSUMERS

If anything, the social media and information availability Surowiecki wrote about in the *New Yorker* was a wake-up call for brands that had been skating by without trustworthy products. Now, there's nowhere to hide. If consumers are going to go directly to other people's reviews, why not make it easier for them to do so?

This was a central pillar of the legendary Domino's Pizza Turnaround campaign described in the third commandment. Beyond simply admitting their pizza sucked and improving the recipe, Domino's put its faith in the new formula on the biggest stage. For four weeks in 2011, the brand broadcast online reviews and customer comments on a 4,630-square-foot billboard in Times Square – positive, negative, or neutral. A static camera captured images of each review as it ran, which were sent to the original commenters to prove that the brand really lived up to its promise.

Since that high-visibility stunt, we've seen other brands cut out the middleman in creative ways. For example, in 2015 Inspired by Iceland, a partnership between the Icelandic government, the City of Reykjavik, the Icelandic Travel Industry Association, Icelandair and several other Icelandic tourism companies, invited people to avoid Google and instead use a 'human search engine'. Noting that 98 per cent of the world's people named Guðmundur or Guðmunda live in Iceland, the campaign recruited would-be visitors to ask questions to seven of the people bearing the name. People could ask queries using Twitter, Facebook and YouTube and the hashtag #AskGudmundur, and the volunteers would answer based on their own knowledge and experiences in Iceland. Brooklyn Brothers, the agency that worked on the campaign, reports that Ask Guðmundur generated £3.5 million in earned media, and 298 million social and PR impressions. The campaign film was viewed 1.8 million times and the campaign reportedly generated an ROI of 1,500 per cent.

Another Nordic nation made waves by going direct to its audience a year later. In 2016, to celebrate the 250th anniversary of the country abolishing censorship, Sweden got its very own phone number. The Swedish Number campaign, created by the Swedish Tourist Association, Stockholm-based agency INGO, Grey PR in New York, and Cohn & Wolfe PR in Stockholm, enabled anyone in the world to call a single phone number that would then connect them at random with a Swede who had opted into the initiative.

At its core, the campaign was about the brand relinquishing control of the message and cutting out the middleman to build faith in the message. 'We decided we didn't want to control it,' Björn Ståhl, executive creative director at INGO, told Contagious.

Of course, we knew from the beginning that there would be a few people who wouldn't praise Sweden. But people should be allowed to express their views. Imagine if a Swede goes on holiday and starts talking negatively about Sweden to someone – we can't control that. It's the same thing.

We kind of made the digital interaction analogue again. You know, people can talk badly about places, things and others on social media and they can hide behind screens. But we facilitated a personal, real interaction between people.

In three months, the Swedish Number registered more than 170,000 calls from 186 countries, generating more than 9 billion impressions and $146 million of media value with zero media spend. Sweden's prime minister, Stefan Löfven, even signed up to answer some calls. 'Wait, how do I know you're really the Swedish Prime Minister?' asked one incredulous caller. 'Well I believe you have to trust me,' he replied.

Still other brands are working to put potential customers directly in touch with the people who might otherwise write online reviews. In 2017 Subaru worked with Minneapolis-based agency Carmichael Lynch to create the Meet an Owner hub, where potential buyers can ask ambassadors any questions related to the brand and its cars. 'I think, recently businesses have come to realize that if you're not honest about your products and services people will call you out,' Subaru's digital and social marketing manager, Jack Kelly, told Contagious. 'Everyone has an opinion and they're able to influence a lot of people to think positively or negatively about the things you're doing based on their experience with your brand.' By becoming the conduit for information from third parties, brands show they're not afraid of their reputation, bolstering trust among prospective customers. As Mandy Yoh of consumer review management firm ReviewTrackers told the *New York Post*, 'Online reviews are the second most-trusted source when someone is buying a product or trying a restaurant, and that's only second to family or friends.'

#NOFILTER

In other cases, brands have attempted to eliminate third parties entirely, going directly to the final consumer without any mediator. In 2016 cruise line Royal Caribbean leveraged live-streaming platform Periscope to beam advertising directly from its ships back to out-of-home ad spaces in New York City. Part of a larger 'Come Seek' campaign created by Boston-based agency MullenLowe, the #ComeSeekLive initiative edited forty-minute films created by influencers into twenty-minute clips and rebroadcast them just ten minutes later.

'The question was, "How do we go about showing something real?",' MullenLowe's lead strategist, Kay Pancheri, told us. 'Especially when we think about how people are consuming media and the increasing distrust of advertising and brands. It was about bringing a level of transparency and trust to a category that is often riddled with perfect images. Periscope seemed like the right thing to do because you can't really hide behind anything.'

According to the agency, the campaign racked up 362,000 engagements on Periscope, including a 4,000 per cent increase in 'heart' counts (the social media measure on Periscope – equivalent to a Facebook like). The campaign generated 7.4 million earned impressions on Twitter and 91.8 million press impressions for the brand.

This sort of unvarnished presentation is often called authenticity. And if you've heard anything about the dreaded millennials, it's that they value authenticity. We'd argue it's why brands have flocked to platforms like Snapchat and Facebook Live, where it's harder to hide your warts. As Taco Bell's senior manager of social strategy, Ryan Rimsnider, told Contagious in 2016: 'Snapchat is a platform where you have to be your true self. It's not heavily curated, it doesn't need to be polished.' Winston Binch, then the chief digital officer at Deutsch, who worked with Taco Bell, noted that the south-of-the-border brand saw a five-times increase in conversion when using 'real' unretouched photographs versus professional photographs in social posts.

In 2017 Volvo came up with a clever campaign based on this authenticity by streaming live footage of test drives directly to billboards in São Paulo. Cameras were installed in new Volvo XC60s to film test drivers' reactions, while quotes were pulled out in real time and splayed onto the videos (alongside a giant image of the car). Over the course of two days, twenty-three test drives were conducted and broadcast to 1,000 billboards in the city. The agency, Grey Brazil, estimates the short campaign generated 40 million media impressions.

We'd bet it generated some word of mouth, as well. Facebook, for its part, says that people comment ten times more on live videos than on pre-produced videos. In a world full of CGI and post-production, there seems to be a growing hunger for content straight from the source. When they see the sausage being made, people are more likely to trust both the sausage and the sausage-maker.

In early 2018 vodka-maker Absolut took the idea of the naked truth to its ridiculous extreme. Created by BBH London, a three-minute video called The Vodka with Nothing to Hide features employees at Absolut's distillery in Åhus, Sweden, wearing nothing but a smile.

Pitched as an induction video for new employees, the film features an Absolut employee named Gunnar walking, while wearing nothing at all, through the process of making Absolut vodka: growing wheat, adding water, distilling, packaging, and even dealing with spent grains – all while encountering other naked workers.

'Every single drop that goes into every single bottle of Absolut vodka anywhere in the world comes from here in Åhus,' says Gunnar, as twenty-seven other actual Absolut employees (including the CEO!) play music behind him, buck naked. 'And that's why we're the vodka with nothing to hide.'

TRUST THROUGH TRANSPARENCY

At 2017's Natural Products Expo West conference in Colorado, Campbell's Soup CEO Denise Morrison noted: 'Transparency is the single most important ingredient for earning consumer trust.' We'll pardon the ingredient pun, because she makes a great point. There is likely no better shortcut to trust than transparency. A study by Label Insight called 'Driving Long-term Trust and Loyalty Through Transparency' supports this statement; the firm's research found that 39 per cent of people would switch to a new brand and 73 per cent would pay more for a product if it offered complete transparency.

Recently, a spate of start-ups have used this movement to their advantage, leveraging to disrupt more established competitors. In the clothing space, Belgian start-up Honest By claims to be the first company to offer a full cost breakdown of its fashion products. Since 2012 the brand has provided consumers with a raw checklist of each item's cost, including materials, packaging, labour, storage, and shipping – down to the €0.03 it costs for the safety pin used to attach the price tag! 'Honest By offers products with complete transparency in price and manufacturing, creating a new paradigm in fashion and retail,' the brand states on its website.

Similarly, e-commerce clothier Everlane touts its 'Radical Transparency', displaying the cost of materials, hardware, labour, taxes, transport, and even what the mark-up is for every item for sale on their site. The brand even goes so far as to offer a 'Choose What You Pay' option on some sale items, where customers can choose between three prices – 10 per cent margins for Everlane (enough to cover development and shipping), 20 per cent margins (enough to cover development, shipping, and salary overhead), and 30 per cent margins (enough to cover all of the above plus R&D).

Similarly exposing overheads is American e-commerce retailer Brandless, which purports to save customers from the costs that come along with buying established brands, which it calls 'BrandTax':

> BrandTax is the hidden costs you pay for a national brand. We've been trained to believe these costs increase quality, but they rarely do. We estimate the average person pays at least 40 per cent more for products of comparable quality as ours. And sometimes up to 370 per cent more for beauty products like face cream. We're here to eliminate Brand-Tax™ once and for all. Our team has benchmarked pricing across five major retailers (in-store and online). With that information, we've calculated the average BrandTax™ for each item across our entire everyday essentials selection.

Brandless publishes this information on its shop pages, showing customers how much they're saving in real time by avoiding costly mark-ups.

Direct-to-consumer make-up brand Beauty Pie is using a similar model for cosmetics. Members of the service pay a monthly fee to get access to products at factory prices. Then, each lipstick, foundation, or blusher is broken down into its constituent elements and accounted for – packaging, testing, warehousing, VAT, and more. *Allure* went so far as to dub the brand a 'Netflix-level disruptor'.

And in California, start-up Alit Wines is similarly bringing transparency to the mystery-shrouded world of the vintner. Customers receive a precise breakdown of costs per bottle, including how much money goes to grape pickers, how much barrels cost, and how much gross margin the company bakes into the final sale price.

The list of start-ups using transparent pricing to disrupt industries goes on. As Rachel Saunders from the Cassandra Report told us: 'Young people are gravitating towards brands that can save them time by being transparent upfront. Transparency feels more genuine and less likely to be a sales tactic, and is thus a more relevant way to earn their trust.'

Perhaps our favourite example of this is Lemonade, a renters- and home-insurance company based in New York City that employs behavioural economist Dan Ariely as its 'chief behavioural officer'. 'If you tried to create a system that would bring out the worst in people, you would end up with something that looks a lot like the current insurance industry,' Ariely told Contagious in 2017. Customers distrust insurers, so they inflate claims about belongings that have been lost or stolen. Consequently, insurers distrust customers, and investigate claims in search of fraud. It's a vicious cycle of distrust. In fact, the FBI estimates that the anticipation of fraud costs the average US family $400 to $700 in additional insurance premiums.

'There's a lack of transparency that makes the relationship between company and customers really frustrating. That's why we're showing everyone exactly who we are and how we operate,' says Yael Wissner-Levy, Lemonade's director of strategic communications. So how do they operate? Rather than taking profits as a percentage of leftover premiums, Lemonade takes a 20 per cent cut up front. It then pays out claims from the remaining 80 per cent. At the end of the year, any leftover cash is donated to charities of customers' choosing – from multinational NGOs down to local libraries.

Lemonade uses machine-learning algorithms to evaluate and

adjudicate claims, allowing it to settle super quickly (in one case, a customer's $729 claim for a stolen down jacket was approved and paid in just three seconds). And to top it off, the brand claims to have premiums 82 per cent lower than legacy insurers.

In its first year of business, Lemonade gave back 10.2 per cent of its revenue – a number that's easily viewable on its website. 'If year one is anything to go by,' the brand writes on its website, 'we expect that amount to dramatically grow.' It's a Public Benefit Corporation and a Certified B-Corp. And, we'd imagine, a walking nightmare for wildly distrusted business-as-usual insurers.

TRUST THE PROCESS

So that's one way to prove your trustworthiness: open up your accounts and show them to the world. But what if your prices are higher than the competition? Or you're in a sector so commodified that price doesn't play a role? Another way we've seen brands use transparency to bolster confidence is by pulling back the curtain on process. How do we make what we make? And how do we get it to you?

In 2010 McDonald's made waves not by showing how the sausage is made, but showing how the nuggets are made. The Our Food Your Questions campaign in Canada invited customers to ask any questions about McDonald's processes, including some difficult ones for the brand to answer. 'Does your Egg McMuffin use real eggs?' customers asked. Also: 'Why do you microwave so much of your food?', 'Why does your food look different in your advertising than in the store?' And even the dreaded: 'Do you use so-called "pink slime" or "pink goop" in your Chicken McNuggets?'

It was a valuable exercise for McDonald's, forcing the brand to be more transparent and accountable. In the first two years, McDonald's responded to 23,000 questions and registered more than 2 million visits to the campaign site. Videos made in response to some of the most interesting questions, like a behind-the-scenes tour of a burger photo shoot, attracted more than 15 million views. The campaign was such a success that it still runs today and has been adapted for other markets, including the US.

Of course, McDonald's wasn't completely open about all of its processes, and couldn't necessarily answer every question it received in a way that would pacify environmentally conscious eaters. As *Time* writer Naomi Starkman noted in 2014, 'while it's angling for the farm-to-table crowd, as the world's largest buyer of beef and pork with hamburgers for as low as one dollar, McDonald's current practices will probably still be considered factory-farm-to-table'. But even a somewhat obfuscated peek into McDonald's processes was enough to instil some trust in the brand. A study by Canadian market research firm Environics Research found the campaign improved perception of food quality by an average of 61 per cent, and increased positive responses in its 'company I trust' metric by 46 per cent – the biggest-ever increase recorded by the McDonald's brand.

Another food brand using process transparency to build trust and increase customer satisfaction is tech-forward turnarounder Domino's. (Yes, them again. Hard to ignore a brand that has so closely tied product, marketing, and innovation while skyrocketing up the stock market charts.) Since 2009, customers who order Domino's online have been able to use its Pizza Tracker to receive updates as their pie is made, baked, sent out for delivery, all the way up until it's in their hot little hands. It was a feature born out of happenstance; the brand already had a system called Pulse that tracked orders internally, which it used to monitor efficiency and quality of service among its franchised stores around the world. Boulder-based agency Crispin Porter + Bogusky simply worked with Domino's IT group to create a user-facing interface that turned the tool into a trust-building exercise in process transparency.

A slightly more upscale brand, Audi, took a page out of Domino's book in 2012, with the myAudi Tracker, a real-time tool to help keep Canadian customers informed about a newly purchased, customized vehicle as it journeyed from design in Germany to its eventual home driveway. The tracker featured behind-the-scenes video, images and information specific to their particular vehicle's manufacturing process as it was assembled, painted, and shipped across the Atlantic. Just like the Pizza Tracker, the campaign leveraged existing tracking technology that already monitored vehicle progress and status, bringing customers into the process through content built on top of that technology. Emails containing the updates generated 64 per cent open rates and

58 per cent clickthroughs, with an astounding 90 per cent of customers clicking through to hear a recording of their new car's engine revving for the first time after manufacturing was complete.

KNOCK IT OFF

It's one thing to show your process to your customers. It's another thing entirely to give an intimate look at your production processes to scammers trying to profit from counterfeiting your brand. But that's exactly what luxury leather goods company Saddleback Leather did in 2014 with its How to Knock Off a Bag video. The twelve-minute film features Dave Munson, the company's president, detailing precisely how to rip off one of its most popular products, the Saddleback Leather Briefcase. With a sarcastic lilt, Munson makes cracks at counterfeiters' poor quality materials, questionable labour practices and economical shortcuts, all while providing a thorough look at the painstaking process and high-grade materials that go into making Saddleback's best-selling product.

'You were probably wondering, when you were cutting all the seams apart and reverse engineering everything,' Munson says at one point, addressing his hypothetical counterfeiter audience, 'why did he do these things? Tell you what: I'm going to walk you through this bag and the construction so you can make it just the way we do it exactly. And you'll understand a lot of the things and the areas that you can cut some corners on and save some money on.'

The video has received nearly 600,000 views on YouTube – not too shabby for a twelve-minute film from a niche luxury brand selling a $700 bag. Saddleback reported 1,170 new customers in the weeks after the video launched.

'What this video is about is: we make really high-quality bags. That's it. That's our number one thing,' Munson told Contagious. The video wasn't just compelling branded content, it served as a product demo. Not only does the film justify the high price of a Saddleback original, but explains exactly how and why the product is superior to cheaper alternatives, appealing to consumers who want to invest in something that is built to last. By showing its process, Saddleback establishes its trustworthiness with consumers, confirming that paying less for a counterfeit version will bite them in the long run.

STRAIGHT FROM THE SOURCE

Imagine pulling into a supermarket parking lot and seeing someone selling boxes of cereal out of the back of their car. The boxes look exactly like the ones inside the supermarket, they're priced a little bit lower, and – wouldn't you know it – cereal is on your shopping list. Are you going to buy them from the bloke in the car?

No, of course you're not. Because of a third P-word, beyond Price and Process, that contributes to trust building: Provenance. You don't know where that fella got those boxes, so you probably don't trust the transaction. Particularly when it comes to food, where something comes from matters more than ever before. Research by Opinion Matters in the UK on behalf of the Co-Op grocery chain found that 84 per cent of people believe that, behind sell-by dates, origin is the most important information in their food-buying decisions. Once you know it's not going bad, the next question is where it came from. Earlier research from the European Consumer Organization had similar findings. When asked *why* origin matters, respondents frequently cited provenance as helping to assess the quality, safety, environmental impact, and ethics of a given item.

The rise in provenance's importance can probably be chalked up to three developments: the complication of global supply chains, increased consumer access to information, and misbehaviour by brands in the past. We've moved away from systems where we know the person who grew our food or made our clothes. Meanwhile, consumer expectations around information continue to rise. And with brands like Ikea and Tesco getting caught with horsemeat in their burgers and meatballs, it's no wonder customers are anxious to verify the stories behind their purchase's provenance.

One recent effort we love comes from French supermarket co-operative Système U. Setting out to prove the freshness of its fish, U stores worked with TBWA\Paris to create a campaign called La Route du Frais (Fresh Stories), utilizing Snap Spectacles and Snapchat stories to prove provenance. The brand gave a pair of Snap Specs – which have a built-in camera directly connected to a Snapchat account – to a fisherman, a buyer, and a fishmonger so that they could record themselves catching, buying, and preparing fish for sale. When the fish made it to stores, scannable Snapcodes were placed next to each fresh catch so shoppers could watch the videos of how their fish got from sea to store. And because Snapchat stories last for only twenty-four hours, the labels were proof that the fish were indeed fresh – caught within the past day.

The U campaign is reminiscent of another 2017 effort from Kettle Chips in the US. Each bag was imprinted with a 'Tater Tracker' code that linked consumers directly to a biography of the farmer at whatever farm the potatoes in that bag were sourced from, including information about how the farm is run and how long it has been a supplier for Kettle. For some farms, the webpage even includes a 360° video and a tour of the farm in question.

Both campaigns remind us of an earlier effort to similarly show off provenance, from Unilever-owned condiment brand Hellmann's in 2014. Working with São Paulo agencies The Kumite, Doubleleft, and FLAG/CUBOCC, Hellmann's launched the Grow With Us website, where customers could stream live videos from cameras placed in farmers' hats, as they cultivated crops that would end up in ketchup and other sauces. To get potential consumers even more involved, Hellmann's partnered with Spotify to enable the audience to crowdsource a playlist that was blasted out to the fields – a reference to the idea that plants respond to soundwaves – and the tomatoes grown while listening to those tunes were made into a limited-edition range of ketchup.

The agencies report that more than 30 million people were impacted by the initiative, resulting in a whopping 78 per cent increase in brand consideration post-campaign. Hellmann's reports that a follow-up survey revealed a 24 per cent boost in customer perception about Hellmann's use of sustainable tomatoes.

In 2012 New Zealand cider brand Monteith's put some proof of provenance into its bottles as a PR push. 'When quality control fails, it gets all over the news. Everyone starts talking about it,' said the brand in a case-study video. 'Which made us think, what a great idea.' The stunt was simple: when boxes of cider bottles were rolling off the production line, Monteith's warehouse employees slipped small apple tree twigs into the packages.

When customers commented on the twigs and media took notice, the brand followed up with an apology campaign. 'Sorry About the Twigs' proclaimed billboards, while newspaper ads contained more formal apologies, followed by a way to avoid twigging out in the future: 'If you really did take offence, perhaps you could try one of the many other cider brands on the market made from concentrate. You won't find any twigs in their packaging. Or any fresh apples and pears in their cider for that matter either.'

The agency, Colenso BBDO, reports that sales increased 32 per cent after the campaign, selling the brand out of cider.

SUPPLY CHAIN ON THE BLOCKCHAIN

Start-ups are emerging to help brands tell an honest story about where their product comes from. One such company, London-based Provenance, has worked with retailers in food and fashion to use technologies like blockchain and scannable labels to give consumers more information about the purchases they're making.

'I think it is going to be a key ingredient of empowering a future where businesses will no longer gain a competitive advantage from information asymmetry. But in fact it's businesses that use transparency and share information about what they're really doing behind closed doors that will rise,' Provenance founder Jessi Baker told *Unlimited*, a brand publication created by UBS and Vice. 'We're banking on a future where transparency is your best marketing tool.'

A quick primer on blockchain, the de rigueur technological development positioned by some as a game-changer on a par with the internet (although we won't claim to be anything but armchair amateurs).

As Robert Hackett described in *Fortune* in 2016, blockchain is a coding breakthrough, most famous as the backbone of cryptocurrencies like Bitcoin, that 'allows competitors to share a digital ledger across a network of computers without need for a central authority. No single party has the power to tamper with the records: the math keeps everyone honest.' Think of it as a decentralized and immutable ledger of transactions – ideal for using transparency to build trust.

As provenance becomes a differentiating factor – and a trust-building opportunity – brands are seizing on the uneditable nature of the blockchain to prove their products' legitimacy. San Francisco start-up Ripe.io, for example, is applying blockchain technology to food and agriculture supply chains. In 2017 the company started working with US salad chain Sweetgreen, which prides itself on being transparent about its use of sustainable and local ingredients.

Ripe.io monitors the ripeness, colour, and sugar content of fruits and vegetables while they're growing, assigning each crop a 'quality factor', down to the individual piece. Once harvested, the company uses sensors to track conditions along the supply chain until the fruits and veggies reach their final destination. The data allows everyone involved in the process – farmers, shippers, restaurateurs, and customers – to see the quality of the produce, as well as how it fares on the journey from farm to fork.

'The promise of blockchain is that it can collect all this information about the supply chain and give a degree of validation of claims around sustainability and/or organic and/or fairtrade,' Ripe.io's founder, Phil Harris, told Contagious. 'There's a lot of rich data in supply chains, but it doesn't always get shared and it doesn't always get validated and certified, and the promise of this technology is that it can do it relatively cheaply and at scale.'

In another sector, legacy photography brand Kodak is leveraging the blockchain to trace the provenance of not food but photographs. In January 2018 the brand announced a partnership with WENN Digital to launch KodakOne, a database that records photographers' image rights and helps them secure payment when their work is used. Photographers who register their work on KodakOne can then license their work to buyers within the platform, with all transactions executed by smart contracts on the blockchain, making payment instant and secure. Plus, Kodak pledges to track the use of registered images across the internet, protecting photographers' intellectual property rights and chasing payment when necessary.

Of course, blockchain is not a panacea. Already the technology has been exploited by scammers trying to make a profit on phony cryptocurrencies and pump-and-dump schemes. Gartner, which tracks buzz vs reality for emerging technologies on its famous 'Hype Cycle', says the technology is somewhere between the 'peak of inflated expectations' and the 'trough of disillusionment'. In one humorous demonstration of the blockchain hype, beverage brand Long Island Iced Tea Corp. changed its name to Long Blockchain Corp. in December 2017 and saw its stock jump 182 per cent on the NASDAQ the following day. But the potential for the technology to bring true transparency to the supply chain, and consequently to product provenance, could be instrumental for brands hoping to build trust with consumers in the future.

GET TRUST QUICK

In his book *The Speed of Trust*, Stephen M. R. Covey writes, 'When trust is low, speed goes down and cost goes up. On the other hand, when trust is high, speed goes up and cost goes down.' Trust between two parties allows them to skip time-sucking processes like research and quality assurance, making interactions (and purchase decisions) faster and less resource intensive.

Unfortunately, speed factors into another dimension of trust: it often takes time to build. It requires consistency, communication, reliability, and transparency. While there are indicators that help build trust more quickly, true trustworthiness usually doesn't come overnight.

There is, however, one hack that psychology professor and influence expert Robert Cialdini shares. 'It turns out to be possible to acquire instant trustworthiness by employing a clever strategy,' he writes in his book *Pre-Suasion*. 'A communicator who references a weakness early on is immediately seen as more honest.'

Admitting weakness can be a shortcut to trust and authenticity. It's a tactic that has been used in some of the most iconic advertising campaigns of all time. In 1962 Avis proclaimed 'When you're only No. 2, you try harder.

Or else.' and had its first profitable year in a decade. A funny Marmite ad acknowledged the yeast spread's divisiveness in a campaign to 'end Marmite neglect' in 2013, rescuing jars from the dusty cabinets of people who hate it. Guinness acknowledges the annoyance of waiting for its double-poured stout in a pub with its 'Good things come to those who wait' tagline.

This tactic has been proven time and time again outside of advertising. In a famous 1966 study titled 'The Effect of a Pratfall on Increasing Interpersonal Attractiveness', psychologist Elliot Aronson and his Harvard colleagues showed two videos to students. In both, a man took a quiz and got 92 per cent of the answers correct. In one version, though, the man spills a cup of coffee on himself after acing the test. The study showed that students believed the man to be more likeable if they saw the version in which he spilled the coffee. A small pratfall, it seems, can humanize a person.

The same goes for brands. A phenomenon called the service recovery paradox finds that customer satisfaction with a brand after said brand has fixed a problem with their product or customer service is often higher than it was *before the problem occurred*. The ability to address an issue engenders more trust than not having an issue in the first place.

Similarly, we are sceptical of perfect performance. In a study titled 'From Reviews To Revenue', researchers at Northwestern University's Spiegel Research Center analysed 111,460 product reviews and linked ratings to probability of purchasing. Likelihood to purchase did not peak with perfect scores but at 4.2 – 4.5 out of 5. The researchers believed that perfect ratings had less impact because they were seen as too good to be true. 'As counterintuitive as it may seem, negative reviews have a positive impact because they help establish trust and authenticity,' they wrote.

This type of shortcut may work in the short term, but it must still be followed up with the other core ideas that lead to trust – reliability, expertise, honesty, transparency, and organizing principle.

TRUST INSPIRES LOYALTY

People, generally, trust auto pilot. We sit in metal birds that somehow lift into the sky, confident that we'll get to our destination safely even if a human pilot rarely touches the controls (auto pilot is behind the wheel some 90 per cent of commercial flying time). Why? The computer has shown it can fly safely, every time. Over many years auto-pilot technology has proven both its reliability and expertise, without a doubt. The ability to perform well repeatedly is the critical first step to establishing trust.

In established sectors, quality can become commodified. Sure, there are slight variations in reliability and expertise – and personal taste or experiences that might influence your perception of one or the other – but generally if you're not making a product with a quality and consistency befitting its price, you won't make it too far in the marketplace.

Beyond this commodified level, however, we have brand preferences. Which are often influenced by facets of trust. We trust companies with generous exchange policies, because it's a signal that they believe in the quality of the product they produce – they are honest about what they are selling and fair in their interactions (think John Lewis's 'Never Knowingly Undersold' slogan, or price-match guarantees offered by other retailers). We trust brands that recover from customer service snafus with speed and generosity, because it's a signal that if something else goes wrong in the future it will be addressed quickly and appropriately – they organize around customer service and respond fairly. We trust products that openly show where they're from and how they're made, because it's a signal that the company has nothing to hide – they are transparent about their prices, processes, or provenance.

All of these types of trust allow us to make decisions faster, to avoid choice paralysis, and to feel confident about our selections. This confidence leads to loyalty. As Byron Sharp notes in *How Brands Grow*, 'Buyers restrict their purchases to a personal repertoire of brands . . . Buyers keep returning to their favourites.' Sharp notes that this loyalty is a direct result of risk avoidance. 'Rather than thinking of loyalty as a market imperfection, it is more appropriately considered to be a sensible buyer strategy, one of many developed by human beings in order to balance risk and avoid wasting the precious commodity of time.'

Through transparency, honesty, and a customer-first organizing principle, backed by a reliable and expertly produced product or service, brands don't just build trust, they *become trustworthy*. And those trustworthy brands have a head start on their competition.

MAKE TRUST SACRED / ESPRESSO VERSION

Communications marketing giant Edelman conducts an annual survey of trust called the Edelman Trust Barometer, analysing the trust people around the world have in media, NGOs, businesses, and governments. In 2010 their report proclaimed that trust was an 'essential line of business to be developed and delivered'. The world, it said, was 'stakeholder, not shareholder'. In 2017 the Trust Barometer bore a more sinister title: 'Trust in Crisis'. It outlined a 'growing storm of mistrust' affecting media, NGOs, businesses and governments alike.

This is problematic for marketers, who rely on trust to build brand affinity. Trust is a lubricant for economic interactions. We trust that our currency won't be devalued overnight. We trust that the contract we sign will be upheld in court. We assign trustworthiness scores to people based on whether we think they'll pay off their credit card, or whether they'll default on their mortgage. It is a shortcut that allows us to trim time and effort from interactions.

Before anything else, brands should believe themselves to be trustworthy. Ask this potentially heretical question:

  // What reason have we given consumers to actually trust our
     brand, our products, and our communications?

If you can't answer the question, you've probably stumbled across an area of great opportunity.

At Contagious, we believe trust – particularly for marketers – is made up of five key pillars. We share the diagram overleaf with our clients.

The expertise and reliability pillars are, admittedly, often outside your control as a marketer, as product quality and consistency decisions are handled higher up the food chain or earlier in the processes. The other three, however, are squarely in your wheelhouse.

We discussed organizing principle at length in the first

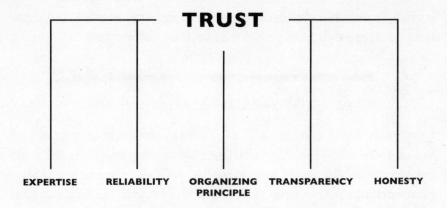

commandment. It's why you show up to work each day, and why your company exists in the lives of its customers. The other two are opportunities. By pulling back the curtain and being utterly transparent, start-up brands like apparel-maker Everlane and insurance company Lemonade have disrupted industries and changed customer expectations. Established brands like Domino's and Audi built trust – and even excitement – by being communicative about their supply-chain processes to take products from assembly to delivery. And brands that have embraced an unvarnished approach to messaging, like Royal Caribbean and Taco Bell, have seen that risk rewarded by consumers who appreciate honesty.

With Contagious's five trust pillars in front of you, ask yourself the following questions:

// How can we improve in each pillar to instil more trust in our brand?
// Can we communicate our expertise, reliability, organizing principle, transparency, and honesty better so that customers will feel confident in their purchase decisions?
// How can we be more trustworthy when it comes to each pillar?

Give your company a score out of ten in each of the five categories. Circle the lowest score, start there, and get to work.

BE BRAVE

I t all comes down to this: be brave. That's what this entire book is about, after all. Ten steps to brand bravery. Ten strategies to incite bold decision-making and convention-challenging work. Ten reminders to serve customers in the smartest way possible, even if those methods have never been tried before.

But what is bravery? Often it's a catch-all term with a definition that is contextually defined. For one person, bravery might mean getting on a plane. For someone else, it's sitting still while a wasp buzzes around their picnic table. For some, it might mean crying.

Bravery is, in large part, undefined. It's variable. And that's exactly why it's perhaps the most relevant commandment for every single business in the world. No matter what bravery specifically means to your company and its clients and customers at this moment in time, we firmly believe that you must do it, or else be lost in the slipstream. Bold action and courageous ideas give consumers a reason to believe and enable brands to stand out from the pack.

Great ideas have never been more essential and yet have never been harder to put into action. Budget cutters, short-termism and our own fears and biases threaten the one thing proven to deliver effective marketing: creativity. But risk-aversion isn't just putting pressure on marketing. It is an anti-creative juggernaut careening down the high-way, with entire businesses caught in the headlights.

Truly creative ideas are rarely predictable. They're often difficult to keep on deadline and under budget. Writing in *The Armed Forces Comptroller*, management expert Lynne C. Vincent writes, 'Creativity is inherently risky. A creative idea by definition is novel and useful. If the idea is truly novel, it will have some risk attached . . . Because of this risk, people often feel more comfortable maintaining the status quo.'

At Contagious, we're allergic to the status quo. We believe that brave, innovative creativity is the best means to gain an unfair advantage over the competition. Ideas are democratic, after all, and even the biggest brands must continually earn consumers' trust and respect. All other things being equal, the braver brand will make more creative work and will win in the long run. This has particularly been proven true in the world Contagious concentrates on: marketing. Simply put, we hold that creative work kicks the shit out of non-creative work when it comes to selling stuff. And plenty of people have confirmed that hypothesis for us already.

WE'RE NOT MAKING THIS UP

Perhaps best known among the research into the link between creativity and effectiveness is a study by Les Binet and Peter Field of the UK's Institute of Practitioners in Advertising (IPA) titled, er, *The Link Between Creativity and Effectiveness*. Binet and Field analysed 1,000 case studies in the IPA effectiveness database and found that creatively awarded campaigns were eleven times more efficient than non-creatively awarded campaigns from 2000 to 2011, when standardized for excess share of voice (how much of the conversation a brand owns versus its competitors, accounting for share of market). Creative ads resulted in a 2.34 per cent growth in market share versus a 0.2 per cent growth for non-creative ads. From 2011 to 2016 the effectiveness multiplier for creative vs non-creative work dropped from eleven to six, largely due to an increasing focus on short-term results. (Remember the emphasis on agile long-termism in the first commandment?)

In another study, titled *The Long and the Short of It*, Binet and Field point the finger directly at the thirst for short-term results tracking in the digital era: 'Even more worrying is the drive to develop real-time campaign management systems driven by these short-term response metrics: unless such systems are heavily counter-balanced by long-term metrics and activity, they could prove to be a death-sentence for brands.'

Other researchers have looked at the value of creativity in spurring advertising effectiveness. In his long-running study 'Do Award-Winning Commercials Sell?', Donald Gunn, the worldwide director of creative resources at Leo Burnett, found that creatively awarded television ads resulted in 5.7 per cent growth in market share per 10 per cent excess share of voice. Non-creative ads, against that same media spend, resulted in growth of just 0.5 per cent.

In the *Journal of the Academy of Marketing Science* in 2014, Jiemiao Chen, Xiaojing Yang, and Robert E. Smith published research that showed that the effects of creative work also last longer than the effects of non-creative work, as consumers are less likely to get tired of the message. 'When an ad has both divergence and relevance, it resists wearing-out even at high levels of repetition,' they write, citing their definition of creativity (divergent yet relevant). 'Only creative ads were able to resist wearing out at high exposure levels. Thus, the positive effects of creative ads are *more* pronounced over multiple repetitions.' So you can go ahead and add 'cost savings' to the list of creativity's benefits. The longer your ads last before diminishing in impact, the fewer ads you need to make.

Finally, creativity has been shown to result in bottom-line success for companies brave enough to commit to it. In the 2016 edition of his book *The Case for Creativity*, James Hurman notes that companies that win the title of Cannes Creative Marketer of the Year outperform the S&P 500 by a factor of 3.5, with annual share price growth of 26.1 per cent vs 7.5 per cent on the S&P from 1999 to 2015. 'Effectiveness is most efficiently driven by campaigns that create fame,' he writes. 'Fame is most efficiently achieved with creativity.'

Without a doubt, our goal as marketers and brand builders should be to get the most creative work possible. So what's stopping us?

POISON, VOMIT, AGONY

Unfortunately, *we* are what's stopping us. Human brains aren't wired to embrace the uncertainty of creativity. We're wired for consistency, predictability, and minimizing risks. We say we want creativity, but when confronted with actual fresh ideas, our brains rebel against us.

In 2010 researchers Jennifer S. Mueller, Shimul Melwani, and Jack A. Goncalo published a paper through Cornell University's ILR School called 'The Bias Against Creativity: Why People Desire But Reject Creative Ideas'. It confirmed our brains' unwillingness to embrace creativity, even when we say we're open to it. 'People often reject creative ideas even when espousing creativity as a desired goal. The results demonstrated a negative bias toward creativity when participants experienced uncertainty. Furthermore, the bias against creativity interfered with participants' ability to recognize a creative idea,' they wrote.

The researchers put study participants into two mindsets, high tolerance for uncertainty and low tolerance for uncertainty, by instructing them to write an essay supporting the statement: 'for every problem, there is more than one correct solution' (high tolerance for uncertainty) or 'for every problem, there is only one correct solution' (low tolerance for uncertainty). They then used what's called an 'Implicit Association Test' (IAT) which instructs people to press keys on a keyboard in response to specific terms and then measures their reaction times. Using four sets of categorized words (positive, negative, creative, and practical), the IAT tested participants' subconscious linkages between the different feelings. They found that participants in the low tolerance for uncertainty group associated creative words with the negative batch – words like poison, vomit, and agony. When asked to rate a creative idea, the same low-tolerance group rated it as less creative than their more-tolerant compatriots.

'Our results suggest that if people have difficulty gaining acceptance for creative ideas especially when more practical and unoriginal options are readily available, the field of creativity may need to shift its current focus from identifying how to generate more creative ideas to identifying how to help innovative institutions recognize and accept creativity,' wrote the authors. That is to say, we don't need to focus on coming up with more creative ideas. We've got that part under control. Instead, we need to work on recognizing and nurturing those ideas to make them into reality.

Everyone knows the Christmas holidays are no time for selfishness. The soft-focus ads that dominate television toward the end of the calendar year hammer that point home, chock full of warm fuzzies, random acts of kindness, and gushing generosity. To do anything else would be risky. It would also be brilliant. In 2013 British metropolitan retailer Harvey Nichols took that risk, breaking from seasonal norms and risking a customer backlash to an anti-generosity campaign at the most selfless time of the year. The Sorry I Spent It On Myself campaign featured ads showing gift-buyers giving mundane items like rubber bands and paper clips to their loved ones, while happily holding on to a costly new purchase they'd made for themselves with the leftover cash. The retailer took the campaign one step further as well, creating a real line of the same 'Ultra Low Net Worth' items featured in the spots. Within a single day of going on sale, the range of products sold out.

The campaign zagged while everyone else zigged, and stuck out as a result. With its cheeky tone and excellent craft, Sorry I Spent It On Myself took home four Grand Prix awards at the Cannes Lions Festival of Creativity. But it was far from accidental. 'A lot of the comments at Cannes were about how it was so brave to fly in the face of Christmas,' says Richard Brim, an ECD at adam&eveDDB who worked on the campaign. 'That's how we've behaved with Harvey Nichols all along; we just pushed it to the *n*th degree.'

Indeed, Harvey Nichols (which has an organizing principle of 'Fearlessly Stylish') hasn't shied away from bravely creative campaigns in recent years. In 2015 it launched a mobile-first refresh of its loyalty programme with a campaign consisting of security camera footage of real shoplifters in Harvey Nichols stores, superimposed with cartoon faces. 'Love freebies?' the strapline asked. 'Get them legally. Rewards by Harvey Nichols.' Another winter campaign saluted the 'walk of shame' with people leaving one-night stands in their going out clothes. And the brand's 2015 Christmas advert showcased the 'Gift Face' put on by people who have just received a less-than-desirable gift, another shot across the bow at the Spread Christmas Cheer establishment. 'There's a playfulness to Harvey Nichols when you put it against all the other retailers who, at that time of year, are incredibly schmaltzy,' Jessica Lovell, a planner at adam&eveDDB, told Contagious. Swimming against the current breaks through the clutter of a crowded advertising period, and it takes some chutzpah to do it.

RECOGNIZING AND ACCEPTING CREATIVITY

Most companies are wired the same exact way as those study participants. They're wired for consistency, predictability, and minimizing risks. When presented with both a practical solution and a creative one, the majority will take the practical to market and save the creative idea for a rainy day. And they do this while talking about creativity as an important part of their business. It's a difficult talk to walk.

There's an inherent contradiction in how businesses tend to be run. Senior leaders are expected to approve bold creative ideas that have the potential for exponential impact, but at the same time are pressured to meet deadlines, stay within budgets, and keep the company away from risks. We reward and motivate people based on certainty and dependability. Instead, marketers should force themselves to push past their instinct to cling to safety. Progress requires growth, and as the old maxim goes, without change there is no growth.

Being brave does not mean being foolhardy, though. Aristotle, that famous brand strategist, cited Courage as one of the four cardinal virtues back in the fourth century BCE, but noted that too much could lead to recklessness. 'The courageous man withstands and fears those things which it is necessary and on account of the right reason, and how and when it is necessary,' he wrote (though we're relying on others to translate the ancient Greek for us, so best to treat it as a paraphrase). Be brave, but in moderation. Companies must have a systematic approach to achieving creative ideas in a way that tolerates, but minimizes, risk.

At Contagious, a cornerstone of our business is helping clients hone this approach. To recognize, accept, and encourage creativity, while constructing guardrails that prevent wasted effort and unnecessary risk. We strive to turn accidental (or against-all-odds) creativity into a deliberate practice of creative excellence. We encourage our clients to take a well-informed step into the unknown, away from what has worked thus far if necessary. We inspire them to follow convictions into uncharted waters. We tell them not to anticipate failure, but not to fear it either.

As poet Robert Frost once wrote, 'Freedom lies in being bold.'

BRAVE WORKS

We've spilled lots of ink in this book (and a few extra drops in the boxed sections of this commandment) citing examples of work that could be considered brave. In most of those cases, the brands were emboldened to be courageous because they adhered to the commandments. Patagonia was brave to tell people not to buy its jacket, but was emboldened because of its crystal-clear organizing principle. It was brave of Kenco to invest its marketing budget in moving at-risk Honduran youths from gang-filled areas to coffee plantations, but it followed through on the idea because of a mindset that prioritized generosity. Art Series Hotels' bold decision to give away hotel rooms for free was empowered by asking intriguing, heretical questions about its fundamental business model.

Every creative campaign in this book was the result of brave decision-making on the part of people inside agencies and clients, working together to push for something better than the status quo.

But all of those examples – and all of the commandments you've read thus far – don't amount to much if they're not put into action, with bravery and conviction. Marketing, after all, isn't an entirely theoretical exercise. While you're at the office reading the latest research, your advertising is out on the town, carousing and trying to snag a date. To make these ideas work, companies need to build a culture where creativity is safeguarded and bravery becomes a working practice. Sure, brands with a maverick creative flag flyer may be able to sneak through some moments of creative brilliance. But we want you to champion, or to systematize, creativity as an entire organization. And to do so, you're going to need a few tools.

A CREATIVE LEXICON

The first arrow in your bravery quiver (there's an oxymoron for you) is a common language. Too often, creativity is mired in the fluffy talk of inspirational lightning strikes and flashes of brilliance in the shower. Creative ideas, legend has it, come from putting creative people in a room and letting them 'noodle on it' for a few days (and, often, a few drinks). This takes creativity out of the hands of the masses, creating two classes – the creatives and the create nots. We firmly disagree. Creativity is a muscle, to be exercised and strengthened through challenge and repetition. Sure, some people have a natural knack for it, just as some people are naturally more athletic or more musically inclined. But even the most astringently left-brained among us can be taught to be creative, or at the very least to become open to the idea of creativity and persevere against our unconscious biases.

To help move the creative conversation from qualitative and subjective to quantitative and objective, we need a common language that allows us to communicate, rationally and with a shared purpose.

During his tenure at Leo Burnett, Paul was a member of the network's Global Product Committee, which evaluated creative campaigns against an acclaimed 1–10 system known as the 7+ Scale. Contagious first put a similar idea to work with global brewer Heineken in 2015, via an advisory project aimed at scaling great creativity throughout the organization. Together with the Global Commerce University (Heineken's internal training and development unit), we devised the Creative Ladder, an assessment tool ranging from 1 (destructive) to 10 (world-changing) designed to help everyone within the organization put words against subjective feelings. Beyond the top-level descriptors, each rung of the ladder has a detailed explanation of what work fits under what rating, applying clear evaluative language to move from qualitative to quantitative conversations.

Rather than saying 'I don't like this' or 'I think this is fine', marketers inside Heineken were enabled to quantify their feelings – 'I think this is a 5 (ownable), because it uses unique executional cues to rise above a cliché' or 'I think this is a 7 (ground-breaking), because it provokes a change in the perception of the category.' The term 'ladder' was deliberately chosen; it's impossible for an idea to score a 7 without being built on the foundations of an 'ownable' idea, executed in a 'fresh' (rung 6) creative manner. One of the main drivers was to avoid deploying advertising that scored a 4 (cliché), and would therefore be uncompetitive in the category.

'If you want great creativity you need to be able to talk about it and to give it a language, because more often than not, creativity is very subjective, it has a lot to do with gut feelings, and the experience and legacy of the different individuals,' Cinzia Morelli-Verhoog, then Heineken's senior director of global marketing capability, told *Fast Company* in 2015. 'By introducing the creative ladder we created a language within Heineken.'

In the same interview, Morelli-Verhoog observed that it's riskier to play it safe, because safe marketing blends in and is ignored. 'The biggest risk in this case is if Heineken were an organization that sees anything that has not been done before as risky,' she said. 'Actually, for us, the creative that is most risky is clichéd because you know for sure it will not make an impact and be part of the wallpaper, where we don't want to be.'

Arif Haq, who led the Contagious creative capabilities practice at the time and worked with Heineken to develop the ladder, comments:

> The hardest task in this industry falls not to the individuals whose job it is to come up with brave new ideas, but to the clients who risk their jobs in approving them. I'm not sure why we ever thought it was a smart idea for people with no formal creative training to be able to provide expert feedback on creative ideas, and yet that's exactly what we expect of brand managers on a regular basis.
>
> Many assume the ladder's power lies in the scoring numbers. But its real value is in the language, not only in the titles of each rung, but the accompanying descriptions which explain in detail why, for example, a 7 is a 7 and not a 6 or an 8 (contagious). It's essentially a dictionary of creative language designed for brand

managers to articulate advanced creative ideas to their bosses, and also their agencies, peers and, critically, themselves.

The ladder is a tool that helps to transform the corporate perception of creativity from an accidental, 'magical', and therefore risky idea to something that can be predicted and replicated, thereby allowing it to be scaled.

Yuval Harari, in his book *Sapiens*, which tracks the evolution and eventual domination of humans on earth, ascribes our success as a species to the ability to communicate quickly and clearly – essentially scaling through language. 'How did we manage to settle so rapidly in so many distant and ecologically different habitats?' he writes. 'The most likely answer is the very thing that makes the debate possible: *Homo sapiens* conquered the world thanks above all to its unique language.' In a similar way, language enables us to unpack the complexity of creativity and make it accessible for people with different skills in different jobs in different areas of an organization.

Much of this conversation about creative lexicons stems back to the ideas above about why we reject creativity. When we have trouble fully grasping an issue or an idea, it is easier to say no than to understand whether we should or shouldn't follow it to its potentially impactful conclusion. Remember that talk of objective disqualifiers in the third commandment? Creative discussions are full of *subjective* disqualifiers. Feedback like 'I don't get it' and 'I don't like it' – or, worse still, 'the client/audience won't like it' – are mired in subjectivity – whoever is highest on the org chart or shouts the loudest in the meetings gets final say. A common lexicon around creativity moves subjective disqualifiers into the realm of objectivity, where it is easier to pinpoint actual issues with work – and then hopefully move on to figuring out ways to make it better.

CREATE ADVOCATES TO ADVOCATE CREATIVE

Our work with Heineken, and the other clients with whom we've shaped creative excellence guides and curricula, goes beyond simply crafting a list of ten grades and calling it a day. In addition to building the lexicon, organizations must promote these new languages, and teach people how to use them constructively. It needs to become habit. For Heineken, this meant a series of local and regional creativity masterclasses to educate marketers on the ground and to embed the language of the ladder into practical conversations, and the founding of a creative council of senior leaders to review and judge the company's creative output.

At Contagious we advise our clients to select internal advocates tasked with leading the charge for creativity both at the senior level and throughout the organization. We help to build creative councils, which routinely review work to see how the brand's work, both internally and outside its walls, stacks up against an objective scale. We develop continuing education programmes, to help marketers understand the evolving challenges in the marketplace, as well as hone their skills as brave advocates for ideas that will break through.

At its core, bravery is a struggle between mind and matter. If you have a fear of bees or heights or clowns, you might call it an 'irrational' fear. Your mind tells you there's nothing to be afraid of, but you break into a cold sweat whenever you're in a phobia-inducing position. Having language in these scenarios – logical, rational language that can deconstruct a situation – is a powerful tool. And when fighting for brave creativity, it can sometimes be the only tool that works.

Picture an ad for a feminine hygiene product like a tampon or pad. Now let us take a guess at one of the key components. Is there a mystery blue liquid involved? It's an entrenched cliché that has come to define the category's comms themselves. Rather than show blood, ads opt for a generic replacement liquid. It's a rule no brand dared to break. Until Bodyform came along, at least. In 2012 the brand (which is owned by Swedish health and hygiene firm Essity) released an ad called The Truth, in which an actress playing CEO Caroline Williams reveals the truth about periods to a male Facebook commenter. 'I'm sorry to be the one to tell you this, but there's no such thing as a happy period,' she said, citing 'the cramps, the mood swings, the insatiable hunger, and yes Richard, the blood coursing from our uteri like a crimson landslide'. Rubber Republic, the agency behind the work, reports that the video received 6 million views, nearly entirely through earned media, and increased Bodyform search traffic by 1,000 per cent.

In 2016 the brand built on that success with a series of three campaigns across Europe that sought to destigmatize periods and break category norms with bold messaging. After polling 10,000 men and women in ten countries, the brand found that a third of people had never seen a woman openly discuss her period in film, television, or books. 'We're more likely to see blood in scenes of horror in popular culture than we are to see something as normal as a woman talking about her period,' Essity global brand manager Martina Poulopati told Contagious. The campaigns, aimed at women between eighteen and thirty-five, talked openly about how periods affect women's health and energy levels, addressed cultural taboos about buying feminine hygiene products, and – most critically – swapped out the blue liquid for a more realistic red.

The third spot, called Blood Normal, generated 796 million PR impressions, 80 million social impressions, and 6 million video views within three weeks. The longer-running campaign, called Red.Fit, achieved 90 per cent of its reach through earned media, and resulted in improvement across all brand equity pillars measured by Essity – both functional and emotional – as well as increased product trial levels.

'Working in feminine care, one of the first things you realize is how many taboos are in this category and that most of the brands follow these norms. Bodyform was brave enough to be the first to break from that and from the huge response it was clear that there was something there for the brand,' says Poulopati.

KNOW THE BARRIERS TO CREATIVE WORK

Next time you're bored at work, do an experiment: ask any of your industry friends if they feel like they are empowered to take wildly creative risks in their day-to-day jobs. Unless you're friends with the luckiest people in the world, almost all of them will say, 'Well, not exactly.' When you ask them why, familiar themes will start to emerge. They are too busy managing people or projects to have time to think. They have to hit budgets and deadlines. They can't afford to fail. When they've pushed for out-of-the-box creative in the past, someone in the C-suite has shut it down. They might get laughed at.

Then, ask the same question inside your own company. What is the biggest barrier to creativity in your organization? Is it knowledge? Time? Encouragement? Resistance to change? Focus on the short term at the expense of the long term? Knowing where your creativity gets bottlenecked is the first step to confronting that issue.

By addressing those bottlenecks, companies can create a culture that thrives on new ideas and encourages people to take the time to find them. Maybe it's a leader giving an award for failures, to show that great ideas often rise from the ashes of aborted attempts. Maybe it's setting aside time for experimentation. Or maybe it's something as simple as encouraging people to ask questions and share off-the-wall ideas in judgement-free sessions.

Because, ideally, creative bravery isn't brave at all. It's smart, fresh, and as risk-insulated as you can possibly make it. It's good business practice. As Phil Adams, strategy director at agency Cello Signal, wrote in a 2017 article for *The Drum*, 'I have worked with clients who didn't need the crutch of pre-testing research in order to approve an idea. And I have worked with a few who have ignored negative research feedback to press ahead with advertising that they believed in. I wouldn't describe these people as brave. I'd say that they knew what they were doing. Good ideas aren't dangerous or risky, they are disproportionately effective.'

In practice, the ecosystem trends more toward the old axiom that 'no one ever got fired for buying IBM'. Even if we know in our hearts that creative ideas win out, our minds seek ways to not rock the boat. To keep the ship afloat until it's time to retire. To focus on the quotidian minutiae rather than confronting the big scary challenges looming on the horizon. But this is a fast track to a slow decline. As Dwight Eisenhower once said, 'What is important is seldom urgent and what is urgent is seldom important.'

HIRE (AND MANAGE) FOR BRAVERY

Bravery cannot be the domain of a single person in an organization. It cannot be a departmental pursuit. Yes, a specific person or persons or department may lead the charge. And companies with a single creative catalyst may occasionally find a needle in a haystack. But repeatable brave creativity requires an environment designed to foster it. And that (surprise!) also requires moving away from the all-too-status-quo. As usual, it requires being slightly uncomfortable.

'The worst kind of group for an organization that wants to be innovative and creative is one in which everyone is alike and gets along too well,' wrote team performance expert Margaret Ann Neale, the Addams Distinguished Professor of Management at Stanford University, in 2006.

Organizational behaviour expert Barry Staw, in an essay titled 'Why No One Really Wants Creativity', echoes that idea. 'From what we know about organizations, they work very hard to recruit and select employees who look and act like those already in the firm. For those who might have slipped into the organization without the proper skills and values, socialization is usually the answer,' he writes. 'Creating clones of existing personnel is generally what management wants and gets.'

These homogeneous cultures do not lead to great ideas. They lead to organizational blinkers that leave companies open to fading into obscurity at best and creating destructive work or being disrupted at worst. Homogeneous groups lead to homogeneous ideas.

Recent research from McKinsey shows that companies in the top quartile of gender diversity are 15 per cent more likely to have financial results above their industry medians. What's more, companies in the top quartile for racial and ethnic diversity are 35 per cent more likely to have financial results above their industry medians. And every little bit counts. Writes McKinsey London director Vivian Hunt: 'In the United States, there is a linear relationship between racial and ethnic diversity and better financial performance: for every 10 per cent increase in racial and ethnic diversity on the senior-executive team, earnings before interest and taxes rise 0.8 per cent.' These are incredible numbers, and proof that inviting different people into conversations pays dividends in the form of well-rounded companies that can produce sharp ideas.

Beyond just hiring those people, organizations must strive to empower them to make bold decisions without penalty – assuming the risks they entail are measured and minimized as far as reasonably possible. As General George S. Patton said, 'Don't tell people how to do things. Tell them what to do and let them surprise you with the results.'

It's an idea echoed by Teresa Amabile in her 1998 *Harvard Business Review* essay 'How To Kill Creativity':

> Autonomy around process fosters creativity because giving people freedom in how they approach their work heightens their intrinsic motivation and sense of ownership. Freedom about process also allows people to approach problems in ways that make the most of their expertise and their creative-thinking skills. The task may end up being a stretch for them, but they can use their strengths to meet the challenge.

You'll recall the conversation about adaptive versus tactical thinking from the first commandment; a similar principle applies here. Give people the space to be creative, and chances are they will take you up on that offer.

Not many brands have an in-house mischief department. But then again, not many brands are like Irish bookmaker Paddy Power. The gambling company has offered odds on the next pope being black, faked cutting down a Brazilian rainforest, and sponsored an egg-and-spoon race in the French town of London so it could bill itself as the 'Official sponsor of the largest athletics event in London this year' during the 2012 Olympics. Leprechaun-like mischief is a part of the company's DNA.

'It's important to understand that we are the underdog in this industry,' Paul Sweeney, head of brand at Paddy Power, told Contagious in 2014. 'We are outspent four-to-one by some of our traditional competitors, so every pound we spend must go four times further.' The aforementioned in-house mischief department has worked closely with agencies like Crispin, Porter + Bogusky, Lucky Generals, Chime Sports Marketing and WCRS (as well as the Paddy Power legal department) to craft big box-office stunts that keep the brand in the news. 'The one rule is that we can't risk anyone in the company going to jail,' says Sweeney. 'Apart from that, it's fair game.' The offline stunts are supported by a sophisticated online editorial team tasked with listening to what gamblers are saying and creating relevant content that cuts through and connects on an emotional level.

Led by this underdog sense of necessary bravery, Paddy Power has made headlines – and a dent in the competition. In 2014 the brand wrapped up a decade of 30 per cent year-on-year growth, with 49 per cent of their bets taking place via mobile, far above the 9 per cent average in the industry. It's a symptom of smart thinking and bold action following through on the words of the brand's first CEO, Stewart Kenny: 'We're going to take your money, so we'll make damn sure you have fun while we do.'

INTRINSIC AND EXTRINSIC MOTIVATIONS

You can lead a horse to water but you can't make it drink, or so the saying goes. What if you hire a horse in a creativity-conducive environment? Can you make it be creative?

Equines aside, companies attempting to spark creativity often come up against this nature vs nurture type discussion. Can you build a creative culture that truly encourages employees to make brave decisions and develop creative ideas? Or is it simply a question of hiring 'rockstars' who have creativity coursing through their bloodstreams?

In reality, two sets of motivating factors drive us to complete any task: intrinsic motivations and extrinsic motivations. Intrinsic drivers come from within a task, and motivate people to do something for the sheer sake of doing it. Full stop. We go for a run because we want to go for a run. In a job setting, intrinsic motivators have been described by St John's University assistant professor Rajesh Singh as 'psychological feelings that employees get from doing meaningful work and performing it well'.

Extrinsic motivations, on the other hand, happen outside the task itself. Think: promotions, financial rewards, prizes.

We often think of intrinsic and extrinsic motivations as happening inside or outside the individual – either someone is a 'self-starter' or they're working for the weekend. And research is divided as to whether extrinsic forces alone can actually motivate employees to create good work regularly. As we discussed in the first commandment, 'making a profit' is not a sufficient organizing principle to drive a company forward.

Recent research, however, suggests that extrinsic and intrinsic motivations may be more closely linked than previously thought. 'Mechanisms Underlying Creative Performance', a study by Hye Jung Yoon, Sun Young Sung, and Jin Nam Choi published in the journal *Social Behavior and Personality* in 2015, found that when it comes to creativity, extrinsic rewards (assuming the reward is something valued by the employee) influence attitudes toward a task and consequently inspire more creative work:

> In the case of extrinsic rewards for creativity, although rewards of this type did not have a significant direct effect on creative performance, extrinsic rewards were significantly related to commitment to creativity, which, in turn, had a meaningful effect on creative performance. Our results showed that extrinsic rewards had a significant indirect effect on creative performance via commitment to creativity, suggesting that the intermediate psychological condition is critical for extrinsic rewards to influence creativity.

So what does this mean? If you can, hire people with an intrinsic drive to be creative and develop brave ideas. Then, incentivize them to do just that, with something they'll actually value. And finally, turn them loose on a task. As Erik Sollenberg, the former CEO of stellar

Swedish agency Forsman & Bodenfors, said of his employees: 'The only boss they have is the task itself.' The agency has a list of principles it enforces as employees work on those tasks:

- // Show your colleague what you're working on.
- // Listen to their critique.
- // Learn.
- // Be prepared to change your mind.
- // Share your success.
- // Engage in other people's work and give your opinion.

We don't claim to be psychologists or behavioural scientists, but these principles seem to blur the line between intrinsic and extrinsic motivations, creating an environment where employees are driven by the task at hand and extrinsically rewarded through opportunities to fulfil their intrinsic drive. As in one example Sollenberg cited: 'One of the copywriters on [two high-profile projects] is a newly hired quite young creative. In order to do that type of work in a traditional agency you would probably have to wait quite a few years.' The extrinsic reward, in this case, is the ability to work on high-profile campaigns, which spurs intrinsic drive and results in exemplary creativity.

BRIEF FOR BRAVERY

Perhaps the worst-utilized implement in the marketer's toolkit for cultivating a creativity-inducing environment is the brief. For readers unfamiliar with the advertising world, think of the brief as marching orders for developing a campaign, typically given to an agency by a brand client, laying out their key objectives. When Contagious conducted a survey among some of the industry's leading creatives about the briefing process in 2017, we heard it time and time again. 'The worst thing is when people give you a brief with an outcome they've already got in their head and they don't want you to deviate off that path and become irritated if you do,' Nick Worthington, creative chairman at Colenso BBDO in New Zealand told us. 'They're limiting the opportunity to do something extraordinary.'

When talking about bravery and creativity in the context of advertising, it is impossible to ignore this delicate dance between agency and client. The briefing process is an opportunity for a brand to establish its thirst for bravery, while defining the parameters and measurable objectives for a campaign.

'You do your best work when people ask you to do your best work,' Andy Nairn, founding partner of agency Lucky Generals, told us. 'Clients can frame the brief and make it stand out by saying that they want something brilliant. I know that sounds like stating the obvious, but some of the time you don't get that impression. Some of the time you get the impression that people just want something OK, that will continue and evolve what they've already been doing.'

'To get contagious work, the briefs are just the beginning, and making that work come alive is something completely different,' says Worthington. 'Pretty much anyone can have a brilliant idea, and they often do, but very, very few people are capable of executing those ideas brilliantly.'

The fact of the matter is that agencies will, most of the time, follow the brief they are given. Occasionally they'll break away and create something off-the-asked-for-path, but even in those cases it's rare for the client to agree to go along with them. Jim Carroll, former chairman at BBH UK, put it this way: 'Extraordinary work often correlates less directly with the brief, breaks conventions and uses unfamiliar reference points . . . Extraordinary work is ordinarily very easy to reject. In nearly all aspects of business, intelligence represents a competitive advantage. But in the judgement of creativity it can represent a curse, a competitive disadvantage.'

And when clients buy ordinary work, they get ordinary work. They send a message to their agency that they're not interested in truly creative ideas. Consequently, talented creatives at those agencies choose to work on different accounts. It's a self-fulfilling prophecy: unless you're asking for great work, you won't get it.

As Marc Pritchard, global marketing and brand-building officer at the world's largest advertisers, Procter & Gamble, said at the Cannes Lions Festival in 2012: 'I like to tell people you need to inspire creative work that is so brilliant you're willing to bet your career on it.'

'This is all or nothing. This is death or glory. This is one giant gamble to turn the beer scene on its head.' So stated Scottish brewery BrewDog in February of 2018, when it announced it would be giving away 1 million free pints in its branded taprooms. The brewery, whose founders once famously proclaimed that they would rather light their money on fire than buy traditional advertising, paradoxically used posters created by London agency Isobel to dare consumers: 'Don't buy the advertising. Make up your own mind.'

BrewDog has always been a rebellious brand – the word punk adorns almost all of its messaging, including its flagship Punk IPA and its 'Equity For Punks' crowdfunding campaigns. It even described itself as a 'post-punk, apocalyptic, motherfu*ker of a craft brewery' before the UK's Advertising Standards Authority rapped its knuckles. And its messaging has certainly lived up to that counterculture ethos. The brewer has three times brewed the strongest beer in the world (most recently in 2010, with a 55 per cent ABV IPA called 'End of History' served in bottles inside taxidermied squirrels and stoats), has distributed free posters for fans to illegally 'fly post' all over the UK, posted all of its own recipes online, and even released a beer laced with steroids to mock competitor Heineken's sponsorship of the 2012 Olympics. A crazy streak runs through its DNA.

'The fact is, big brands say no to that kind of thing because they see perceived risks, but actually the opportunity of taking a stand far outweighs any risk. Because it's true to a purpose, people can disagree, but we can't be wrong,' Alex Myers, founder of long-time BrewDog PR agency Manifest, told Contagious. Within the brand, marketers ask themselves if any other brand could produce a campaign they're considering. If the answer is yes, they move on to the next idea.

In 2010, when Contagious first profiled the aggressively independent beer-maker, it brewed 1.58 million litres of ale annually and had just opened its first bar. In 2017 BrewDog expanded to the US with a second destination brewery that increased its brewing capacity to 1.64 million hectolitres, more than a hundred times that 2010 number. That was good enough to make it the fastest-growing craft brewer in the world, valued at over £1 billion. Its portfolio now includes eponymous bars and hotels, and the punks are reportedly even planning to launch a craft beer TV network, of all things.

DON'T JUST SIT THERE, DO SOMETHING

Creativity is only useful if you're brave enough to deploy it. You'll recall Tom Raith, portfolio director of brand experience design at IDEO, and his concept of 'back of the deck ideas' referenced in the seventh commandment. When agencies pitch a client, he told the audience at Contagious's 2015 event in San Francisco, they often come with presentations that are mostly the same – generally similar ideas and tactics make up the majority of the pitch deck from agency to agency. Where the agencies differentiate themselves is toward the back of the deck, where they stick their exciting, creative, risky ideas. Clients often choose their agency based on these back-of-the-deck ideas, said Raith, but then pay them to execute only the front-of-the-deck concepts.

This is akin to buying a Lamborghini and only ever driving it to church.

We firmly believe that in today's competitive landscape, bravery isn't optional. It is a strategic imperative. In fact, working with marketing and sales consultancy OxfordSM, Contagious developed a framework for brands to activate many of the commandments explored in this book. We use that framework, called Fit for the Future Now, to encourage brands to take stock and prioritize according to what's needed to grow today. 'There's so much noise and complexity that commercial teams have to cope with that it's easy to lose sight of the few things that really matter,' says Peter Kirkby, head of the capability practice at OxfordSM. One of those things that 'really matter'? Acting with bravery.

The diagram of Fit for the Future Now will look familiar to anyone who has made it this far into this book, although a few of the words are different. There are two anchor points ('Live your purpose' and 'Own a simple experience'), four behaviours and two enablers ('Simplify' and 'Break through the data').

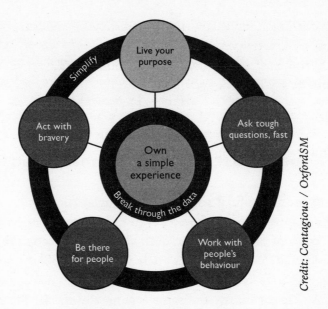

Credit: Contagious / OxfordSM

None of the circles in the Fit for the Future Now diagram – and none of the commandments in this book – are more important than the others. You must do all of the above (and then some) to be a successful brand for the decades to come. But if we had to pick just one, you can probably guess which one it is by glancing at the cover of this book. You can have all the incredible ideas in the world, but if you don't attempt to make them a reality and put them out into the world, if you don't take risks in how you articulate your values and reach your consumers, if you don't defy conventions and stick out from the crowded masses, the rest of it may not even matter.

'There's strong evidence from Peter Field's analysis that a combination of great strategy and real creative bravery is up to six times more effective than great strategy and averagely creative work,' says Kirkby. 'This is down to what Peter Field calls the "fame effect" – creatively brave work gets talked about so has a multiplier effect that less creative work doesn't.'

In the framework, Contagious and OxfordSM encourage brands to ask themselves a few simple questions around bravery:

// Do you have creative work that's getting talked about?
// Do you have a way of asking agencies for it, and evaluating

and selling it internally, that reflects how the odds are stacked against creativity in large companies?

II Do you have testing and learning about 'next practice' baked into how you work and budget?

Answering these questions can start to give you a process for bravery, and sense-check your ways of working to make sure they're not defaulting to the tried-and-true.

IT ALL COMES DOWN TO THIS

Our hope is that this book can serve as a rallying cry for creativity. A practical guide to ignite exceptional ideas. We hope that when you set this book down you'll walk away with nuggets of wisdom, practical case studies, and one or two dumb jokes you can't quite get out of your head. But most of all, we hope that these ten Contagious Commandments give you the courage to follow your creative convictions and set ambitions above and beyond the status quo.

It's far from easy. Defining your organizing principle requires soul searching for your company and its employees. Crafting services and communications that are useful, relevant and entertaining requires a deep understanding of your customers and the capabilities to deliver on that knowledge.

Asking heretical questions can be uncomfortable and challenging, even when they lead to breakthroughs and opportunity. Aligning with behaviour necessitates constant commitment to putting the customer at the centre of the way you work.

Giving generously and allocating budget to experiments can feel counterproductive to profits. But both make brands stronger and more valuable in the long run. Prioritizing experience over innovation in a world focused more on 'latest' than 'greatest' can feel out of step.

Making people a central part of how you both develop and disseminate messages is often unpredictable. Building trust takes time and transparency, both of which can be challenging (the former more for upstarts, the latter for legacy brands).

All of these challenges lead up to the last: bravery. Having the stomach for creativity requires courage to do what has never been done, or to break away from what has worked in the past, or to put something into the world without knowing how it will be received. But if you take the first nine commandments to heart, the last should be the easiest. Bravery isn't a blind leap into the unknown, it's a measured step into the unwritten future. Persevere in the face of uncertainty, because uncertainty isn't going away. Although, really, who can even be sure of that?

Creativity is infectious. It connects to something primal in our DNA – to hunting legends painted on the walls of caves and tales told around campfires or in the bustle of marketplaces. There's something fundamentally human about contagious ideas. People need to share, to relate, to connect, to persuade, to feel like we're part of something bigger than ourselves. We believe brands can earn the right to add their voice to that cultural conversation, enriching the human experience in this fantastic but frenetic world of ours, if they stay true to these ten commandments. At the heart of each of the ten lies a simple truth: make people a priority. Understand and celebrate their needs, their whims, their desires, their fears, their frustrations and, above all, their brilliant idiosyncrasies. Be generous with your creativity, be brave with your vision. And, if you like what you have read, pass it on.

BE BRAVE / ESPRESSO VERSION

CONDITIONS		MOTIVATIONS	OUTCOME
Common Language	Diverse Viewpoints	Intrinsic	
		X	**=** CREATIVE BRAVERY
Strong Partners	Creativity Valued	Extrinsic	

Nothing ventured, nothing gained. You miss all of the shots you don't take. Shoot for the moon; even if you miss you'll end up among the stars. Whatever your favourite cliché about bravery, in the marketing world it's probably more true today than it has ever been. The fracturing of audiences and evaporation of barriers to advertising entry means that creativity is the last true long-term competitive advantage in the modern marketplace. Creative work is, simply, more efficient and more effective than non-creative work.

Creative work is also scary. It takes effort to approve bold ideas and challenge conventions. After all, people rarely get fired for playing it safe. But if we want not just to survive but to thrive, we have to fight against our every instinct to retreat to safety and skate by with 'good enough'. We're hardwired to avoid risk, and consequently we need to dig deep to find the courage to go with our gut and to invest in our instincts.

But there's a thin line between bravery and foolishness – a line we'd like you to stay on the correct side of. That's exactly why we advise you to think of bravery in terms of measured risk. Some experiments succeed and some blow up the lab. Create the right ecosystem for intelligent bravery, and hopefully you'll avoid the latter outcome.

So how do you create an ecosystem for bravery to thrive? We think it boils down to establishing the right starting conditions, and catalysing them with a combination of intrinsic (driven by passion) and extrinsic (driven by reward) motivations.

To make sure you have the right conditions in place, ask yourself the following questions:

// **Do we, as an organization, have the terminology to talk about creative ideas in concrete and universal language?** You can gather the smartest beings in the universe in a single room, but unless they can communicate with each other, it won't amount to a hill of beans.

// **Are we inviting new voices to take part in our conversations, and attempting to involve as many different perspectives as possible?** Without fresh eyes and different viewpoints, you're only getting a thin slice of what's possible.

// **Do we have a strong working relationship with partners who are also willing to be brave?** Think of brave creativity like a nuclear decision – two parties need to turn their keys to make it a reality.

// **Have we bought into bravery at a core level?** If your bravest ideas get spiked at the end of a long journey to the top, you can say goodbye to getting similarly brave work in the future.

If the right ecosystem is in place, you need to motivate people to take advantage of those environmental effects. Ask yourself:

// **Are we hiring people who are driven by a passion for bold, creative ideas?**

// **Are we creating an environment where that passion is fuelled and encouraged?**

// **Are we motivating people to make truly creative work by offering rewards that they actually want? What could we offer that would be even better?**

Occasionally, creative bravery can happen overnight. But more often it's the result of months or years of work. Bravery is a muscle. Creativity is a muscle. Marketing is a muscle. Sit back, and it will atrophy. Push your organization to be stronger, and it will develop.

We hope this book has given you a set of tools and strategies that will help you get closer to your audience, understand why and how your company can best serve those people, and to grow your brand by creating exceptional ideas that will enhance and enrich their lives. Push yourself to do those things. We think you'll find it's contagious.

ACKNOWLEDGEMENTS

Although there are two names on the cover, the Contagious Commandments are truly a collective effort, and we owe a debt of gratitude to everyone who has contributed over the years. This book is the product of brilliant brains convening in Contagious offices around the world since 2004, where they have crafted smart stories, formulated insightful theories, and stayed true to our mission of championing creative innovation.

Special thanks to Georgia Malden, Alex Jenkins, Katrina Dodd, Patrick Jeffrey, and Dan Southern, whose insightful notes on the draft of this manuscript were essential for helping us hone and articulate the ideas within. Thank you to Nick Parish, for working with Paul to push the very idea of this book forward in the first place, and helping to make it a reality. Thank you to Will Sansom, Arif Haq, Janaina Borges, Silvia Antunes, Arwa Mahdawi, and Jess Greenwood for developing and road-testing many of the strategies we outline in these pages. Richard Newman, Noelle Weaver, and Amar Chohan also deserve a special mention, for supplying the rocket fuel that helped to launch Contagious in the first place.

And while we won't name every single person who has ever worked at Contagious, we'd be remiss not to mention the writers who have made up the engine room of our editorial products over the past fourteen years – many of whose reporting we relied on to write this book. To Emily Hare, Chloe Markowicz, Kate Hollowood, Sophia Epstein, James Swift, Kristina Dimitrova, Alice Franklin, Sian Bateman, Gina Rembe, Raakhi Chotai, Jeremy Edwards, Gabby Lott, Louise Potter, Lucy Aitken, Ed White, Robin Leeburn, Greg Copeland, Stacey Jacobs, Jamie Madge, Chris Wall, and John Ridpath: THANK YOU.

And, while we have the opportunity, may we please sneak in a big shout to designers Dean Dorat, Garvin Hirt, Smita Mistry, Charlotte Sallis, and Rich Spencer for making *Contagious* magazine, our online platforms, live events and marketing materials look suitably fabulous over the years.

The Contagious Commandments could not have happened without the enthusiastic support of the Contagious board: John Gordon, David Forster, Charles McIntyre, Paul's long-time collaborator and co-founder, Gee Thomson, and our extremely patient CEO, Karl Marsden.

Chris couldn't have done this without his wife, Ashley, who makes him smarter and more thoughtful every day of the year. It feels weird to thank your wife in a book, so instead I will say: Ashley, I'm incredibly glad you're my person and I'm excited for the adventures to come. Thanks to Mom and Dad for giving feedback on an early draft and, much more importantly, for raising me and teaching me everything I know. Thanks to Caroline for being my first writerly influence and the best sister in the world. Thanks to all of the friends and family members who have encouraged and challenged me over the years. Thanks to Nick for bringing me into the Contagious family and the so-called 'dirty church of advertising'. And, of course, thanks to Paul for going on this journey with me, and for putting up with me when I asked him to take out obscure Britishisms, even though I only succeeded about half the time.

Paul would like to return the thanks to his co-author, the super-human Barth, whose energy and expertise taught this old dog some new tricks. On a personal level, Paul is deeply indebted to his wonderful wife, Su, who has been his rock and mentor ever since they met at Goldsmiths College in 1986. She will also find it weird being thanked in a book, but her husband will insist on saying: Thank you, from the bottom of my heart, for always believing in me, for showing me what's important in life, and for being brave enough to let me turn down a comfy corporate job in order to sail into uncharted waters with a precious little idea called Contagious that Gee and I had scribbled down on the back of a beermat in a pub. I hope that in some small way, this book repays the countless late nights, long trips, lost weekends, creative strops and occasional overdrafts that you have had to endure along the way. To my incredible children, Lois, Hayden, and Kristen: I know that I have always encouraged you to reach for the stars, but occasionally you're allowed to look downwards, to pick all that stuff off your bedroom floors. I'd like to pay homage to my wordsmith father, Ray, for giving me the journalism bug and sneaking me into the press room at Middlesbrough matches as a kid, and to my ace sister, Simone, for being Snowy in our games of Tintin. I would like to dedicate this book to the memory of two strong and selfless women who brightened my life: my lovely mum, Joan Robertson, who would be proud beyond reason to see my name on the cover of something you can buy in a shop; and my similarly superb mother-in-law, Margaret Kemp.

Our sincere gratitude to our agent, Toby Mundy, for calming our nerves and making this remarkable experience possible. To our esteemed editor, Martina O'Sullivan, our copy-editor Trevor Horwood, our publicist David Over, and the entire team at Portfolio Penguin, thank you for making the process smooth and collaborative. It has been a pleasure and an honour, and we are childishly excited to be associated with that iconic little black-and-white bird.

And finally, thank you to everyone who has supported Contagious over the years. Our ideas have travelled around the world and back again via readers like you, subscribers, clients, and advocates at brands and agencies, small and large. You have enabled us to chronicle brave, passionate, infectious creativity as it changes the world around us, and for that we say, 'Cheers!'

FURTHER READING

On their first day of work at Contagious, we give every one of our researchers, writers, and strategists a list of books that have informed or reinforced the company's outlook on the world of marketing. As this book was sparked by the strategic insights and creative intelligence of the entire team, we polled them to develop a similar list to share with you. Now that you've finished *The Contagious Commandments*, here's a collection of additional books that we think will make your brain a better place . . .

Dan Ariely – *Predictably Irrational: The Hidden Forces That Shape Our Decisions*
Phil Barden – *Decoded: The Science Behind Why We Buy*
Linda Bernardi, Sanjay Sarma, and Kenneth Traub – *The Inversion Factor: How to Thrive in the IoT Economy*
Les Binet and Sarah Carter, *How Not to Plan: 66 Ways to Screw It Up*
Les Binet and Peter Field – *The Link Between Creativity and Effectiveness: The Growing Imperative to Embrace Creativity*
——— *The Long and the Short of It: Balancing Short and Long-Term Marketing Strategies*

Rachel Botsman – *Who Can You Trust? How Technology Brought Us Together – and Why It Could Drive Us Apart*

Claire Bridges – *In Your Creative Element: The Formula for Creative Success in Business*

Erik Brynjolfsson and Andrew McAfee – *Race Against the Machine: How the Digital Revolution is Accelerating Innovation, Driving Productivity, and Irreversibly Transforming Employment and the Economy*

Ed Catmull and Amy Wallace – *Creativity, Inc.: Overcoming the Unseen Forces That Stand in the Way of True Inspiration*

Robert Cialdini – *Influence: The Psychology of Persuasion*
——— *Pre-Suasion: A Revolutionary Way to Influence and Persuade*

Jim Collins – *Good to Great: Why Some Companies Make the Leap . . . and Others Don't*

Tyler Cowen – *Average is Over: Powering America Beyond the Age of the Great Stagnation*

Elizabeth Currid-Halkett – *The Sum of Small Things: A Theory of the Aspirational Class*

Pedro Domingos – *The Master Algorithm: How the Quest for the Ultimate Learning Machine Will Remake Our World*

Nir Eyal and Ryan Hoover – *Hooked: How to Build Habit-Forming Products*

Michael Farmer – *Madison Avenue Manslaughter: An Inside View of Fee-Cutting Clients, Profit-Hungry Owners and Declining Ad Agencies*

Paul Feldwick – *The Anatomy of Humbug: How to Think Differently About Advertising*

Adam Ferrier – *The Advertising Effect: How to Change Behaviour*

Richard P. Feynman – *Surely You're Joking, Mr Feynman!*

Lisa Goldman and Kate Purmal – *The Moonshot Effect: Disrupting Business as Usual*

David Heinemeier Hansson and Jason Fried – *Rework: Change the Way You Work Forever*

Yuval Noah Harari – *Sapiens: A Brief History of Humankind*
——— *Homo Deus: A Brief History of Tomorrow*

Steve Harrison – *Changing the World is the Only Fit Work for a Grown Man*

James Hurman – *The Case for Creativity: Three Decades Evidence of the Link Between Imaginative Marketing and Commercial Success*

Bernadette Jiwa – *Difference: The One-Page Method for Reimagining Your Business and Reinventing Your Marketing*

Laura Jordan Bambach, Mark Earls, Daniele Fiandaca, Scott Morrison – *Creative Superpowers: Equip Yourself for the Age of Creativity*

Daniel Kahneman – *Thinking, Fast & Slow*

David Kelley and Tom Kelley – *Creative Confidence: Unleashing the Creative Potential Within Us All*

Kevin Kelly – *The Inevitable: Understanding the 12 Technological Forces That Will Shape Our Future*

W. Chan Kim and Renée Mauborgne – *Blue Ocean Strategy: How to Create Uncontested Market Space and Make the Competition Irrelevant*

Verlyn Klinkenborg – *Several Short Sentences About Writing*

Ray Kurzweil – *The Singularity is Near*

Anne Lamott – *Bird by Bird*

Judie Lannon and Merry Baskin – *A Master Class in Brand Planning: The Timeless Works of Stephen King*

Heather LeFevre – *Brain Surfing: The Top Marketing Strategy Minds in the World*

Steven D. Levitt and Stephen J. Dubner – *Freakonomics: A Rogue Economist Explores the Hidden Side of Everything*

Cara Alwill Leyba – *Girl Code: Unlocking the Secrets to Success, Sanity, and Happiness for the Female Entrepreneur*

Brian McDonald – *Invisible Ink: A Practical Guide to Building Stories That Resonate*

Rita Gunther McGrath – *The End of Competitive Advantage: How to Keep Your Strategy Moving as Fast as Your Business*

Karen Nelson-Field – *Viral Marketing: The Science of Sharing*

David Ogilvy – *Ogilvy on Advertising*

Adam Pierno – *Under Think It: A Marketing Strategy Guidebook for Everyone*

Daniel H. Pink – *Drive: The Surprising Truth About What Motivates Us*

Richard Rumelt – *Good Strategy Bad Strategy: The Difference and Why It Matters*

Byron Sharp – *How Brands Grow: What Marketers Don't Know*

Byron Sharp and Jenni Romaniuk – *How Brands Grow: Part 2: Emerging Markets, Services, Durables, New and Luxury Brands*

Richard Shotton – *The Choice Factory: 25 Behavioural Biases That Influence What We Buy*

Kevin Simler and Robert Hanson – *The Elephant in the Brain: Hidden Motives in Everyday Life*

Simon Sinek – *Start with Why: How Great Leaders Inspire Everyone to Take Action*

Dave Trott – *One Plus One Equals Three: A Masterclass in Creative Thinking*

Sam Walker – *The Captain Class: The Hidden Force Behind the World's Greatest Teams*

Matt Watkinson – *The Ten Principles Behind Great Customer Experiences*

Amy Webb – *The Signals are Talking: Why Today's Fringe is Tomorrow's Mainstream*

Rick Webb – *Agency: Starting a Creative Firm in the Age of Digital Marketing*

Tim Wu – *The Attention Merchants: The Epic Scramble to Get Inside Our Heads*

Faris Yakob – *Paid Attention: Innovative Advertising for a Digital World*

INDEX

PENGUIN PARTNERSHIPS

Penguin Partnerships is the Creative Sales and Promotions team at Penguin Random House. We have a long history of working with clients on a wide variety of briefs, specializing in brand promotions, bespoke publishing and retail exclusives, plus corporate, entertainment and media partnerships.

We can respond quickly to briefs and specialize in repurposing books and content for sales promotions, for use as incentives and retail exclusives as well as creating content for new books in collaboration with our partners as part of branded book relationships.

Equally if you'd simply like to buy a bulk quantity of one of our existing books at a special discount, we can help with that too. Our books can make excellent corporate or employee gifts.

Special editions, including personalized covers, excerpts of existing books or books with corporate logos can be created in large quantities for special needs.

We can work within your budget to deliver whatever you want, however you want it.

For more information, please contact
salesenquiries@penguinrandomhouse.co.uk